Bertrand Hallward
A Biography

[handwritten inscription]
July '98
Karli BA

BERTRAND HALLWARD

First Vice-Chancellor of
The University of Nottingham
1948-1965

A Biography

Derek Winterbottom

THE UNIVERSITY OF NOTTINGHAM

First published in 1995 by
The University of Nottingham
University Park
Nottingham NG7 2RD

ISBN 0 85358 045 6 hb
ISBN 0 85358 046 4 pb

Printed in Great Britain by The Alden Press Limited, Oxford.

To the memory of
Margaret Hallward

Contents

Preface

I first met Bertrand and Margaret Hallward in October 1987, shortly after I had been commissioned to write an official history of Clifton College, which Bertrand had sponsored. I visited them at Gretton Court and wrote in my diary: 'They are both 86, and, in his case especially, it is difficult to believe. I was given tea and there was an immediate spate of genial but intense conversation, now on, now off the immediate point. Reminiscences of Clifton; anecdotes about people and events; observations about politics, philosophy, religion, current affairs; quotations from a wide variety of literary and academic sources — all poured forth as he lay upon a sofa as at a Bacchanal, though this posture was actually dictated by a painful back caused by years at the helm of a large yacht in the Mediterranean. Margaret cooked and served supper, and, despite her frailty, was very much abreast of affairs, interjecting occasionally to provide a fact or a name that had momentarily escaped her husband's memory. It was all remarkable; even, indeed, inspiring.' When, therefore, it was suggested that I should write this biography, I needed little persuading: since then there have been several more visits to Gretton Court, many long conversations, dozens of early-morning telephone calls and about 200 letters, all in a lively, lucid style, neatly written and instantly legible. My main debt of gratitude, then, is to the subject of this biography, for his generous co-operation, constant encouragement and buoyant sense of humour.

I am also very grateful to the authorities at the University of Nottingham for making it possible for me to spend several months on campus. The Warden and tutors of Rutland Hall gamely took me into their midst for nearly a whole term and patiently answered my endless questions about the University and its mysteries. Later in the academic year, Beverley Shotton and the administrative staff at Cripps Hall looked after me most hospitably during my stay there. I also received a great deal of help from the offices of the Vice-Chancellor and the Registrar. A good deal of my time was spent in the Manuscript and Special Collections department at the Hallward Library where Dorothy Johnston and her staff were very patient in dealing with my frequent enquiries and requests. Also, my thanks go to members of the Boat Club for allowing me some fresh air and exercise on the towpaths of the Trent.

In the quest for information farther afield I was lucky that Gertrude Nunns was prepared to seek out details of the young Bertrand Hallward's career at

Warden House, and I am grateful also to the librarians at King's, Cambridge, Peterhouse, and Haileybury. The Master of Haileybury (David Jewell), Robert Turnbull, Alastair Macpherson, Susan Ablett and Peter Rendle have all helped with different aspects of the book.

One of the pleasures of writing this biography has been to make the acquaintance of Bertrand Hallward's immediate family, who have offered me help, friendship and hospitality, for which I am very grateful. In the section on sources there is a list of the many other people who, either in interviews or in letters, have provided important material for the book, and I thank them for their trouble and, in many cases, their generous hospitality.

I owe a particular debt of gratitude to the former Registrar, Alfred Plumb, and to Frank Barnes and Brian Tolley, all of whom read the Nottingham section of the manuscript and made important suggestions: they are not, of course, to blame for any mistakes I may have made.

A word about Sir Francis Hill. I happened to meet him in April 1976 when researching a biography of the diminutive, yet formidable, Dr Fry, who was Dean of Lincoln from 1910 to 1930. Sir Francis gave me lunch at his splendid house, The Priory, and then took me on a highly informed tour of the cathedral, terminating at Fry's grave in the Cloister Garth. Hill was by then Chancellor of the University of Nottingham, a fact of which I was vaguely aware; but, of course, I had no reason then to quiz him about Bertrand Hallward, more's the pity. However, the fact that I had once met Hill and formed a distinct impression of this 'nicest sort of septuagenarian' (my diary), helped a great deal while I was writing this book. Hallward was lucky to find so perfect a foil to be his President of Council.

I wrote the manuscript during a three-month stay in sunny Tenerife, looking in one direction at the volcanic peak of El Teide, and in another at the glittering Atlantic: in a very literal sense, therefore, my warm thanks go to Joan and Harry Sawbridge for making this possible.

Derek Winterbottom
The Isle of Man
October 1995

Part One

Youth 1901-1919

Parents and Family

'Who are these Hallwards or Halvards?' asked Margaret Tait in 1926, about to become Mrs Bertrand Hallward. 'Aren't they brutal, blue-eyed Vikings who go marauding abroad and rape nuns?'[1] According to her husband the name derives from *Halle-Vard*, Warden of the *Halle*, the long communal house of the Vikings. 'After their rampages abroad,' he explained, 'they returned home and kept wassail and got very tight so they needed a Hallvard as a bouncer to keep order.'[2] Notable early Halvards include the patron saint of Oslo, a young man slain in 1054 and cast into a fjord with a millstone round his neck. In 1185 one Ricardus Halwardus appears in England in the Templar records for Warwickshire.[3] All this is justification enough for the insistence of Bertrand's branch of the family that despite the spelling with *two* l's the name should be pronounced to rhyme with 'shall' rather than 'shawl' — a brave, but losing battle, worthy of any Viking.

We are interested in the Hallwards who descend from Thomas Hallward of Worcester, born in 1720. His son, grandson and great-grandson were all styled the Reverend John Hallward but the tradition was broken with his great-great-grandson Norman, born in 1859 the son of the Rev. John Leslie Hallward, and destined to be Bertrand's father. The eldest child in the family of seven born to this Victorian Anglican clergyman, Norman was at thirteen packed off to boarding-school — in his case Haileybury, near Hertford, where his three younger brothers followed in due course.

Haileybury was only ten years old in 1872 but it was making good progress and Norman was a successful pupil, leaving in the summer of 1877 for King's College, Cambridge, where he had won a Classical Scholarship. He was a tall young man by now with rather a long face and the distinctive Hallward nose. He arrived at Cambridge in the same year that a Royal Commission had been set up to modernize the ancient customs and traditions of the University, and he arrived at King's the year after Oscar Browning was appointed a Fellow.

Norman Hallward,
Bertrand's father.

Browning is one of those legendary characters in whose career it is impossible to disentangle truth from fiction. He had been a housemaster at Eton but the Headmaster, Dr Hornby, was suspicious of his friendships with some of the boys, particularly the young George Nathaniel Curzon. Hornby eventually used a technical excuse to sack Browning, an event that caused a national controversy. As a Fellow of King's Browning made it his business to know the undergraduates as personal friends — there were only about 100 in those days — and he was 'at home' every Sunday evening in his spacious rooms on 'A' staircase. 'Round the elegant gothic balusters, up the forty-six steps, under the coved and plastered ceiling, and through the fluted, mediaeval doors came colleagues, pupils, friends and strangers from every corner of the University. There, before them in spacious rooms, lined from floor to ceiling with books, and filled with pictures, clocks and knick-knacks, they found a portly, mincing host never failing to be pleased to see them. The air was soon thick with smoke, and every chair and settee occupied. In the then extremely bohemian fashion later arrivals sat on the floor. Some talked, a few sang, others strummed the grand piano. Conversation and whisky warmed them. By ten o'clock, if not before, the noise was positively "indescribable".'⁴

Norman Hallward, like hundreds of Kingsmen, was befriended by Browning, and there are in King's College library about fifty letters sent by him to 'O.B.', as the don was universally known. The earliest date from soon after his going down from the University in 1881, and the last is dated 1908. The tragedy of Norman's life, according to Bertrand, was that he gained only a poor second class degree and found it very difficult to secure the kind of job he had begun to think was his by right. 'My guess is that he did tutoring in noble families,' wrote Bertrand in his *Memoirs*, 'using his bicycle for transport (he was a passionate cyclist in the early days of cycling), and he became enchanted with the easy, cultured life of the rich and noble, and he did no work in the terms at Cambridge and so came down disastrously.'⁵

Norman Hallward's early letters to Oscar Browning reveal him to be uncompromisingly demanding of favours. Can O.B. put in a good word with Mr X, the Headmaster of Y School? is the theme of most of them. Browning must have done his stuff, because Hallward was appointed to about a dozen schools, though he did not stay long at any of them: clearly he was not cut out to be a schoolmaster. In 1889 he accepted a post in the Indian Educational Department, lecturing in English Literature, and set sail for the sub-continent, where he worked diligently, though grumbling in many letters to O.B. about his low pay. He returned to England from time to time on leave, and on June 16th 1898 he was able to write an ecstatic letter to Browning from Lansdowne Place, Brighton.

> My dear O.B.,
>
> … I am so intoxicated with happiness at this present moment that I can't make any plans or engagements for the future … Three days ago, after seven years of waiting and two years of wooing, I have at last been so supremely fortunate as to win the love of my pearl of great price. I had hardly dared to hope that it would ever be. She is very fair and sweet and accomplished, and so honourable and true-hearted; although she would not give me up, she refused to give me any encouragement for a long time, while she was not sure of her own feelings, knowing how much I loved her and feeling that she must give me all or nothing.⁶

The pearl of great price was Eva Gurdon, daughter of Major-General Evelyn and Mrs Mary Gurdon. Born in 1833, Gurdon had entered the army in 1852 and fought in the Indian mutiny of 1857, when he was mentioned in despatches. Later he became a Commissioner and Divisional Judge in the Punjab, and he was promoted to Major-General in 1892 just before retirement to Hove, in Sussex. In 1858 he had married Mary Sanderson, daughter of another Indian

Eva Hallward, née Gurdon, Bertrand's mother.

Army general; they had three sons, but Eva was their only daughter. She was exceptionally good-looking, so Norman Hallward might well have counted himself a lucky man.

Oscar Browning did not attend their wedding, but he sent a handsome inscribed cigarette-case as a present for the bridegroom. 'I have worn the gold links you gave me ever since I had them, and now in the cigarette-case which will be almost, if not quite, as constantly about my person, I shall keep your kindness and friendship faster fixed in memory than before. I am so sorry to learn that you will not be able to give us your blessing at our wedding,' Norman wrote in thanks.[7] They were married on September 14th 1898 and drove down to Dover the same day to cross the Channel on the 15th. Then followed a honeymoon in the Alps and Italian Lakes before they boarded a ship bound for India at Brindisi. But by the end of 1899 the Hallwards were back in England recovering from a tragic experience. 'You may perhaps have seen in the newspapers', wrote Norman to Oscar Browning, 'that we lost our first child, a boy, at birth. My wife has gone through a terrible time of suffering, both physical and mental. It was a great grief and a bitter disappointment to us both.'[8]

Silhouettes of Norman and Eva Hallward.

When another child was expected Eva travelled alone to England to stay with her parents in Hove, and it was there, at 12 Norton Road, that her second son was born on 24th May 1901. He was named Bertrand Leslie Hallward; Leslie because that was a Hallward family name, and Bertrand because the Gurdons nourished a tradition that they were descended from Bertrand de Gurdon, a defendant on the walls of the castle at Chalus whose poisoned arrow had killed King Richard I back in 1199. It would have saved a lot of trouble if the Gurdons had been content to translate *Bertrannus* as Bertra*m* rather than Bertra*nd*, but Bertrand it was to be. Eva took the baby back to India with her that autumn and gave birth to another son, Philip, out there in 1903.

In the summer of 1904 Norman Hallward wrote in jubilant mood to Oscar Browning. 'Since I last wrote to you I received quite unexpectedly the offer of the acting appointment officer in charge of the Imperial Records, under the Government of India, together with the Secretaryship of the Patent office. I sent in an application for it when it was temporarily vacant in 1901, while you were out here, but heard no more of my application. I do not think I can be wrong in supposing that you said a good word for me to Lord Curzon at the time; and if so, I think I must be partly at least indebted to you for your kind help in obtaining this promotion.'[9] The bright schoolboy who had caused Browning's downfall at

Eton had become Viceroy of India, fount of all honour, and Browning was not slow to bathe in the glory.

> From Timbuctoo to distant Downing,
> Who has not heard of Oscar Browning?
> In shape he is something like a roller,
> He wears a most impressive bowler.
> He'll give you a lot of useful tips
> On emperors, and ghosts, and gyps
> Abroad he's very widely known;
> His smile would melt a pumice stone.[10]

According to his biographer, Browning would rise 'every morning at six o'clock to drink tea and write twenty or thirty letters of great length, swiftly and illegibly, before he began the normal work for the day.'[11] He received vast numbers of letters in return, 50,000 being deposited in Hastings Public Library after his death, from some 10,000 correspondents. The letters of Norman Hallward to his old tutor should be seen in this context: he was just one writer among thousands, yet for the best part of thirty years Browning, whatever his critics might say, proved a loyal friend and true mentor. It is a sad irony that Browning was never able to use his alleged influence over the great to secure honours for himself. Hints that a knighthood might be a worthy reward for his labours were ignored. In the end he became O.B., O.B.E. which gave cause for delighted laughter among friends and enemies alike.

Warden House

In the tenth decade of the twentieth century Bertrand Hallward, recently a widower, broke the habit of a long lifetime and wrote a few pages of memoirs to his daughter Christabel. They will be quoted at length from time to time, partly for the details they provide and partly because they reveal something of the style and character of the man. Turning his attention to the first decade of the century he encountered quite a blank. 'My earliest memories as a child are exceptionally bad. I have wondered whether this blockage of youthful memory was due to some trauma I suffered. Although I am told that I spoke fluent Hindustani, better than my child's English, I do not remember a word, and I remember nothing of what must have been the exciting journeys by steamer from India. At the age of six I was brought back, and in fact I only begin to remember things a little clearly when I was probably eight or nine.'[1]

In the summer of 1911, when Bertrand was ten years old and his brother Philip was eight, they were both sent to a small boarding-school in Deal, Kent. It was called Warden House, and was described with pride in a splendidly Edwardian publication entitled *Deal, Walmer and Sandwich, their attractions as sea-side and holiday resorts*. 'Mr Mullins,' the article ran, 'the Principal of Warden House, who is the son of Lieut-General Mullins, R.E., was educated at Charterhouse and afterwards at Magdalen College, Oxford ... Under his careful direction Warden House School is rapidly advancing into a recognized position among the best preparatory schools. The whole system of education here aims at the formation of character and the development of the full intellectual, moral and physical powers of the pupil. From the moment he enters the school every pupil receives individual attention, and there is no possibility of shy or backward boys being neglected or prejudiced in the interests of the more forward. In this high pressure age the first essential to success in life is undoubtedly a strong constitution, and consequently special attention is given to the physical health and development of the pupils at Warden House, which is a large, handsome edifice standing in its own grounds, close to Deal and Walmer, and

Warden House, Deal.

in one of the most salubrious spots on the Kentish coast. The grounds, which are about six acres in extent and well sheltered by trees, afford every facility for cricket, football and outdoor recreations of all descriptions, while splendid sea-bathing is available at Sandown, where there is a safe and sandy beach. There is a good gymnasium attached to the school, besides carpentry shops, play-grounds, recreation rooms, library and reading-room, etc. The sanitary arrange-ments throughout are excellent, and the domestic arrangements, which are of a very superior class, are under the personal control of a lady superintendent, Miss Edith Bode, who has also had great experience in nursing. About forty pupils are received, and a thoroughly sound preliminary education is given to boys destined for the public schools, the universities, the Royal Navy, etc.' This has all the makings of a Dotheboys Hall, an impression strengthened by the illustration of a rather gloomy-looking late Victorian house that accompanied the article. However, Bertrand liked it. 'Warden House was certainly an excellent preparatory school under the Headmaster Mr Mullins with Miss Bode as his Lady Manager,' he recalled.[2]

Moreover, it was at Warden House that the young Bertrand was effectively schooled in the intricacies of Greek and Latin grammar by Mr Sawyer, 'a very crusty old teacher whose methods were old-fashioned but remarkably sure and effective. Any mistake at even quite advanced Greek syntax ... and you were called up to his desk, held out your hand and received two raps from a ruler — nasty and not very severe in pain, but enough for the purpose. There never was any mention of the beauties of Greek or Latin literature but only the need for accuracy in grammar and syntax and the perfect memorization of Greek accents. Of course we were very afraid of him. He was an ogre, but never a terrible or unpleasant ogre. And we owed our scholarships entirely to him and to his extremely effective style of teaching.' In addition to his methodical learning of Mr Sawyer's Greek and Latin preps, Bertrand was already showing a typical interest in current affairs. 'I remember distinctly knowing the names, number and tonnage and guns of the new German battleships and battle cruisers which the Kaiser was building to challenge the British Navy and the British Command of the Seas.'[3]

It is quite clear from his record at Warden House that Bertrand Hallward was the sort of person who would prosper in a competitive environment. In a small school of forty boys his presence was soon felt. By 1912 he had won his cricket first XI colours and on the soccer field 'Hallward's kicking was sometimes brilliant.' In 1913 he became Head Boy and took the part of King Buonocore (who was fond of making jokes) in the Christmas play *Princess Zara*. By 1914 he was winning academic prizes for all subjects except Scripture, while as captain of the cricket XI he 'fulfilled his task nobly and his batting at critical moments seemed without nerves, which was certainly not the case.' By the time he left, nothing short of eulogy was deemed appropriate. 'We feel we cannot let [Hallward] leave without some small appreciation of his services. During 1914 he managed to be captain of the football, cricket and hockey teams, to win the Sports' Cup, to be well up in the Drill Corps, to be Head Boy and finally to crown his efforts by being top scholar at Haileybury. His keenness in everything he took up was wonderful and he has left behind him a reputation which present boys may envy.'[4] Can he have been popular too?

For most of their time at Warden House, Bertrand and Philip saw little of their parents, who were still out in India. In 1910 Norman Hallward had enjoyed a whole year's leave of absence in England and had leased a small manor house at Brendon in Devonshire. Here, according to Bertrand, 'we had a cook, a butler and two other servants and my father was happy, perhaps for the only time in his life, walking the glorious Devonshire woods and cliffs, because he hated India and had no sympathy for, or understanding of, Indian culture and religions.'[5] But he had to go back there for another four years, and during this time the boys spent the school holidays with either the Gurdon grandparents or the Hallward uncles and aunts. General Gurdon lived in a tall house in Hove with a large basement filled with shooting trophies. 'Everything seemed to have antlers of one strange shape or another, and there were leopard and tiger skins. My grandfather the General was a slight, kindly and not formidable figure, usually away at his India Club during the day. Mrs Gurdon was a very large laughing person with the tears streaming down her face for laughing, but she ruled the roost and I remember the firm "Do this" or "Do that Evelyn" (her husband's Christian name), or "Fetch my spectacles".'[6]

The other holiday home was 21 Pembroke Gardens in Kensington where lived Norman's siblings Maud, Herbert and Clement Hallward, all at that time unmarried. 'Maud had her own independent Hallward income, Herbert was in finance in the City, and Clement imported New Zealand frozen meat.' Another brother, Lancelot, would make occasional visits from Africa where he was a missionary and, eventually, Dean of Umtata Cathedral. These Hallwards 'had a cook and a maid and lived in considerable Edwardian comfort, though far from rich. The two Uncles and Aunt never quarrelled, had a special "You're a duck Sir," "You're a Pet Sir" form of courtesy address to thank for passing the salt or the pepper. When the Uncles came back from the City there were always card games, and on special occasions Velma Suchard chocolates in the red paper wrapping. But during the day the wonderful walking Auntie Maud took us two boys to the theatre — incredible excitement — or to the Tower or Hampton Court — and was educating us in the historical sites of London. But one must also recall the wonderful summer holidays with the Uncles and Aunt Maud in Cornwall. They were all three tremendous sea-bathers, or certainly Maud and Clement were. I remember Auntie Maud's full coat and skirt Edwardian bathing dress and Uncle Clement's fine striped blue and white gentleman's bathing dress, sandcastles and playing in the sand, Cornish cream and Cornish pasties. Much more remarkable was the elaborate hamper which had been ordered and came down, I think, by special courier service from Fortnum and Mason. Those were the days! Food mattered a great deal — and rightly — perhaps sometimes too much — in those last glorious days when Britain ruled the seas.'[7]

Haileybury

Early in 1914 Norman Hallward returned from India, having retired from his position as Director of Public Instruction and Member of the Legislative Council of Bihar and Orissa. In March he acquired, for £750, a house named 'Westcote' in the village of Dunsfold in Surrey and this was to be the family home until his death in 1934. Bertrand speaks of this home rather slightingly: 'It was a poor villa type of house with two floors and rather small rooms, a front door opening into a hall room which was my father's study and considerable library, a small drawing-room, one bathroom and one interior loo, and a very poor ill-lighted kitchen and scullery: there was no electric light or gas but only oil lamps. The

Westcote, Dunsfold.

house had quite a lot of land, a kitchen garden at the back, a garage, and at the side a considerable part of a field in which a tennis court was made with very ample surround.'[1] In 1994 the house was relatively unchanged except for the addition of a Victorian-style conservatory, and in the opinion of the young City businessmen playing weekend cricket on the village green it could be expected to change hands very rapidly at £350,000, even in a depressed market.

Dunsfold was, and still is, distinctly off the beaten track, the sort of village associated with calendars and rose-covered cottages. For centuries this part of the 'Weald' was covered in impenetrable forest and even now the place appears to be simply a clearing among the woods. The parish church of St Mary and All Saints lies a good mile's walk from the main houses, surrounded by trees, and according to the pamphlet on its history, William Morris considered it 'the most beautiful country church in all England',[2] though to a less aesthetic observer in 1994 it seemed a crude, rustic affair, albeit venerable, dating from the late thirteenth century. The village itself boasts a pub, a few shops, several quite grand houses, and a village green. For the rest of his time as a schoolboy and undergraduate, Dunsfold was home to Bertrand in the holidays.

His father had retired at 55 from a position of moderate importance in a country which, by all accounts, he disliked. Moreover he had contracted an Indian disease called sprue, 'a slow, wasting disease showing itself in great thinness and anaemia', according to Bertrand. 'And the treatment in those days was to eat masses of liver. Imagine my mother's job in cooking and serving those masses of liver in the hot weather in Dunsfold!' The outbreak of war in the year Norman retired to Surrey imposed certain duties on the Hallward household. A party of Belgian refugees came to stay for several months, and they were followed by 'a series of distressed gentlewoman ladies'. According to his obituary in King's College Annual Report, Norman 'served as a private in the Volunteer Army of Defence, took all measures to qualify as an efficient soldier, and found no little interest in the contrast between civil and military manners in imparting instruction. After the War, he served for a year under the Food Control Board.' In his early years as an English teacher and lecturer, Norman had written a two-volume edition of Lamb's *Essays of Elia*, as well as his own poetry. In retirement he produced what the King's obituary calls 'his one serious piece of research, *William Bolts: A Dutch Adventurer under John Company*. This book contains the result of much arduous work. It is primarily intended as material for the future historians of India, but it is interesting to the general reader for the lively insight it gives into the working of the East India Company and the reactions of Europe and India on one another in the latter half of the eighteenth century.'[3]

The obituary goes on to suggest that Norman Hallward would have preferred a life of academic scholarship to his career in India. Certainly Bertrand gives a picture of an embittered man and a strained marriage. 'My mother was never really in love with my father, who was a difficult, almost typical Victorian father. "Don't argue!" he would say to me. I well remember him saying to my Margaret arriving at Westcote, engaged to me, when she asked him sweetly, "Did you watch Mademoiselle Lenglen at Wimbledon Centre Court?" "My dear, I *never* watch women's tennis!" "My dear, always remember to pick up the bath mat and place it on the back of the chair".'4 'I think one must say that my mother had a very difficult life living with my father. She had sick headaches which stopped when he died. I remember when the first Labour Government came in after the War my father "went into Coventry" for three days and would not speak at meals. During the War, when there was double summer time he would not change our clocks from Greenwich time. The consequence was that when Philip, my father and I bicycled the ten miles into Guildford, taking an hour, leaving at 10.00 am, we arrived at one o'clock and the shops were all shutting for lunch.'5 Norman also had very fixed ideas about how eggs should be boiled. 'I remember as if it were yesterday my father and the problem of the correctly boiled egg which in his view no one seemed to be able to achieve except himself. So he demanded that a very small saucepan filled with water and a spirit lamp stove be brought into the dining room, and one egg. We watched entranced, almost in silence for the three and a half minutes and saw him take his knife and slice off the head of the egg. Lo and behold! It was all runny and undercooked because of course it was a very fresh and newly laid egg!'6

It may well be that Bertrand's arrival at his public school provided a welcome change from family controversies over boiled eggs. Although he *did* win a scholarship to Haileybury, the Warden House *Valete* eulogy had concealed a previous failure because the first choice had been Charterhouse, only a few miles away from Dunsfold, a far more ancient and possibly more prestigious school at that time. In the late autumn of 1914 he sat for the scholarship at Charterhouse, but 'the arrangements were chaotic; it was piercingly cold weather and I had sickness and diarrhoea (from nervousness). Later in my life when I was a Fellow of Peterhouse I was sent on behalf of the Fellows to visit Frank Fletcher the Headmaster of Charterhouse and to offer him the Mastership of Peterhouse, which he smilingly refused. I said to him "I once sat for a scholarship at Charterhouse." He quickly went to his filing cabinet and after a few moments read out "Looks intelligent but no performance".'7 The wheel turned full circle later still in his life when in the late 1940's the then Archbishop of Canterbury approached Bertrand with a view to his becoming the Headmaster of Charterhouse, and it was his turn, smilingly, to refuse.

Wilkins' façade at Haileybury: a model for The University of Nottingham's new buildings?

After the failure at Charterhouse Bertrand sat the scholarship exam for Haileybury, a school attended not only by his father but by his uncles Clement, Herbert and Lancelot. They had all been there in the 1870's when Haileybury was still in the process of establishing itself as a great public school. It had been opened in 1862 in the magnificent buildings of the former East India College designed in the Greek revival manner by the architect William Wilkins, situated very close to the county town of Hertford. From 1806 to 1858 the College had instructed future administrators of India in the languages, religions, history and culture of the region, as well as other relevant subjects. In many ways it was run on university lines and several Fellows of Oxford and Cambridge colleges served on the staff, including the famous economist Malthus who was Professor of History and Political Economy at the College from 1806 to 1835. However, most of the students were of schoolboy age and they led their academic teachers a merry dance. Rioting was a frequent problem and ill-discipline a daily fact of life. In 1858 the East India College closed when it became government policy to institute competitive exams for the Indian Civil Service rather than continuing the privileged system of nominations upon which the College operated.[8]

In 1861 the buildings (which had cost over £50,000) were sold for £18,000 to a group of local people who were keen to establish a new boarding-school based on recent foundations like Marlborough (1843) 'rather than the old foundations

such as Eton and Winchester where the education was still firmly and exclu-
sively classical'.[9] This was to be a modern school, following the high standards
set by Dr Arnold at Rugby; to ensure this the Revd. A.G. Butler, a former pupil
at Rugby, was appointed the first Headmaster. Starting with 54 boys in 1862, he
proved popular and successful, attracting 255 pupils after only three years. He
found the post a strain, all the same, and resigned after five years, though he is
revered at Haileybury as the effective founder of the school's success. He was
replaced by another Rugbeian, the Revd. Edward Bradby, who was Norman
Hallward's headmaster, and in whose time the new chapel was built, as well as
three new boarding-houses. By the time Bradby retired in 1883, Haileybury had
been securely established as a major public school. Bertrand's headmaster was
F.B. Malim, a hard-working and efficient administrator as well as an enthusiastic teacher whom Bertrand undoubtedly admired, both as a schoolboy and later,
in retrospect, when he himself took over the responsibility of running a school.
At Sedbergh, Haileybury and later Wellington, Malim was acknowledged as
being one of the most successful headmasters of his time. Bertrand thought him
brilliant and witty though a member of his staff saw him more as 'a quiet,
sensible scholarly man, who saw Haileybury through the tribulations and
shortages of the War, and reconstructed it in the post-war years.'[10] Bertrand was
at the school for four years and two terms, from January 1915 to July 1919. The
outbreak of war in August 1914 meant that this was not a comfortable time.
According to the school's historian, 'When the Autumn Term of 1914 started,
thirty boys who should have been back, four masters and twenty-six of the
college servants had already joined the army and this was only the trickle at the
start of the watershed. Fifteen masters, or half the strength of the staff, joined the
forces, as did the Bursar, and the Medical Officer. Immediately, masters who
were due for retirement and some of those who already had retired, were
pressed back into their old jobs.'[11]

One of these was A.A. Lea, housemaster of Thomason House where Bertrand's
father and uncles had been boys and where Bertrand and Philip naturally
followed. Lea had been housemaster since 1899 and was due to retire from the
House after so many years' service but was required to stay on during the War
when younger colleagues left to join up. Lea has been described by one of his
colleagues as 'essentially a retiring and unassuming man ... the very soul of
fairness and efficiency'. Lacking any athletic distinction, Lea was 'at first sight
rather a negative kind of man, but when you saw more of him you began to
realize that there was a great deal more to him than you had imagined.
Outwardly [he was] rather prim and old-maidish, but in reality a man of
sparkling wit, and good company.'[12]

One of the most notable features of Wilkins' design for the original East India College was that the buildings were arranged around a vast quadrangle that has been described, perhaps with exaggeration, as 'the largest academic quadrangle in Europe'.[13] When Haileybury became an Anglican public school, Arthur Blomfield was employed to construct a huge chapel, which he designed in Byzantine style and managed with considerable success to graft on to Wilkins' Greek colonnades. Immediately across the quadrangle from the chapel lay Thomason House (named after a student of the East India College who rose to be Lieutenant Governor of the North-West Province), occupying a ground floor section of the building. All the forty-odd boys in the house, from the most junior to the most senior, slept in one large dormitory (as they were still doing in 1994), though senior boys enjoyed the privacy of a study.

There were three new boys at the beginning of the January term of 1915, taking their place in the lowliest part of the dormitory. Two were scholars, Bertrand Hallward and A.R.W. Harrison, who, by virtue of their awards, went straight into the fifth form. The other new boy was H.J.W. Scarr, who started in the Juniors. At the top of the House (and the other end of the dormitory) was the Head of House, D.M. Lang, and two School Prefects, A.S.G. Colthurst and P.M.R. Innes.[14] Although Haileybury was founded with the intention of making it more modern and up-to-date than older foundations, like many of the new Victorian schools it had conformed to a distinct pattern by 1914. The cult of games had taken a firm hold, as had a sense of group loyalty (or patriotism) which demanded devotion first to the House, then to the School, and ultimately to King, Church and Country. Within the House, younger boys were subject to the discipline of House and School Prefects, and this could be severe. Stepping out of line was not tolerated. The boys who fared worst in this kind of environment were the sensitive souls who did not conform to the expected pattern. Those who fared well were good at games or work. Those who fared best were good at both.

Bertrand's Prep School record as a games player should have got him off to a good start at Haileybury but he broke his right arm in the first term playing rugby. 'It was set badly and although I had been a demon fast bowler at Warden House, I could bowl no longer at Haileybury, and it affected my serving for the rest of my life at lawn tennis. In a tournament my service grew weaker and weaker. I was therefore off games for a year and A.G. Colthurst sent me for solitary and ghastly long runs practically every afternoon.'[15] To be off games for a year when he knew he could excel at them must have been a severe trial. Fortunately he became firm friends with the other scholar new-boy in Thomason, Robin Harrison. They were both classical specialists, both good games players and both destined for academic careers. Robin Harrison eventually got a first at

Oxford, taught for a while at Westminster School, became a Fellow of Merton College, Oxford, was seconded to the Ministry of Food during the War, rose to be Under-Secretary there, and was elected Warden of Merton in 1963. He died in 1969 but Bertrand swears he saw him again after this when he went to meet his widow at an airport. Robin was apparently walking behind, a ghost by auto-suggestion.[16] There was a strong spiritual bond between the two. In his *Memoirs* Bertrand noted that 'when we were perhaps both sixteen and a half, Robin put his arm round my shoulder. I had been reading about Socrates and Alcibiades and Platonic love and friendship. I very gently released his arm from my shoulder and looking at him said "Let us have in our friendship love of the eyes and the heart, but no touching or physical contact." This was the beginning of a rule which I have kept all my life in my male friendships.'[17]

One of the first things Malim had done after his arrival at Haileybury was to restructure the curriculum to take account of the criticisms of the School Inspectors of 1911, who considered that the provision for science teaching was unsatisfactory. The effect of Malim's reforms was to ensure that boys in the fifth form, even though they might be classical scholars, all studied one year's science, something that would serve Bertrand well in the future.[18] At the beginning of his second academic year, the September term of 1916, he moved into the sixth form, even though he was only fifteen. As a member of the classical side he came strongly under the influence of an outstanding teacher, C.H. Garland. 'Very few had the rare privilege of being taught by this fine scholar,' wrote R.C. Ashcroft in his book of memoirs about the school, 'but I imagine the others knew from hearsay that they were missing something of special quality. C.H.G. was not really known to any but the senior classics, except as Hall Master or as the "tall, silent, grim figure" striding down XX-acre path, reputed to have suffered a terrible personal disappointment, and now a lonely, friendless man eschewing all social engagements. To a denizen of Formroom 25 he was everything: he was first feared, then respected, and finally loved. He epitomized pure scholarship; he stood for accuracy, taste, meticulous attention to *minutiae*, the search for perfection... As a teacher, he was probably the greatest living at the turn of the century. Anyhow, he served Haileybury well, and turned out a succession of boys who won renown for the school. "Inexorable to the idle, not gentle to the dull", he imposed his impeccable taste and cultured mind on all who submitted to his discipline.'[19] A worthy successor had been found to Warden House's Mr Sawyer, who would make the most of Bertrand's natural academic talents.

When the time came for Bertrand to be confirmed, he discovered that his classical studies served as something of an intellectual obstacle when it came to embracing the doctrines of the Anglican Church. 'I was confirmed at the age of perhaps fifteen and a half. The preparation of the doctrine and the service made a slight, but not at all deep impression upon me. I think it seemed like joining another, more special, club and my mind, trained in all this Greek and Latin literature and Greek rational thinking found it very difficult to give a mystical, holy, sacred meaning to the service, though I tried to.'[20] Religion was always to present him with something of a problem, not least as Headmaster of an Anglican school. A Master of Peterhouse (Lord Chalmers) put it rather well when he suggested Bertrand could at least consider himself 'one of the flying-buttresses of the Anglican Church.' As for issues of sex, often tackled at confirmation time, this 'was fortunately of very little trouble or anxiety because I had read one or two sensible books and this was anyhow all a purely private matter which in those days was completely secret and one never discussed with anyone else.'[21]

In time Bertrand's broken arm mended and he duly appeared for the Thomason House cricket XI in 1916. He had also taken up rackets and played for his House's Junior Pair. In 1917 he reached the School Second XI and in the House photograph of that year he alone wears a white blazer, though his collar and tie look scruffy and his eyes are screwed up. The flaxen mop of his early years had started to mature to the gold colour for which he was so frequently remembered, but the faded black-and-white prints do not shown us that. This year, we are told, he played 'almost brilliantly' in the junior rackets, but Robin Harrison had overtaken him as a rugby player, being chosen for the House 1st XV while Bertrand was not. By the January term of 1918 the Head of Thomason (Conner), who was also Head of the School, wrote proudly in the House Records that 'this term was one of the most successful the House has known for some years.' He then went on to explain why. Thomason boasted that term the Head of School (himself), the Captain of Rugger (Carr), the Captain of Agriculture (Young), the Hair-Cutting Prefect (Harrison) and two other School Prefects, making six in all (Bertrand was one). There were nine N.C.O.'s, a Company Sergeant Major, four rugger colours and one cricket colour (Bertrand), a member of the Fives Six, and one of the School Rackets pair (Bertrand).[22] For one House to harbour six School Prefects was indeed unusual.

Bertrand was a School Prefect for five terms and this spanned two cricket seasons during which he played for the School 1st XI. Fixtures were held against other schools, such as Wellington, Felsted, St Paul's and Uppingham, and with a number of clubs. The high point of the year was the match against Cheltenham at Lord's, but on both these occasions Bertrand scored a duck. In general he was a capable, though not brilliant, school batsman. He was probably a more distinguished rackets player but this was a less high-profile sport. In 1918 he began to take an interest in the School Debating Society, until then dominated by Nevill Coghill, later a well-known English scholar. In the 601st meeting of the Society in the Bradby Hall he seconded the motion that 'Women between the ages of eighteen and thirty-five should be conscribed for work of national importance'. 'In melodious and ecclesiastical tones', we are told, he 'informed the thronged rows of eager faces that he was not a misogynist, for all he might say. He said that we still had to face the worst of the War, and that we needed the help of every man, woman and child. Women have the franchise and so must be expected to bear some of the burdens. In the last century women were mere puppets, but "aliud tempus, alii mores", so it is not strange that work should be expected of them today; anyhow, let us kick over the traces of convention and cut out a new line for our own age.'[23] A little later he is to be found proposing that 'It is better to be born lucky than to be born rich.' This was an impromptu debate, and he gained time to think what to say by beginning 'I will just tax you for half a minute to think over the subject.' In the end he decided that 'it is self-sacrifice and not wealth that brings happiness.'[24] In another debate on 'A third class railway carriage is the church of the future', he insisted that an excursion train really *would be* the church of the future. His next contribution a few moments later was described as 'a little paradoxical'. 'We are here,' announced the future headmaster, 'to provide employment for about forty lazy schoolmasters, and have to pay for this privilege'. This may have lost him a few admirers in the Common Room.[25]

Bertrand's younger brother Philip appeared in Thomason House two years behind his brother, and, though he laid no claim to his senior's academic or sporting talents, he settled in well and it is pleasant to find both brothers playing in the House 1st XI towards the end of Bertrand's time. Moreover, 'there was a good system which allowed seating for the supper meal to be by choice, and by families, so that Philip could sit with Robin and myself. Robin and I loved having Philip and hearing what the Lower School was thinking and I think Philip liked being with us. I once asked Philip whether he would have preferred to be sent to a different public school but he was quite firm in his opinion that he liked being with me at Haileybury, and of course we had so much in common to discuss in the holidays'.[26]

Holidays for both boys were generally spent, during these war years, in Dunsfold, and in his *Memoirs* Bertrand provides a colourful picture of his life there which is well worth reproducing in full.

> Dunsfold was a typical widespread English village. The church was one mile away from the main village with its very lovely green, school building, universal shop and post office, butcher's shop and I think two main pubs. Famous people such as the Mudies of lending library fame

Bertrand and his brother, Philip.

lived there, and the wealthy retired jute merchant from India, Mr Walsh. We were never asked to his mansion, I suspect because it had got to his ears that my father had called him contemptuously a JUTE WALLAH. This irked me because his beautiful daughter, Sylvia, lived there! I was only allowed to fish with a float in his carp pond. Then there were the Simpsons, in a glorious rambling farmhouse and property. The father was a well-off non-functioning parson, once a great cricketer; the son George, a particular friend of mine, became the famous submarine admiral of the Mediterranean, who played a large part in the defence of Malta and the defeat of the Italian Navy in World War Two, and wrote a remarkable book *Periscope View*. There were two sisters, Joan, who trained as a nurse and went, I think, to Nova Scotia, and Doris, whom my mother liked especially and encouraged to feel she might be the right girl for BLH. Hers was a sad, slightly neurotic life, and when she knew she was dying she suddenly came and visited Margaret and myself and I had a long intimate talk with her about old times. There were the two brash Canadian Slater ladies with a huge garden and a vintage early motor car with brass fittings, wonderfully maintained. Their brother was an admiral in the British Navy.

But as I look back I can see that the great event of my life was attaining the age when it was legal to ride a motor-bicycle. I had saved up all my

Christmas and birthday presents, and was able to buy for £46 a new A.J.S.
motorcycle, a marvellous machine. I suddenly became mobile and could
visit houses to play tennis. The special house to which I was often invited
was that of the Buzzards at Godalming. Sir Farquhar Buzzard later
became Regius Professor of Medicine at Oxford. But in those earlier days
he regularly attended a race meeting on Saturday and then played tennis
quite well on their hard court on a Sunday afternoon. Marty and Sylvia
were good players, and Anthony who went into the navy got a Blue at
Oxford. From a distance I much admired Marty, but she married an
eminent rising doctor.

It was on Boxing Day that we regularly had meetings of the *Jeunesse
Dorée* for mixed hockey matches and I have splendid group photographs
of tousled hair, shorts and breeches. At this distance of time they still look
very good healthy specimens of English country middle-class families.
For Philip and myself on Sunday there was the longish walk with my
father and mother to Matins. I never remember any question for my father
of Holy Communion. I don't think he could ever have got up or dressed
in time; and I fancy that he regarded H.C. as papistical. At any rate it was
a subject never discussed.

It is noticeable in all this account that I have said nothing about dances.
The fact is that for us teenagers during these four years (1915-1919) to the
best of my memory there simply weren't any. I had no sisters, and I have
really no memory of mixed social parties at Christmas time. To modern
ears it must seem that we lived an extraordinarily deprived and dull life.
And yet it didn't seem to me so at the time. My father had a good library
and I read voraciously English novels, Dickens, Thackeray, Scott, Buchan,
Harrison Ainsworth, Wilkie Collins, Fenimore Cooper and of course Jane
Austen, Trollope and the historical novelists Charles Reade, George Eliot,
Robert Graves, etc., etc. And this stood me in good stead later in life
because I had a richly furnished mind and memory with the splendid store
of English novel character and plot.[27]

Idyllic and innocent though this picture of English village life might be, a
dark and menacing threat grew for Bertrand with every passing year. This was
the grim fact that the War that had begun in 1914 even by 1918 showed no signs
of ending, and that the numbers of young lives it had demanded already
exceeded all known proportions. To be at a school like Haileybury as either a
pupil or teacher during the Great War was truly a desolating experience.
Generally speaking, the English public schools lost about as many Old Boys
killed in the War as there were pupils in the school in any one normal year. When
the final toll was counted, it emerged that 2,825 old Haileyburians had fought

in the War, and 586 had died. Four Old Boys won V.C.s and 87 reached the rank of Brigadier-General and above, while an old Haileyburian, Edmund Allenby, was the hero of the campaign in Palestine. Four Haileybury masters were killed, Robin Harrison's father and two elder brothers died in the first three years of the War, and many boys known to Bertrand in the House and School were lost, including P.M.R. Innes who had been at the top of Thomason in his first term. There were frequent memorial services in the chapel, and the ever-lengthening list of the dead was a constant and depressing factor. 'All our week-days have become Sabbaths' *The Haileyburian* recorded in a striking phrase in 1915; 'it is not unnatural to wonder whether anything will ever be the same again.'[28] The Editorial of April 1916 discussed the arguments for and against conscription, which had just been introduced, and decided that 'whatever the opinions concerning the justice of any measure may be, there is no justification for a denunciation on the sole ground of lack of precedent.' If the War continued, Bertrand could expect to be called up within months of leaving school.

Unlike the Second World War in which, as Bertrand was to discover to his cost, air raids were a serious menace to schools, there was little immediate danger to the boys of Haileybury in this War, though there were occasional raids by Zeppelin airships to worry about. On June 12th 1916 an audience of over a hundred heard E.T. Chaplin lecture in the Bradby Hall on Count Zeppelin and how he had built his first airship in a floating shed on Lake Constance in 1898, and how it was 420 feet long, 30 feet in diameter and contained 400,000 cubic feet of hydrogen in seventeen separate compartments. Turning to the use of improved Zeppelins in the War, the lecturer explained that 'there were no raids during the first four months of the War because the Germans had not anticipated our entry and therefore had no Zeppelins prepared to cross the North Sea.'[29] Within weeks of this talk a Zeppelin was shot down over Potter's Bar. 'It was quite frightening,' Bertrand recalled, 'you heard the Zeppelin's engines a-whirr, a-whirr, a-whirr, as it went overhead, and then the loud shatter of the bombs and the windows all rattled. We watched the amazing sight of the Potter's Bar Zeppelin come down from the dormitory windows.'[30] 'Those who saw the Zeppelin brought down in flaming ruin on the night of Sunday, October 1st,' warned *The Haileyburian*, 'will never again need a reminder of the presence of the God of War.'[31] The other reminder which was a constant problem throughout the War was the effectiveness of the U Boat campaign in preventing food supplies reaching Britain. According to a historian of Haileybury, 'boys at school at this time were very often really hungry. Mr Malim urged on them the patriotism of abstinence and suggested voluntary reductions in bread rations. Beer, which had been drunk in a diluted form known as College Swipes, disappeared for ever. Potatoes were planted on XX acre, which also supported crops of hay. Tending these became a form of exercise as did munitions work turning shell bases and 'bolsters' for Woolwich Arsenal. Economy was carried to extraordinary lengths. Soft collars replaced stiff ones since starch was a form of food and should not be wasted. A letter-writer to *The Haileyburian* even inquired whether straw boaters should not be given up, "as straw provides food for horses".'[32]

In April 1918 *The Haileyburian* warned its readers about Ludendorff's great offensive. 'Serious news is reaching us from the Western Front. And the emotion that is uppermost in our hearts is a blind, unreasoning anger. Anger first with the Kaiser; then with the state of things that lets us sleep on a bed at night and rise to grumble at our breakfast, while men not two years older than us are thanking God for a bed of mud and what scraps they can get to eat, and then turn to face the hordes of devils loosed upon them. And last, though not least, we cannot help almost hating the engineers and miners, who crouch safe at home in grimy pits and greasy shops and whose warcry is "Down tools!" The next few days will be, in the words of a great statesman "heavy with the fate of nations," and we at home feel powerless. But this at least we can do; we can help to bury the hatchet of internal disagreement; now is our chance to prove to the world and our enemies that Britain's glory is not a thing of the past, that adversity only makes our spirit more indomitable. Let us show again the stern and stubborn character of our race, facing reverses, disappointments, even disasters, fear-lessly, unflinchingly.'[33]

The Allies withstood the great offensive but in its June issue *The Haileyburian*'s Editorial again concentrated on the War, because 'it is so constantly in our thoughts. And yet it has been with us so long now that there seems nothing new to be said. Indeed, the War is almost a commonplace, impossible as it may sound; it has come to be an integral part of our lives, and we have now become so used to living under the shadow of the black war-cloud, that we find it hard to imagine what the blue sky of peace would look like. Those days are like some dream long past, unreal and half-forgotten, when there were rarely more than half-a-dozen corps parades a term and uniforms were cleaned once a year for the inspection in the summer, when the "grubber" still sold "victorias" and "cherry-creams", when the windows were not all disfigured with brown paper and the sunblinds daubed a sooty black.'[34]

In October 1918 that much maligned strategist Field Marshal Haig planned a counter-offensive that effectively swept the German armies from the field and led to a request for an armistice, prompted by Ludendorff's realization that he could not carry on. Ten days after the armistice the young man whose last editorials had been full of 'backs to the wall' sentiment could write in joyous relief: 'An epoch has closed with the most wonderful news that war can give us

— Peace. For four long years Might has striven with Right, for four long years the awful flame of war, kindled by the brain of a megalomaniac, has engulfed our dearest and our best. And now it is all over. The supermen are slinking to their lairs, whining and cringing like thrashed dogs. The world is rejoicing, happier and cleaner by the purging of the fire.'[35]

The news of the abdication of the Kaiser and the Crown Prince had been given to the school by Malim on November 9th at a school concert. He then went on to sing, solo, *Land of Hope and Glory*, and when he had finished 'he asked for three cheers for King George V, which were given with more than usual enthusiasm'.[36] With the news of the armistice, however, a great plot began to hatch among the lower orders at Haileybury. After the Relief of Ladysmith in the Boer War, Haileybury boys had celebrated by cutting afternoon school and marching jubilantly to Hertford and Ware. The Master of the day had caned about seventy offenders, which caused quite a stir. Now, according to Bertrand, the boys were determined to try something similar. 'Malim had bad toothache and had summoned Robin Harrison, who was Head Boy, and told him to take responsibility and to deal with the matter. Well, we six Senior Prefects (the ultimate élite, called *Elysium*) did. The ringleaders were summoned to the Bradby Hall and a public beating was enacted. I still remember how when this was finished we six Prefects filed out of the Bradby Hall and walked between two vast rows of Lower Boys in silence and hatred. I thought then and since how easy it would have been to tear us to pieces. But I marvelled how AUTHORITY triumphed!'[37]

Robin Harrison, it can be seen, had won the race to be both Head of House and Head of School. This did not put a strain on his long friendship with Bertrand. 'Malim preferred to make him Head Boy rather than me, though I was slightly ahead in work, and Malim was quite right in his choice which I recognized then as right and proper and never resented. Our friendship was always perfect and complete. And Robin was a very good Head Boy whom we called by the nickname "The Crow", but it was said with a smile as a term of respect and affection.'[38] They had gone up the House and School together, pooling their intellectual resources in Classics and working together for all preps 'which undoubtedly gave us a great advantage because in Classics you spend part of your time looking up words in the dictionaries and two pairs of eyes for alternate words gives you this double time advantage and two brains on a difficult passage have two chances of getting at the right meaning quickly.'[39]

In December 1918, with the excitement of the Armistice celebrations still a fresh memory, Bertrand sat the scholarship examination at King's, his father's College at Cambridge. He was seventeen years and seven months old, and he won a Minor Scholarship of £60. One incident in the scholarship exam stood out

The quadrangle at Haileybury, showing Thomason House in the right-hand corner.

in his mind. 'A grammar school boy from Southampton (A.D. Nock) sat near me in the seating list and I got talking with him as we came in and went out. After the General Paper he walked with me and said "Did you feel that you did yourself justice on that paper?" Justice be blowed! I had struggled to find enough to say in answering two or three questions on a paper which I found very taxing and difficult.'[40] Shortly afterwards Robin Harrison won an award to Merton, Oxford.

After that, it should have been all plain sailing. With the War over, and a Cambridge scholarship assured, Bertrand could look forward to an enjoyable last two terms at school, and a second season in the cricket XI (66 against St Paul's, 82 against Wellington). He had been a successful and distinguished pupil, a regular public school Apollo. Yet his last memories of school were clouded by a tragic incident.

> At the end of my time at Haileybury a strange and very terrible thing happened to me. A temporary master appeared on the staff. He was a good tennis player and during the last Easter Holidays from school he invited me to play tennis on some court (I can't remember where). At the

end of the term when I finally left Haileybury he invited me to go to London to see a theatre show with him. I was of course utterly ignorant of the ways of the world and accepted his invitation. When I got to London and met him I found that he had booked a double room for the night in the Strand Palace Hotel. Well, to cut the story short, that night he lost control and made a physical assault upon me which I repulsed very firmly with expressions of disgust. I slept through the night in my bed alone. Ten days later there was a notice in the papers that a named person had committed suicide by putting his head on a railway line. Had I been the cause of a human being's death, one of God's creatures on this Earth? These and other such thoughts were with me then and have been since. It was a horrific psychological experience. But perhaps it was a very salutary experience for me before going up to King's College, Cambridge.[41]

Part Two

Cambridge 1919-1939

Undergraduate at King's

Of all the reigns in English history, that of King Henry VIth might be considered the most tragic and pathetic. Born to a glittering inheritance, Henry was crowned as an infant not only King of England in Westminster Abbey, but King of France in Nôtre Dame. But when he assumed power after a long minority it soon became clear that he had no skill or judgement as a ruler: worse still, he suffered bouts of insanity. Piece by piece the fabric of his kingdoms fell apart: France returned to the allegiance of its own royal house, while overmighty subjects laid claim to Henry's throne in England. Bullied by his barons, henpecked by his wife, the king was dragged unwillingly from one battlefield to the next while civil wars raged round him. Deposed and imprisoned, he was then restored as an uncomprehending puppet. Finally, he was dethroned for

King's College, Cambridge.

good and quietly murdered. Luckily, before the mayhem of his reign had taken root, he had founded, in 1440, a school for poor scholars at Eton and, the next year, a college at Cambridge where they could go on to study at the University. Surprisingly, his generous benefactions to these institutions were not irrevocably despoiled and the twin colleges grew over the centuries to become, contrary to their founder's wishes, the most exclusive educational establishments in England. In the case of King's, the College's prestige was particularly enhanced by a superb late 15th-century chapel which is by general consent one of the architectural marvels of Europe.

King's was governed by a self-electing group of academics, called Fellows, headed by a Provost, who was elected, usually from among the Fellows. The link with Eton was very strong and a large proportion of the 200 or so undergraduates were Old Etonians. Indeed, the Provost in Bertrand's time, Sir Walter Durnford, was a grandson of the legendary Headmaster of Eton, Dr Keate, and had himself been a housemaster at Eton. The Dean, responsible for the ecclesiastical life of the College, was Eric Milner-White, who, returning to King's from being a Senior Army Chaplain, introduced six weeks after the Armistice of November 11 1918 the Service of Nine Lessons and Carols from King's Chapel that has found its way into English national life. Many of the Fellows in 1919 were young and comparatively new. Oscar Browning, now in his eighties, had retired and his rooms had passed to John Sheppard who in many ways continued the Browning tradition. Bertrand Hallward would come under his influence, as well as that of F.E. Adcock and F.L. Lucas, two young and lively Classics dons.

At first, however, Bertrand did not take to King's. For one thing, he seemed absurdly young compared with many of those who, deprived of a university education by the War, returned to Cambridge to take up their studies. They were not only much older than Bertrand but they were, as he put it, 'men of wide experience of administration, command and often of danger. They were all determined at first to have a very good time. But they all had goals in front of them and before long they mostly settled down to get good degrees and they lived without financial anxiety on their war gratuity and post-war study allowances. I, on the other hand, arrived very young for a university student, a mere boy: and hence the sobriquet "the Babe".'[1]

Nor was Bertrand impressed with his rooms or his tutor.

> Although as a scholar of King's and therefore on the Foundation of King Henry VI and entitled to rooms in College, I was placed in dreadful rooms in Little St Edward's Passage with an appalling landlady, who even controlled the putting on of coal on my fire, which I was paying for. After

being a Prefect and rather grand at Haileybury, I was suddenly nobody, very bored, because my Classical tutor was Mr Sills, an utterly boring man, and I was very lonely. I bought sixpenny booklets on popular science and read widely in physics, chemistry, and biology but especially evolution, human physiology and medicine, sexual psychology, etc. I had realized that as a result of the extreme specialization in the sixth form at Haileybury there were vast oceans of human knowledge where I hardly understood the meaning of the great subject headings in scientific knowledge. Ever since then, through my life, I have been extremely thankful that I did this reading in this first nine months at Cambridge, because as a result I have had a much better general scientific awareness than most classical scholars and I have retained a very lively interest in the amazing new developments of science.[2]

It was during this rather forlorn and unhappy period at King's that Bertrand read two books which he felt at the time, and continued to feel throughout life, had a special message for him. One was George Eliot's *Romola*, not perhaps a great novel and certainly not her best work. Set in the fifteenth century, it tells the story of young Tito who is adopted by Baldassare as an orphan and grows up to be handsome and clever. However, the two are shipwrecked and Tito abandons his foster-father, believing him dead, and takes from him a purse full of jewels. He reaches Florence and, selling the jewels, gains a high position in society through his intelligence, good looks and fine clothes. He marries Romola, daughter of a distinguished scholar, but also deceives a simple country girl, Tessa, into believing him to be her husband. When Baldassare unexpectedly appears in Florence to claim his son and fortune, Tito denounces him as a madman. Finally, exhausted by a long swim in the Arno to escape a band of ruffians, Tito crawls ashore only to be strangled by Baldassare, the last act of a half-demented old man thirsting for revenge. The simple message, that good looks and high intelligence can pervert the soul, struck home with Bertrand. So too may have lines like 'For where could a handsome young scholar not be welcome? That bright face, that easy smile, that liquid voice, seemed to give life a holiday aspect. Here was a professor likely to render the Greek classics amiable to the sons of great houses.'[3]

The second book had an even more startling relevance to Bertrand. It was Oscar Wilde's *The Picture of Dorian Gray*. Dorian Gray is young, handsome, and the darling of London society. He is painted by a fashionable portrait painter, and takes the picture home. He then embarks on a life of wickedness, and as sin piles upon sin, so the portrait changes with time to reveal an ugly, evil old man yet Dorian Gray himself remains eternally young. Finally, he murders the painter in front of the portrait and has his body cut up in pieces and dissolved in acid. And what is the painter's name? — Basil Hallward! This shocked Bertrand into some genealogical research. 'I found out that my father's first cousin Reginald Hallward, who had been at the Slade, had been a rising painter, living on the edge of London, and a family friend of Oscar Wilde (they were both married, with children) at the time Wilde wrote the book. Oscar Wilde quite simply used the Hallward surname with a new Christian name.'[4] This theory has been corroborated by the actress Gloria Grahame, who, despite her name and a starring role in the film version of *Oklahoma!* (I'm just a girl who Cain't say No!), was in fact born Gloria Hallward, the grand-daughter of Reginald. In a novel about her last few months entitled *'Film Stars don't die in Liverpool'* she is quoted as saying: 'My father's father was a painter and a great friend of Oscar Wilde. He suggested the whole idea of the story to Wilde, about the picture ageing and the beautiful boy remaining young, so Wilde called the artist in the book Basil *Hallward*, which was my grandfather's name.'[5]

Two powerful stories of particularly handsome young men falling prey to the darker side of human nature were taken by Bertrand as an unequivocal message. 'Certainly these two books read at this period of loneliness and lack of success had a profound effect upon me in the nature of a moral warning. Looking back, I can't help feeling that it was an inspired warning. I am very grateful for it.'[6] Throughout his teaching life, one or other of these books was likely to crop up when he was discussing literature with pupils. Certain Clifton boys at Bude were sometimes told, rather to their astonishment, to go off to the library and read *Romola*.

With his classical work not going well, Bertrand turned to the sports field.

> It was the playing of regular games for the College which restored my confidence and happiness though I was still 'the Babe'. Games gave me many friends. In my second year I was Secretary and in my third Captain of Rugger and ditto in the Easter Term for hockey, and I even played sometimes at soccer where we had two Blues.
>
> All this playing of games and solving the problems of the Universe in each other's rooms with buttered muffins in front of the fire meant that I did no work. In the 'Mays' examination at the end of the first year I sat for three hours in front of a set of thirty lines of English verse to be turned into Greek iambics. I got panic and verbal blockage, sweated profusely, and produced at the end three verses. That did shake me to my foundations and I saw failure and loss of career prospects staring me in the face. I think too I wondered whether something of this kind happened in my father's career at King's before me. At any rate the warning was extremely

Bertrand Hallward as an undergraduate at Cambridge.

effective and I did work extremely hard in term and in the vacations for my next two years.[7]

In Bertrand's second year at King's he was persuaded by John Sheppard, the Fellow who had taken over Oscar Browning's rooms and was to become a legendary Provost in due course, to take the part of 'Apollo' in Sheppard's own adaptation of the *Oresteia* of Aeschylus. *The Sketch* (a national illustrated news magazine) reviewed the performance enthusiastically in its issue of March 9 1921:

> It was a bold idea to condense the *Oresteia* of Aeschylus into a single performance, but the Greek Play Committee at Cambridge carried it out courageously, with the result that the production at the New Theatre, acted in the original Greek by members of the University, must be acknowledged to be a success in every way. To condense the *Agamemnon*, *Choephoroe*, and *Eumenides* into one play means ruthless cutting; but the damage done by this is as nothing compared with the absurdity of acting one of the three plays without the others. Mr Armstrong Gibbs' music is a great feature of the production, and the cast — all male members of the University — gave a performance which, with the English verse translation, made it fairly easy for those not conversant with the language to follow the play.'[8]

Bertrand Hallward as Apollo in The Oresteia.

The Ladies' Field (another illustrated magazine) produced a series of photographs of some of the leading players, featuring B.L. Hallward as Apollo and G.W.H. Rylands as Electra.[9] *The Sketch* on March 16 went a little further with an article entitled *Cambridge Men as Grecian Women*, in which 'Dadie' Rylands features again. 'There were no women in the recent production of Aeschylus' Oresteian Trilogy', the caption runs, 'but as our page shows, the University men made dignified and handsome Grecian women, and wore their classic draperies with almost feminine grace.'[10] Sheppard, if anything, flaunted his homosexual tastes and it is very likely that 'Dadie' Rylands and 'The Babe' Hallward were the centre of much attention and gossip in King's. In fact Bertrand had to say comparatively little in the play, but he was expected to stand there and look god-like. This was enough, recalled Bertrand, to bring 'one or two strange letters and invitations. However, by now I knew how to deal with this.'[11]

In his history of King's College, Patrick Wilkinson writes: 'No doubt many Kingsmen who were up between the Wars would protest that they never came across the homosexuality so often alleged. But the fact remains that in (some) circles at least, it was a constant topic both of serious discussion and of gossip. By now it had ceased to have any moral overtones. In the general absence of women in the 'twenties homosexual affairs were natural and common, and passionate relationships were accepted and sympathetically regarded by the friends of those concerned. Of course, there was much jealousy and heart-burning; but in the end most of the participants got married, often soon after going down. It was the same in ancient Greece.'[12]

Indeed the Greek example of platonic friendship, especially between older and younger men, is the key to Bertrand Hallward's crucial relationships with two bachelor dons at King's, F.E. Adcock and A.C. Pigou, both of whom influenced his life greatly, one as an academic, the other as a mountaineer. Bertrand's recollections of Pigou are reproduced here in full from his *Memoirs* because, apart from being informative and entertaining, they are important historical evidence for mountaineering enthusiasts.

> Professor A.C. Pigou, the Professor of Political Economy, to give him his full title, had a beautiful house called Lower Gatesgarth, which he had built at the northern end of Buttermere Lake, where he organized male climbing parties. He was known to us as 'the Prof', and was a quite extraordinary figure. His handwriting only one typist at Miss Pate's could decipher. His mind was so brilliant that it was said that in competitions between fellowship dissertations, his short summary of judgement, what-ever the subject of the dissertation, often proved decisive amongst the

electors. His dress might have been that of a 'down and out', an old tattered sports coat and the inside stuffing of his tie dangling outside; gym shoes with the toe area often slit to make them comfortable.

He invited me to Buttermere to join climbing parties with Willie McLean many times, and then we went for five summers to the Alps (Willie and I as his guests), to climb mountains. I was able to apply for membership of the prestigious Alpine Club and wear its AC button. In order to secure election you had to put forward a fairly stiff record of major climbs and Pigou was our leader in all this.

He was not a natural athlete, but he brought his formidable powers of mind to bear upon the task of mastering the essentials of rock climbing and mountaineering. His friend Philip Baker had been with him when he was learning the techniques. But what was quite exceptional about him was his decision to form his climbing parties from callow undergraduates giving them intensive training opportunities on Scafell, Great Gable and the Pillar by frequent visits to his house, Lower Gatesgarth, Buttermere. And there were Easter chances of exposure to snow and ice conditions with an ice axe in Great End Gully and elsewhere. What is interesting to me is the speed with which we learnt a modicum of competence in rope work, belaying, rappelling and all the arts of the climber. Pigou always gave complete trust to you in your job for the moment, and I remember being amazed to find myself quite soon last on the rope in a descent in charge of securing the safety of the party. All this was of course much frowned upon by the Alpine Club! There was one other similar case of a Winchester master who took boys with him on the mountains.

The Alpine expeditions were planned and financed by Pigou and the route-finding was his concern as leader, since he had mastered the available text books with the detailed Alpine maps, but as leader he would always accept questions and suggestions in the route finding. His method of climbing was always very careful, methodical and safe. I never saw or heard of him slip. No party of his in my time had an accident.

I must now recall that the general conditions of climbing and mountaineering in those years 1920-1925 were very similar to the early great days of Mummery, Whymper and Geoffrey Young in the Victorian and Edwardian periods when Britain largely invented and pioneered the sport. We had a rope, of course. Boots were shod with turn-over hob-nails though tricounis were coming in and crampons for ice work. Gym shoes were always carried in the sack and worn for slab work on dry rock. Helmets were unknown and all the modern ironmongery, pitons, carabiners, slings, etc., etc. The fundamental point is that the leader had to lead each pitch to the full extent of that pitch with his rope, descending to his Number 2, who would have a good belay on a medium standard climb. But the leader *must never fall*, since the extent of his fall in these conditions is obvious.

Conquest of fear, self-confidence and development of personality are achieved and of course it is immensely adventurous and exciting especially in the dark with a fitful moon. You are also very close to Nature, often literally clinging desperately to Her. Mountaineering indeed builds toughness by exposure to adverse and often painful weather conditions and the exercise of good judgement to determine when to turn back. It is carried out in a group which fosters reliance and trust in each other. But its claim as a training of character is universally accepted. Hence the epigram *Great things are done when men and mountains meet*. To sum up, it was athletic vigour and skill, a considerable spice of danger, some of it more apparent than real, exposure to the grandness and wildness of Nature in all weathers, the strange romance of getting to the top, conquering peak after peak. Only mountaineers know the subtle addiction of that sport. Mountaineering became almost a religion to me.

It is fitting that I should conclude this tribute to Pigou by the statement that I was with him through a 'night out' on the *Mer de Glace* near Chamonix when he had a heart attack and fibrillation. He lived on for many years and died at over 80 but never climbed again. He passed his climber's mantle first to Tom Gaunt and then to the famous Wilfred Noyce whose expeditions he partly financed. My own Alpine expeditions included *Mt. Blanc*, the *Matterhorn*, *Aiguille D'Argentière*, *Mt. Combin*, *Becca d'Invergnan*, and the traverse of the *Grepon*; *Charmoz* and *Blaitière*, but there were a great many others in five seasons climbing. It has left a wonderful set of memories.[13]

While Arthur Pigou was developing the 'whole man' in Bertrand, Frank Adcock kept his mind on his classical studies. Born in 1886, Adcock attended the local grammar school at Wyggeston in Leicestershire where he proved so brilliant as a classical pupil that all thought of his entering the family pork pie business was abandoned and he won a scholarship at King's instead. He was not overawed by the place. He found that the Fellows 'were at ease with us, yet securely our betters'. The Head Porter 'knew his place and kept us in ours', while the undergraduates were 'highly varied and permitted to be varied, and no one looked askance at our vagaries.'[14] He got a top double First in Classics, and won the Craven Scholarship, the Chancellor's Medal and the Craven Studentship — all glittering prizes. Off he went to Berlin where he apparently astonished his colleagues by translating Thucydides into German at sight. In 1911 he was elected a Fellow of King's and Lecturer in Classics, and in 1915 he was chosen for naval intelligence work in the Admiralty, where his success in breaking German codes and cyphers won him the OBE in 1917. According to his memorialist and colleague Patrick Wilkinson, 'After the Armistice his mastery of the German language and the esoteric knowledge he had acquired were put to most appropriate and gratifying use, when he was sent, with the temporary rank of Lieutenant-Commander (in full dress uniform, as tradition alleged) to help receive the surrender of the German Submarine fleet. He was to maintain agreeable contacts with the world outside Cambridge in future years through membership of the Savile Club in London, and to travel first-class for the rest of his life.'[15] In 1925, aged 39, he was appointed Professor of Ancient History at Cambridge, a post he held until 1950, and he was knighted in 1954.

Returning to King's from his encounter with the German submarine fleet, Adcock resumed his practice of inviting Kingsmen to read Greek plays in his rooms after Hall on Mondays, and it was here that he encountered Bertrand and realized his academic capabilities. Bertrand, in turn, was impressed: 'One of the best pieces of distinguished classical education in its best sense was Adcock's Greek Play-Reading Society in his large rooms on Sunday evenings in which we all took parts to read. And there was often a strange mixture of pronunciation.'[16] This is a reference to the fact that Adcock was not only a north countryman, but had trouble with his 'r's'. 'Off to chapel then?' this son of a Methodist family is alleged to have demanded of passing undergraduates. 'There lies the woad to Wome.'[17] Bertrand's role as Apollo in Sheppard's production made him appreciate the producer's scholarship also. 'I had been to one or two of his lectures on Homer but had thought them flawed, emotional and based upon brilliant rhetorical acting. But to listen to his explanation and acting of line by line of my part as Apollo, was a revelation of ripe, superb scholarship.'[18]

Bertrand's poor performance in the exams at the end of his first year was not particularly important because these did not count towards his degree. The Classical 'Tripos' was a three-year course divided into two parts. Part One required the ability to compose a great deal of prose and verse and to read widely over the whole range of Greek and Latin. Part Two was mainly concerned with a number of options, including Ancient History. In the last two years at Cambridge — though he did not abandon his sporting interests — Bertrand worked very hard, certainly to the exclusion of social engagements. 'I'm having some girls to tea on Sunday; will you come?', his friend Graham Doggart would ask. 'Too dangerous, I'm too susceptible, I must get my first', came the reply. 'What a prig I was, you ladies must think', concedes Bertrand. 'But what a wise prig! First things first. Career before everything else. Also in those days your chance of attracting a desirable girl depended a great deal upon your prospects of a career. Or certainly I thought it did.'[19] The strategy worked, and he gained a first class in Part One of the Tripos in 1921 and a first class with distinction in Part Two the next year.

Towards the end of his time as an undergraduate Bertrand's mind had naturally turned to the question of a career. One of his contemporaries at King's was Gordon Selfridge who suggested he might like to work for his family's famous Oxford Street store. 'I knew nothing whatever about Industry, Commerce or Finance and was, as far as I can remember, tickled at the idea of Selfridge's but hardly regarded it as the compliment which it was.'[20] His father advised him against the Indian Civil Service and it was thought that a private income of £400 p.a. was necessary for the Diplomatic Service, so the Home Civil Service seemed the answer. Teaching was a real possibility, however, and an opening arose when Lionel Ford, the Headmaster of Harrow, dined at King's on Founder's Day in 1922, interviewed Bertrand the next day and offered him a job as a master at Harrow. He accepted in principle but explained that he could not take up the post for at least a year because he had applied for the one year's Studentship at the British School of Archaeology at Athens. Adcock had recommended him strongly for this because, as far as Adcock was concerned, Bertrand was going to be a Cambridge don lecturing in Adcock's speciality, Ancient History. Therefore he needed experience of the archaeology of Ancient Greece. In the end Bertrand spent six months in Greece, which he found exceptionally beneficial. 'I could write a whole essay about it,' he states in his *Memoirs*, but confines himself to a relatively short, but illuminating description.

> I travelled with Harold Cohen to Greece at the beginning of September and it was characteristic of me to have planned our start in Greece by climbing Mt. Parnassus. We stayed the first night in a monastery on the lower slopes and crossed the many ridges and alternative summits of the plateau the next day, coming down to Arachova near Delphi picking ripe grapes along the track near dusk. The main thing I remember is the huge size of the mountain, its extreme aridity and wildness, and the vast numbers of savage dogs with hardly any shepherds to prevent them attacking you or to call them off. I had heard that surrounded by two, three or four dogs you pick up fairly large stones, two at a time, throw one in the air which the dogs look at and then score a bull's eye with the other. But it was not so easy; and the savage barking dogs with red fangs were fairly intimidating. There had been a story of a student torn to pieces. There were no views at all. I can't say that I enjoyed it except in the sense of Noel Coward's 'mad dogs and Englishmen go out in the midday sun'. We had crossed Parnassus (8061 ft). Next day our first visit to Delphi topped every

expectation. Here was what we had come to Greece to see, to explore and to study. We returned by bus to Athens and found the British School open but not yet in session. There had been a typical Greek political revolution with politicos murdered. Harold Cohen's father had sent a series of telegrams enquiring about our safety to which there had been no replies. We were not popular.

However the American School of Archaeology which is adjacent with an equally fine garden, tennis court and splendid building had begun its session. Professor Blegen was about to lead a party of sixteen American students on a tour of the Peloponnese in two motor vans. Harold Cohen went home to placate his father and I was invited by Blegen to join the Peloponnese expedition. It was certainly for me an extraordinary experience. The party was mixed, male and female, from southern and northern states of America, with the fiercest political disagreements. The Civil War was fought every evening, which makes me so pleased to have an Honorary Degree at Chattanooga University. It was my first total social immersion and adult boy/girl baptism. I learned a lot about America and about male and female. At the same time we visited some intensely interesting archaeological sites with Blegen's superb lecturing in his quiet unemphatic voice. I admired his beautifully fluent and idiomatic Modern Greek. It was my exceptional chance to watch closely for a fortnight a man, who is acknowledged today to have been amongst the very great Greek archaeologists. His excavations produced the Linear B tablets which Ventris deciphered and we gained a completely new view of Mycenaean bureaucratic and political organization.

In my first six months in Greece I did a large amount of touring on foot using trains and buses, often with the invaluable copy of Frazer's *Pausanias* in my rucksack. I had no narrow project of research to pursue and as a result gained a wide first hand knowledge of the topography and ancient sites of Mainland Greece which has been very valuable for me ever since. And I learned quite a lot of Modern Greek staying nights in the villages.[21]

During his time at the British School at Athens Bertrand wrote many letters to his father, several of which have been preserved. In February 1923 he wrote to thank him for a telegram with the news that his brother Philip had been commissioned in the Border Regiment, and he was sad to hear that his grandmother was seriously ill and not expected to live. He also indicated that his sights were now more clearly set on an academic career. 'I'm working up especially a period of History, 4th cent. in Thessaly, the tyrannies of Jason and Lycophron and Alexander of Pherae ... If I can make a success of it I hope perhaps to send it in as a fellowship dissertation. There is very interesting coin evidence for the period and a considerable amount of inscriptional evidence to be picked up from various sources. Not much has been done on it so far and what there is, is in German. So I'm faced with the imperative necessity of learning German, and I think I shall almost certainly go to Vienna for two or three months from May to August and work there. Professor Wilhelm there is very Anglo-phile and has a fine archaeological and classical library and is a friend of Adcock's.'[22]

Before he left Athens for his journey to Vienna Bertrand wrote to his father on May 6th 1923 with some more interesting news about career prospects. 'Must tell you, I have received through an usher at Eton (a great friend of mine at Cambridge) what practically amounts to an offer of a post on the staff there from the Headmaster Alington. For a year I can imagine nothing more tempting as I have so many friends there and have become greatly imbued with Eton spirit. The chance of the VIth form at Eton or part of its work was an additional line in the bait since at Eton Classics is very flourishing and the standard extremely high. Apparently [his friend] mentioned that Ford was offering me a job at Harrow and Alington immediately pricked up his ears and said he could write and tell me that if I was prepared to consider it he might quite likely be able to offer me a job there in September. Astute move of his, trading on the traditional rivalry!'[23] However, Bertrand had given his word to Lionel Ford and was intending to keep it.

The journey to Austria went without hitches. 'I travelled to Vienna with stops at Troy and in Gallipoli, several days in Constantinople and then by a steamer up the Danube through the Iron Gates and three days each in Bucharest and Budapest. In Vienna I lived in a pension with entirely German speaking occupants. I joined the English Seminar in the University. There were weekend expeditions into the beautiful wooded country surrounding Vienna and even-ings listening to Wagner's Ring in the cheap Volksoper with an electric torch and the libretto. I got on fast with my German and much enjoyed this self-education in the language and culture of this wonderful centre of European musical and artistic riches. At the end I went with an Austrian student to the mountains and we climbed the Gross Glockner and one or two other peaks. I was a better rock climber than he was and I thought at times he might fall off because he had much too heavy a sack.'[24]

A letter to his father in July, before he left Austria, was able to convey something of Bertrand's grasp of the German language. 'I went for a long walk with Professor Wilhelm, perhaps the best living Epigraphist — he was fifteen years in Athens and speaks English absolutely perfectly. Very interesting man to talk to as he was an intimate friend of the highest families in the realm during the monarchy and is consequently monarchical in sentiments. His views were an amazing illustration of the tremendous and continuous influence of Prussian Militarism even here in Austria. As another Austrian actually said to me "Es liegt im Blut die Weltherrschaftlust". The Viennese however on the whole have very little of the German character, it seems to me — a good bit of laissez faire about them. One of the students I've talked to said "In England ist alles erlaubt das nicht verboten ist — In Deutschland ist alles verboten das nicht erlaubt ist — In Wien ist alles erlaubt das verboten ist!"'[25]

Reflecting on this journey many years later, Bertrand was in no doubt as to its value. 'Looking back of course I can see how much I revelled in the new freedom which the Parker of Waddington University Studentship plus the British School Studentship gave me to plan and carry out this varied programme of useful self-education. In the eighties and nineties universal travel for the young has become commonplace, but in the twenties it was not so. I was amongst the fortunate by winning these awards. But I must note in amused self-revelation, which must seem extraordinary to our own more recent times, that there is no mention whatever of girls, or mixed parties with girls or of taking girls out to this or to that. And indeed I have left out nothing in my account. I lived a girl-less life and was happy in it, nor was I making up for this deprivation by special male friendships. Life was just so full to the brim with travel, learning German, exposure to great music, reading and reading, that loneliness, the want of the other never reached me. It may be that this was rather a good learning, studying, way of life. There were certainly no distractions.'[26]

By August Bertrand was in Switzerland for the annual Alpine climbs with Pigou, and it was there that a fateful letter reached him. On the eighth of July he wrote in high excitement to his father from the Hotel Montanvent in Chamonix: 'I must plunge at once to give you the really remarkable piece of news I have just received — a much travelled letter four times re-addressed from Peterhouse, Cambridge, with the offer of a Lectureship in Classics at that College.' He then went on to quote the letter of Paul Vellacott, Senior Tutor of Peterhouse. 'I do not know if you have ever met Mr H.J. Edwards who was our Classics Lecturer. In any case, you may not have heard of his rather sudden death about a month ago. It has occurred to us that you might consider the position of Classical Lecturer at this College if we on our side were able to offer it to you.' There then followed details about conditions and emoluments. 'Now I am aware that you are engaged to go to Harrow next term', Vellacott went on. 'It does not seem to me that this must preclude you from considering the suggestion I am making, if you are inclined on other grounds to consider it.'

Not surprisingly, Bertrand was somewhat astounded. 'The financial part of it of course for a man of only 22 — £700 p.a. with part income tax free, with rooms and dinners in a rather charming little College — well one can only gape,' he confided to his father. 'It would mean, I gather, a sole and free hand in the direction of the Classics in the College. It would give me a lot of time during the vacs to work up into something perhaps respectable the results of this year. And lastly from this position I should be certainly able to apply direct for the headmastership of a public school if I desired to. More than one of the most recent appointments of this sort to very big schools have been made direct from dons.'[27]

What is interesting about this letter is the extent to which a young man on the threshold of his first job is already thinking of school headships rather than a permanent university career. He goes on. 'The question is the future offered: in Classics *qua* Classics I am not sufficiently *totus in illo* to think of seeking the highest honours of Professorships: on the other hand it may be I could be a successful lecturer or coach and there would be plenty of openings for College administrative posts perhaps.' He wanted to have a long talk with his father before committing himself but in the end it was agreed by all parties that, though his election as a Fellow dated from 1923, he would take up the post at Peterhouse in October 1924. Meanwhile, he would fulfil his pledge to Lionel Ford by teaching at Harrow for the Easter and Summer terms of that year.

Harrow School resulted from the generosity of John Lyon, a local merchant, who provided the money to build an endowed grammar school for local boys in 1571, at a time when many such schools were founded in England under the influence of Renaissance scholars. Although always one of the 'great' schools, it was only during the headmastership of Dr Vaughan in the first half of the 19th century that it became extremely fashionable. The linking of Eton and Harrow in the popular mind through the famous annual cricket match at Lord's gradually gave Harrow an edge over other rivals to Eton's pre-eminence, such as Winchester, Westminster and Rugby, and Harrow educated more than its share of aristocratic and even royal pupils. When Bertrand arrived there in January 1924 it was a school of some 800 boys, scattered about 'The Hill', yet centred on the famous 16th-century schoolroom of John Lyon.

In view of the fact that he was committed to leaving for Peterhouse after two terms, Bertrand's time at Harrow was seen by both sides as an arrangement of convenience. For him it provided an interesting experience and some money to tide him over; for the school it provided an able young man who could fill in some temporary gaps. His own account of these, his only two terms as an assistant master, runs as follows:

I arrived at Harrow in January 1924 and found that I was to teach the
bottom form of all as form master. Lionel Ford was Headmaster. He had
been good at Repton, especially with his grasp of finance and skill at
attracting good parents and good boys to the school. At Harrow he
seemed to me to be losing grip. Some masters and senior boys would
deliberately turn the other way and fail to recognize each other as they
caught the fast train at 6.15 pm to Baker Street, changing into evening
dress on the way. And these boys had no difficulty in climbing into their
houses when they returned to Harrow, perhaps because it was winked at
in the general atmosphere.

I must have been a very bad form master. After I left, a candid
colleague when asked to relate what the boys of my form said of me as
their master, said, 'Mr Hallward talked a great deal but we only understood about a half of what he said.' However I still remember one success.
I set two alternative subjects for an essay, 'Your favourite sport', and
'Buddha'. I still recall the exceptional account of the sport of skiing by
Jimmy Riddell who later became champion skier of Great Britain. The
other essay was even more remarkable on Buddha by Prince Chula, who
later lost the throne of Siam, later Thailand, by marrying a very beautiful
English girl. In his autobiography he has left an amusing picture of his
form master at Harrow. I also taught an upper fifth class of elderly lags
determined to do no work. Amongst them was a son of the Headmaster
who in the summer term was on the edge of the cricket XI. I'm afraid it
appeared to us younger masters that there was some improper pressure
from the heights above to secure his inclusion in the side to play at Lord's.
The school was really ruled by the great housemasters. Kittermaster and
Inky Stevens are two names I remember. And one particular dinner party
in a House at which the host addressed us as we waited for dinner in tones
of portentous seriousness, 'I have five new boys and not one of them can
hold a bat straight'. This might be taken as a text-book passage to illustrate
the games idolatry of the public schools. So much playing of games has
meant that we have not worked so hard in our school years as the Germans
and the French. The British weekend is another sign of a less naturally
industrious race.[28]

The 'amusing picture of his form master' comes from Prince Chula's autobiography *The Twain have Met*. 'Having obtained low marks for Latin in the
Entrance Exam,' he writes, 'I was placed in the lowest form but one; the form-
master who was also in his first term was B.L. Hallward, a brilliant young man
just down from Cambridge who left the following term to be a don and later
Headmaster of Clifton. He took infinite pains with me, especially with the so-

called English essays, which I had to write for him every Saturday night, and if I have been able to write English at all I owe much to him.'[29] School histories of Harrow corroborate the view that towards the end of Ford's time discipline began to sag: he left in 1925 to become Dean of York. Though Bertrand (and others) found him 'a pompous Headmaster' he had done a great deal for Harrow in numerous ways, not least in overseeing the construction of the War Memorial Building begun in 1921 and completed in 1926. It would not be the last time that Bertrand would watch, day-by-day, the growth of a large and important institutional building.

Fellow of Peterhouse

'King's College was a very superior and in fact snobbish College,' Bertrand admitted, 'and we undergraduates of King's thought that Peterhouse was a small College of lower status.'[1] It was nevertheless a good deal older than King's — indeed the oldest College at Cambridge, founded in 1284 by Hugo de Balsham, Bishop of Ely. Over the centuries it acquired some fine buildings including the ancient Hall, the Perne Library, the 17th-century chapel and the early 18th-century Master's Lodge, one of the gems of Cambridge architecture. There was also a charming garden, and though King's could certainly boast more grandeur, Peterhouse was nevertheless, by the twentieth century, a venerable and distinguished seat of learning. Like other Cambridge colleges it enjoyed a great deal of independence within the University. Governed by a self-electing body of Master and Fellows, it admitted its own undergraduates and was responsible for their welfare and tuition. It made its own appointments internally and was responsible for the College properties and endowments. In 1923 a Royal Commission was set up to inquire into the affairs of Cambridge University and new statutes for Peterhouse came into effect in 1926. They required any future Master to retire at the age of 70 and regulated the number and stipends of Fellows as well as scholars and exhibitioners. Just after the end of the War the College led the fashion for selling agricultural land which it had owned, in some cases, for centuries. At the time of the sale high prices were realized, though in a few years agricultural depression set in. The College was also lucky to be able to make money on its lands at Cherry Hinton, which became a new Building Estate. As a result of all this the College income and especially the Scholarship Fund was in a very healthy state when Bertrand Hallward took up his fellowship in 1924.[2]

That very year saw a change in the Master's Lodge when the venerable Sir Adolphus Ward died in June at the age of 87. The ten Fellows then proceeded to consider who should succeed him. As Bertrand had been elected a Fellow in 1923 he took part in the election of the new Master even though he was still

Peterhouse, Cambridge. Photograph by Martin Golding.

finishing the summer term at Harrow. Naturally he followed the lead of his seniors, especially Paul Vellacott, who was rapidly establishing himself as the guiding hand in Peterhouse affairs. A former scholar of the College, Vellacott returned as a Fellow in 1919 after a distinguished war record. As Tutor and Lecturer in History it was his ambition to advance the reputation of the College in all respects, and especially in History. It was he who had written to Bertrand with the offer of a fellowship (doubtless advised by Adcock and others at King's); another of his protégés was the equally youthful Herbert Butterfield, elected a Fellow (in History) at the same time as Bertrand, and at a similar age. The man who emerged as the new Master after the deliberations of the conclave of Fellows early in July was Robert, first Baron Chalmers of Northiam.

Thought by some to be the most pompous man in England after Lord Curzon, Chalmers came to Peterhouse after a varied and distinguished career during which he had held such posts as Chairman of the Board of Inland Revenue, Governor of Ceylon, Joint Secretary to the Treasury and Under-Secretary for Ireland. He was, according to *The Times*, 'the first peer to be elected head of any College at either Oxford or Cambridge.'[3] The undergraduates at Peterhouse soon produced a jingle that summed him up nicely:

> Last but not least, the cat's pyjamas
> Our venerable oriental Grand Cham Chalmers.[4]

Bertrand liked him, all the same, and certainly during his seven years in office Chalmers made sure that the College was run efficiently and with sound financial sense.

In the early 'twenties Peterhouse was a relatively small community with only ten Foundation Fellows and 126 undergraduates.[5] Bertrand was the only Classics Fellow, and there were at first only about eight undergraduates reading his subject. He settled down in his bachelor rooms at the top of G staircase over the Perne Library to contemplate his duties for the forthcoming academic year. These would consist of giving tuition to Peterhouse classicists in the basic prose and translation work for Part One and in Ancient History for any who chose that option in Part Two. He was not yet a *University* lecturer and his first ambition was to prove himself suitable to that post, which would give him status within the entire University as well as within Peterhouse. So there was much to be done.

However, there were distractions. Not only did he throw himself heart and soul into the sporting life of the College and University, but his attention had focused upon the grand-daughter of the Master of St Catharine's College, a slim, self-possessed, dark-haired girl called Margaret Tait. Six months older than Bertrand, Margaret was the daughter of Canon Arthur Tait, Principal of Ridley Hall, and Jane Drury. Her mother's father had been Bishop of Sodor and Man, then Bishop of Ripon, and in 1920 he was elected Master of St Catharine's. Because he was a widower, he asked Margaret to be his hostess in the Master's Lodge from 1923 onwards, and it was in the social circles of College life that Bertrand and Margaret came to know each other well during 1925. A strong link already existed between them because Margaret's younger brother George had been two years below Bertrand in Thomason House at Haileybury. Margaret and her sister Alice had caught the eye of Hilary Macklin, an undergraduate at St John's College who kept a diary of his Cambridge years. 'Margaret was looking awfully pretty in a blue dress with a white fur which showed off her dark hair to perfection,' he wrote in May Week, 1922. 'By God, Tait is lucky in his sisters; both are perfectly topping.'[6] In fact it was upon Alice that his affections eventually settled while Margaret, after quite a lengthy courtship, became engaged to Bertrand in June 1926.

It was a match of opposites; Bertrand robust, fair, highly intellectual and out-going, Margaret slight, dark, educated at home, reserved. Yet it was a love match, and remained so through sixty-four years of married life. 'You may not be surprised to hear', wrote Margaret to her elder sister Alice, 'that I am engaged to Bertrand, and oh my dear what a consuming thing it is to be in love. Of course I am just incredibly happy, in fact I have found it difficult to believe it's all true. On Saturday I went up to London with him for the day to see the Australians and it came off in the car on the way home. He says he has been contemplating it for months and it's not just the result of May Week! About plans, he is terribly anxious to be married in September, as ever is! Although I am sure of myself, it would be rushing things a bit, but from his point of view I quite realize the sooner the better as the sooner he will be able to settle down to his work, etc. At the moment he is so terribly head-over-heels that I fear he finds it difficult to do much.'[7]

The marriage was fixed for September 2nd, even though some very rapid planning had to be done and the Drury side of the family was affronted that the date fell just inside the six-month mourning period for Margaret's grandfather Bishop Drury, the Master of St Catharine's, who had died earlier in the year. As a result four Drury aunts and two Drury uncles did not attend the wedding. Moreover, with the ending of the summer term at Cambridge Bertrand went off on a cycling holiday in Sicily which had been arranged the year before with the brilliant young King's don F.L. Lucas (known as 'Peter') and which, nearly seventy years later, Bertrand still remembered well.

> We hired bicycles in Palermo and using the railway system which circles the whole of the island we cycled round most of it, almost entirely long ups and often steep downs. It is certainly not ideal cycling country. But we accomplished it with much sweat and some cursing and questioning why we had chosen this method. There were plenty of opportunities for swimming which alone saved one's life in the heat. I shall not attempt to pick out our favourite resting places or visits to classical sites. The fact is that the beauty of Sicily is incomparable and a revelation to the young impressionable mind. My memory is stored with images.
>
> In contrast Peter's exceptionally brilliant mind was often in his most characteristic mood of utter pessimism. 'The desert disillusion of the too intelligent', was the epigrammatic phrase which I remember. He had overworked to complete his edition of Webster's Plays with commentary and he said, 'I will never do such a thing again'. It had been slavery. And certainly his mind was more attuned to writing such charming books as *In the Mountains of Greece* or his definitive book on Greek Tragedy. He was much under the influence of French literature and in particular Proust and he was full of the new psychological theories of the Unconscious. I could not begin to keep up with him in all this, Thank Heaven! We ended our tour in Catania where my brother Philip joined us for an ascent of Mt. Aetna. At that time there was no road except up the lowest slopes and it was a very long way up rough loose cinder tracks with a portion of snow slope at the top and peering over the cliffs into the smoking Hell was intensely dramatic. My brother Philip began to wilt much further down

and I am not sure whether he ever got to the top. Peter showed his extraordinary wiry strength and quickly outpaced me to arrive first at the top. As a trained mountaineer I was much impressed by his far greater stamina in these conditions. The view was nothing because of smoke and cloud. But we had done it. As I look back I think it a little strange that this should have given me such satisfaction. But it was part of the mountain madness of the age. 'If you see a mountain, it is a challenge, and you must climb it!'[8]

By the time Bertrand returned, sun-tanned, from Sicily, details of the wedding had been finalized. The ceremony would take place on September 2nd 1926 in Holy Trinity Church Cambridge, with the Revd. Professor W.E. Barnes officiating, assisted by Canon Edward Woods, the vicar. Bertrand's brother Philip would be best man, Margaret's chums Maisie Anderson and Alison Pollock would be bridesmaids, and the reception would be held afterwards in Ridley Hall. A nine page letter from Alison, written the day after the wedding, has survived to provide a detailed account of the great event, which was indeed a notable society wedding in Cambridge. 'The whole show went off splendidly', Alison thought, 'excepting for weather which was *too* awful. It poured with rain from 12.00 onwards solidly and it is still raining!!!' As for the bridegroom's family, his mother 'looked rather a dear, oldish but obviously was a very pretty woman in her younger days, lovely eyes with grey hair'; his father 'has a huge nose and is rather amusing but until you actually talk to him is apt to be a little alarming'; while Philip was a 'very smart, tall, straight Army-looking man with an amusing smile but unfortunately rather lacking in a sense of humour'. The bride looked '*too* adorable, long train reaching heavily to the ground and her hair looking just lovely. Her lace frock with full sleeves suited her admirably and they had hit off the length wonderfully'.

As Margaret was escorted to the altar by her father, 'Bertrand turned round and slightly bowed to her which was rather nice'. Canon Woods' 'harangue' was rather repetitive, it seems, and when the bridal party moved to the vestry to sign the Register there was much kissing all round. Fortunately Lord Chalmers came to sign the roll 'after most of the kissing was over, so we were spared that!' Then everyone piled into motor cars for the journey to Ridley Hall where there was a 'terrific squash of people'. Eventually the bridal pair left for their honeymoon in a car on whose hood 'awful things' had been written by the young wags present. 'Fortunately Philip had time to rub some of them off and I think the rain would very shortly do the rest', Alison concluded. [10]

The plans for the honeymoon were in theory idyllic: a week's rest in a gorgeous country house in Wiltshire followed by two weeks in the Pyrenees. In

The wedding of Bertrand Hallward and Margaret Tait, 1926.

his third year at King's and during the summer vacation which always included climbing with Pigou in the Alps, Bertrand had been spotted looking rather lost in Venice, Baedeker in hand, by an ex-Kingsman, Geoffrey Fry. Fry, a friend of Sheppard and a private secretary to Stanley Baldwin, enjoyed with his wife Alethea possession of a *palazzo* in Venice as well as a fine Georgian mansion at Oare, near Pewsey in Wiltshire. In Venice he had sent a gondola to rescue Bertrand and ask him to dinner in the *palazzo*, and a friendship was formed. Hearing now of Bertrand's marriage he had offered the Wiltshire house as a honeymoon retreat. A *Country Life* article of 1992 dwells with relish on the architectural charms of the house and the special beauty of its extensive gardens, but it was not a success as a honeymoon home.[11] It was too big, too unfamiliar, and Margaret was embarrassed by the constant presence of the servants, and the ribaldry of telegrams that arrived from her brothers George and Wortley.

However, the fortnight spent in a hotel in the mountain village of Gavarnie in the Pyrenees was a complete success. After a night crossing and a day in Paris visiting the Louvre and Versailles they reached Gavarnie where Margaret was soon introduced to the wonders of climbing. She wrote to her sister Alice on September 15th from the Club Alpin Français Refuge at Bayssellance, 2,670 metres up on Mont Vignemale: 'This morning we started at 10.00 am and

Margaret on her honeymoon in the Pyrenees.

arrived up here at 5.00 pm. The Vignemale is the highest peak in the Pyrenees — 11,000 feet. We have to cross a glacier and then do what B. calls Baby's rock climbing. I am pleasantly frightened by the prospect! ... I just can't tell you how wonderful the scenery is — I have never seen anything like it.'[12]

But October was approaching, and with it the beginning of another Cambridge academic year. Bertrand was able to rent from Peterhouse Number 4 Belvoir Terrace, an elegant Georgian-style house with a fine first-floor drawing-room and plenty of bedrooms. 'Though up and down with many stairs', Bertrand recalled, it 'was a large and comfortable house and not a suburban box. It was five minutes away from my work in Peterhouse on a bicycle. It was opposite to the Botanical Gardens and had a delightful walk across the Coe Fen to the Newnham Shops. Looking back one can see that we had a great many blessings. We were tremendously, miraculously in love, which did not wear off or grow stale, as the novelist likes to insist it must.'[13] Almost at once the joys and the responsibilities of parenthood were upon them. Three daughters, Ruth (1927), Catherine (1929) and Iola (1930) were born in rapid succession, though not without some distress to Margaret, as Bertrand recalled.

> There was first a period of four months when the newly married pair were asked out to dine (Margaret in her wedding dress by command) at Trinity Lodge (Lady Thomson), Peterhouse (Lord Chalmers) and St Catharine's; and then came the closure of social life — the gay Cambridge social life — pregnancy, babies, nappies. Indeed I approach the task of describing this

first period of my married life with Margaret with considerable misgiving. Because inevitably the mother who immediately has children at once after marriage (and Margaret had three children in less than four years) bears an immeasurably greater burden than her husband. First there was the change in her style of life from the security of her life at home to the new necessity of home-making on an exiguous income with this new partner. Then there were all the anxieties of the E.M. (expectant mother) as we laughingly called her and the terrible pains of child-bearing which were excessive for Margaret because with a small pelvis she had to have a frightening, old-fashioned method of induction to produce the child at 8 months and long periods of labour for the actual child-birth. All the children were born at home. Dr Canney, the Cambridge expert gynaecologist for difficult births, was clinically efficient but with no bedside manner and his favourite trusted midwife was to me a caution. She was determined to put me in my place, or one several places lower, indeed as low as she could achieve. At first we had teenage village girls to help with the children in washing and cleaning and it was only later that we had good nurses. Thinking back I marvel how Margaret coped because we had no granny able to take care of the children and she had no modern 'nappy-expert-husband'. Fortunately Margaret and the children kept well apart from the minor children's illnesses.[14]

*Number 4, Belvoir Terrace,
Cambridge.*

Engagement, marriage, the setting up of a home and preparation for parenthood were not the only things on Bertrand's mind in 1926. He was that year appointed a University Lecturer at Cambridge and it would be important for his reputation that his lectures should be well prepared, ready for the October term. Most daunting of all, however, was the fact that Adcock, now Professor of Ancient History, had recently taken over responsibility for editing the *Cambridge Ancient History*, an ambitious work planned to cover the entire field in many volumes. Several of these had already been published, and it was Adcock's task to invite classical scholars of proved worth to write chapters for the next volume (Volume VIII) on *Rome and the Mediterranean, 218 to 133 BC*. There were to be about a dozen contributors in all, including distinguished professors from France, Germany and the United States. Adcock, doubtless keen to advance his protégé's career, invited Bertrand to write chapters on the Second and Third Punic Wars, the story of Rome's continuing struggle with Carthage which included one of the best known episodes from this period of history, Hannibal's crossing of the Alps.

This was not a commission that an ambitious young don could possibly afford to turn down; on the other hand Bertrand was very young, completely inexperienced as an author, and far from being, as yet, an expert on the Punic Wars. He accepted the challenge and the deadlines involved but from now on, both at home and at his work, he was a very busy young man. A clash of interests soon developed when in the Easter vacation of 1927 Adcock offered to take Bertrand on a three week tour of historical sites in Italy relevant to the Punic Wars: again, this was something he could hardly refuse yet he was unhappy about leaving Margaret, who was expecting her first baby in July. Nevertheless, he duly set off with Adcock at the end of March 1927 on what is probably the best documented journey of his life because he wrote to Margaret almost every day, and more than a dozen of the letters have survived. Adcock, who was accustomed to style, had engaged a 'ruffianly driver' whom he 'scandalously overpaid'. They moved via Piacenza to Bologna and on to Rimini where Bertrand 'managed to inveigle FEA into loosening his tongue on the war and his part in the Secret Service'. On the way to Ravenna they encountered 'great preparations for tomorrow, the 8th anniversary of *Fascismo* — hundreds of small boys marching in fours, a sort of Fascist boy scout organization — a most fetching get-up all in black and puttees'.[15] At Foligno he received two letters from his wife and reported 'I can't tell the thrill of getting them — in the nape of the neck and the back of the spine! As we approached the P.O. I had been imagining all kinds of things which might prevent anything being there — and when I presented my card and the man without a murmur handed me two letters I got white with excitement. FEA meanwhile was sending with difficulty a telegram to Hoylake to wish good luck to the Varsity Golf Side.'[16] They moved south to Caserta and intended to reach Naples but had to turn back, defeated by bad roads. In the last few days, spent in and around Rome, Bertrand visited important battle sites such as the Caudine Forks and Lake Trasimene, 'where one of the chief battles of my Second Punic War was fought. Climbing up some height we came suddenly over a pass to a fairly delicate view of the lake in the early soft morning light before lake mists were quite free from the atmosphere — streaks of dark blue like a jagged saw across the waters where an uneasy breeze flickered — a sort of ethereal scene which made the thought of battles and war a devil's pastime, or a joke.'[17]

Bertrand wrote four chapters for this volume of the *Ancient History*: Chapter II deals with Hannibal's invasion of Italy, his passage over the Alps, and his victories at Trasimene and Cannae; Chapter III is concerned with the Roman general Scipio's invasion of Spain; and Chapter IV deals with his conquest of Spain and the conclusion of peace with Carthage after the battle of Zama. Chapter XV gives an account of the Third Punic War, in which the City of Carthage is conquered and destroyed. 'Buildings and walls were razed to the ground; the plough passed over the site and salt was sown in the furrows made', wrote Bertrand with a comparatively rare flourish.[18] Sixty years later, this assertion that the site of Carthage was sown with salt — something that was unquestioningly accepted at the time — was fanned into an academic controversy that enlivened Bertrand's ninth decade.[19] In general the chapters read well though the style is clearly that of one steeped in classical constructions. According to the judgement of distinguished scholars such as Professor Nicholas Hammond and Professor Frank Walbank the four chapters did their job well and have been the basic reading material for anyone studying the period. Bertrand himself drew heavily upon a recently published work, *Storia dei Romani*, by the distinguished Italian historian Gaetano de Sanctis, many of whose charts and maps were modified for use in the Cambridge volume which was published — to good reviews — in 1930. One of Bertrand's best paragraphs recounts the story of the founding of Carthage:

> To the modern world the very name of Carthage stands, and has long stood, as a symbol for mercantilism, for a State in which money was the first pre-occupation, and art or letters the last. Yet, by some curious chance, Carthage can claim one of the most famous and tragic figures in legend and literature. Greek authors, musing on the history of a city that had been so formidable a foe to Greek and Roman alike, demanded for her origin something more impressive than the silent growth of a trading port: if Rome had been the creation of a band of splendid adventurers fleeing

from an unjust ruler, Carthage too must have her saga. And so from the primitive native tradition of Elissa, refashioned by generations of later writers, there slowly grew up the romantic tale of Dido, Princess of Tyre, who had fled from the persecution of King Pygmalion, and with a few faithful followers reached Africa. Here, when she wished to buy land, the natives mockingly offered her as much as a cowhide could cover. To this she replied by cutting a cowhide into thin strips and so enclosed a space large enough to contain her new city; here she welcomed the wandering Trojan hero Aeneas, and here deserted by him stabbed herself to death on her pyre. As history the tale is worthless, a compost of legend, folk-lore, aetiological myth and cult practice, seasoned with the love interest so dear to the Hellenistic heart. In this form it might well have been the subject of an antiquarian chapter in Gellius, but it had the good fortune to be taken over by Virgil, and in his hands the passion and death of Dido was moulded into one of the great stories of the world, and Dido herself has become one of the imperishable names in literature.[20]

Although Bertrand's chapters in the *Cambridge Ancient History* were entirely successful and brought him considerable prestige as an authority on the Punic Wars, he did not particularly enjoy the toil of research and writing. Apart from an article on Cicero as a historian, published in the *Cambridge Historical Journal* in 1931, his scholarly writing ended here, though he was editor of the *Classical Quarterly* from 1935 to 1939. What he enjoyed most was teaching and lecturing, and also organization and administration, for which he had a natural flair. Perhaps this derived to some extent from his father who had often reminded him that 'an item misplaced is as good as lost'.

It is clear that he gave a lot of attention to the careful organization of the teaching of Classics in Peterhouse. One of his pupils, Frank Walbank, later Professor of Classics at Liverpool, wrote in 1994 a five-page article on Bertrand Hallward at Peterhouse, drawn from his own memories as an undergraduate between 1928 and 1932, and from research into College and University records. One feature that is revealed is the Hallward knack of spotting talent. 'Realizing the advantages to undergraduates of contact with a variety of teachers', Walbank recalled, Hallward 'habitually arranged for one or two outstanding young graduates from other colleges (or from Peterhouse itself) to share in the supervision especially of Part One undergraduates. Thus in 1928-1930 I was taught at various times by Walter Hamilton, later Headmaster of Rugby and Master of Magdalene, Donald Lucas, the brother of F.L. Lucas and later, like him, a Fellow of King's, and G.V.L. Heap, a Petrean who later became a lecturer in the University of Exeter.'[21] So buoyant were the numbers of classicists at

Peterhouse that in 1930 Bertrand was able to persuade the College to elect a second Fellow in Classics, Keith Guthrie.

According to Walbank's researches, 'an analysis of the class lists of the Classical Tripos for the period shows that during the years from 1923 to 1939 around 70 to 80 Peterhouse undergraduates came under the supervision and care of BLH, with an average 14 to 15 studying Classics in the College at any one time. Between them they came up with 34 firsts in Part One of the Tripos, and 14 in Part Two, a very commendable achievement. It is also worth noting that, no doubt stimulated by his teaching, a large number of these opted to take Group C (Ancient History) in Part Two of the Tripos.'[22] Bertrand also gave tuition in Ancient History to men from other colleges who had chosen Group C, which is how he first came into contact with Desmond Lee of Corpus and Nicholas Hammond of Clare, both of whom successively followed him at Clifton as Headmaster, not entirely by chance. Professor Walbank writes enthusiastically about Bertrand's 'immediate warmth and welcome, his obvious enthusiasm for Classics, and more important, the impression he gave of concern for his pupils'. 'BLH was a great communicator and inspirer', he recalled. 'He had a special gift of stirring up one's interest for the wide range of subjects in which he happened, at any particular time, to be interested. He would encourage one to leave the beaten track. To him I owe my original introduction to Clive Bell and Roger Fry, with subsequent routes into "Bloomsbury" and also into modern painting generally.'[23]

Bertrand found life as a Fellow of Peterhouse 'stimulating and very agreeable'. He dined in College five nights a week, where 'there was clever conversation at High Table, even alarming from Harold Temperley. I made no intimate friendships amongst the Fellows and felt no need of it, because I saw a great deal of Adcock, playing regular golf with him. The direction of the policy of the College was in the hands of the dominating Paul Vellacott whose administration was brilliant. I was never admitted to his inner circle and felt no wish to be.'[24] In 1931 Lord Chalmers retired as Master, which enabled Vellacott and the Fellows to play again the supreme Cambridge game of Elect-a-Head-of-House. This time their choice was thought by many in Cambridge to be bizarre, namely Field-Marshal Sir William Birdwood, a most distinguished soldier and a charming man, but certainly no academic. However, he made the transition 'from khaki to gown' very smoothly and certainly brought a fine-looking presence and sense of social distinction to Peterhouse — which was partly the aim of Vellacott and his circle. Vellacott had also been in uniform during the War and indeed chose to sit in his uniform for a portrait sketch which the artist Kenneth Green made in the late 'twenties of several Peterhouse Fellows. Green's pencil sketch of Bertrand is one of the best attempts by any artist to portray the

Hallward face and mood: in this case it is a thoughtful, slightly worried mood, as though the sitter had quite a lot on his plate, which in truth he had.

As far as Peterhouse was concerned, Bertrand had four main interests. The first was his Classics teaching. Next came his administrative duties as Steward (1924-26), Praelector (1926-31) and Tutor (1934-39). Then came his role as Treasurer of the College Amalgamated Sports Club which gave him overall responsibility for College sport. Under him a new boathouse was built in 1928, new playing fields were acquired from Trinity College in 1930, and a new sports pavilion was completed in 1933. Finally, from 1930 to 1939 he was Fellow in charge of gardens — a lifelong interest — and he discontinued the Deer Park in 1930 and laid out the Gisborne Court and Fen Court gardens towards the end of his time.

He also had a wide range of responsibilities within the University. He was Deputy Public Orator, Secretary of the Greek Play Committee, Librarian of the Classics Faculty Library, a member of the Faculty Board in Classics, a member of the Classical Archaeology Committee, and a member of the Appointments Committee of the History Faculty. He also, at various times, acted as examiner for both Part One and Part Two of the Classical Tripos. This brought him into contact with the formidable A.E. Housman, Kennedy Professor of Latin. According to Bertrand, Housman did a lot of damage to Cambridge Classics, making personal attacks on other scholars and specializing in clever, acid remarks which were often thinly disguised personal insults. At one examiners' meeting Housman requested Bertrand to come to the next meeting armed with 'a list of the more egregious blunders of the candidates'. Bertrand did produce a short list but it was nothing compared with Housman's. He was rather like a shy girl, Bertrand thought 'with a pink spot on each cheek'.[25]

In addition to all this, Bertrand confessed to 'a positive mania for physical exercise'.

> It became an addiction. There is no doubt that one of the reasons for this was that I got such great enjoyment from it. For three years after becoming a Fellow I played at weekends for the Old Haileyburian XV Rugby side in London and then I started and ran an MA Hockey XI and a Tennis VI to play against the Colleges each week. This I did entirely by myself by the use of the telephone. In cold winters there was English style figure skating on Madingly Pond with Charles Wright, Andrew Gow and Edward Woods, visits to an ice rink in London and superb skating with Margaret on Earith Fen. Margaret became quite good and we were able to Waltz together. I also played a lot of tennis singles at Fenners with Barry Kipping and others and later captained the County Tennis VI. Squash and real

A pencil sketch of Bertrand Hallward as a Fellow of Peterhouse,
by Kenneth Green, 1928.

Bertrand Hallward as a young father with his three elder daughters.

tennis have to be added to the list and golf with Adcock. Of course it is obvious that I was blest (or cursed?) with extraordinary physical energy which I thought it necessary to work off; or rather I enjoyed immensely the exercise and the feeling of physical fitness. But it was also a typical middle-class English habit engendered by the public schools and was widely practised in the Army and in the Colonial Service of the Empire.

I did a lot of swimming in the Cam especially during lunch time with sandwiches and Margaret was fond of swimming too. We discovered Quy Fen and started the children learning to swim in rubber rings. I can still see the scene in memory of a family of five afloat at Quy like ducks on a pond. Then a grass snake swam across the water and our dog started snapping and biting in panic. All on shore quickly.[26]

Among the sporting appointments that Bertrand held at various times and failed to mention in the extract were: Secretary of the Cambridge Alpine Club, President of the Undergraduate Mountaineering Club, President of Cambridge University Hockey Club and Lawn Tennis Club, and Captain of Cambridge-shire Lawn Tennis Club.

Onlookers at games in which Bertrand was taking part would be amused to note how in a hockey team he would shout 'Take, Take, Take!' and take the ball himself, while at the net in tennis he would generally shout 'Yours' for difficult balls. 'We won't bother about history today, we'll go skating', he announced to a pupil in the harsh winter of 1928-29. He skated in the English style, firm back, hands behind him, very scornful of lifting the legs in the French manner. There is little doubt that he had come to be viewed by pupils and colleagues as not only a character, but a phenomenon. He was 'vibrant, never still, physically glowing, overwhelming'.[27] 'I did not know Hallward personally,' a former undergraduate has written in his autobiography, 'but friends at Peterhouse thought him too charismatic by half; tall and good-looking, he had a bewildering tendency to blow hot and cold at the same time. "Come in! Come in!" he would cry heartily at tutorials. "Sit you down! Sit you down! Splendid! Make yourself comfortable! And, by the way, next time you come you might see that your gown is properly cleaned will you? Good! Good! I think we understand each other."'[28]

Frank Walbank recalled that 'around 1930 the Peterhouse undergraduate magazine reproduced a drawing which showed the railings on the Trumpington Street side of the College filled with a serried rank of ladies' bicycles and entitled simply "Mr Hallward will lecture". Bertrand's reputation as a lecturer rested on more than his looks, however. He was not a witty or amusing *extempore* speaker; the lectures were generally read from a text and were accompanied by lengthy bibliographies: but they were very useful. The Rt. Hon. Enoch Powell, who attended some of them, wrote back very promptly in 1994 to say 'I remember attending two courses of Mr Hallward's lectures on Roman history. He was an important lecturer for those taking Part Two of the Classical Tripos and gave students what they needed.'[29] Bertrand was at his best on a one-to-one basis, when, according to Nick Hammond, he was frequently 'inspiring and full of ideas. He was very thorough in reading and criticising essays, very demanding. You had to work hard.' Though not a keen researcher himself, Bertrand had the happy knack of suggesting fruitful lines of research to pupils whom he knew would make the most of them.

In 1932 Bertrand applied to be Headmaster of Felsted School. He was 31 years old at the time, which would generally have been considered very young. However Felsted, though a well-established public school, was not in the first rank and Bertrand knew it from Haileybury days when he had gone there to play cricket. It was an attractive school charmingly located in rural Essex and, perhaps, ripe for expansion by a young dynamo. After only eight years as a don he was attempting to fulfil the ambition he outlined to his father back in 1923; also, with a wife and three young daughters to support, he was aware that public school headmasters were in general better remunerated than dons. Most of all, however, he knew he enjoyed the exercise of power and he sought a suitable stage for his creative urge.

These were still the days when printed testimonials were required for such applications, and a six-sheet pamphlet was produced, containing the recommendations of his three referees, Sir William Birdwood, Professor Ernest

Barker, and Professor Frank Adcock. Birdwood, striking a soldierly note, described Bertrand as 'just the man whom I should wish to see as headmaster in a school at which my own sons might be'. 'Mr Hallward is a very fine athlete', he went on, 'and, though it may not seem opportune to mention personal appearance, he is fortunate in possessing what we all could wish to see in the Head of a great school'. Naturally Ernest Barker spoke mainly of Bertrand's academic stature, and found him 'very, very far from being "the pale anaemic don" of Mr Belloc's imagination: he has a full vigour and a rich field of interests'. He also pointed out that he had known Margaret Hallward for several years and felt 'that it is not irrelevant to mention that she has every gift to fit her for being a headmaster's wife'. Adcock was able to refer to Bertrand's time as an undergraduate at King's where 'he was a leader in College partly because of his remarkable proficiency in games but far more because of his personality and wide interests'. He also spoke highly of his work for the *Cambridge Ancient History* which 'admirable both in scholarship and presentation, has won high praise'.[30] The Governors of Felsted School did not, however, choose Bertrand as their next headmaster. It must have seemed a big risk to them: at 31 he still looked alarmingly like a School Prefect.

The closest any Cambridge don can get to playing the headmaster in the University is to become Proctor. He is the man entrusted with enforcing the

Hallward as Proctor with his 'bulldogs'.

University's rules and with disciplining malefactors charged with gross crimes such as climbing into College after the gates had been locked, or being seen about the University after dark without a gown. Flanked by his 'bulldogs', two bowler-hatted porters chosen for their fleetness of foot, the Proctor would stalk the streets, on the look-out for trouble. Although in retrospect Bertrand considered this 'a complete waste of time', undergraduates knew that there was always a risk of being detected in their illicit revelries. Bertrand became Pro-Proctor in 1933 (the junior partner) and Senior Proctor in 1934 and in these two years gained a good deal of useful experience in administration and the imposition of discipline.

Just at this time, his father died in January 1934, and in due course the house at Dunsfold was sold and Bertrand was able to move from his rented house at Belvoir Terrace to a larger, comparatively modern detached house, Number 75, Grange Road, which he bought for £2,000 in 1935. A fine house with large rooms and an extensive garden, yet very close to the centre of Cambridge, it was then and is certainly today a very valuable property. According to Bertrand he bought it cheaply because the previous owner had committed suicide by slitting his throat in one of the bathrooms. Although he had respected his father as the one who had guided him to Haileybury and King's and as the parent from whom he had inherited his intellectual ability, his father's constant bullying of

Number 75, Grange Road, Cambridge.

his mother had caused Bertrand much distress. After a year spent visiting her younger son Philip, who was with the army in India, the widowed Mrs Hallward came to live with Bertrand and Margaret in her own rooms at Grange Road, and indeed she was to remain part of the family circle throughout the Clifton and Nottingham years. 'For twenty-five years', wrote Bertrand 'my mother and Margaret lived in our different houses in harmony and warm affection. And of course my mother was a perfect baby-sitter. We were now rather better off and we did a lot of entertaining of undergraduates on Saturdays and Sundays.'[31]

The love of gardening was indulged at Grange Road where much planting was done, including the overhanging Judas Tree which was still a feature of the road in 1994. It was at Grange Road , too, that a fourth addition to the family was made when Christabel was born in 1937, the Hallwards' fourth daughter and last child. During these years a pattern of family holidays was established in a farm house at Tyndon near Nefyn on the Lleyn Peninsula of North Wales. The Hallwards were joined there by Margaret's sister Alice, her husband Hilary Macklin, and their two children, as well as by several other members of the family, and friends. Hilary was Secretary to the Joint Board of Examinations in Music and these holidays were a welcome break from life in London. There was golf on the nearby Nefyn course, where Bertrand admired the drives of Margaret's dashing naval brother André, whose swing 'was snake-like and ferocious. You thought as you watched that the ball would go off at 90 degrees, but it didn't, because it was actually a really controlled swing, whereas my own drives had their origin in an off-drive at cricket and had fatal right-wrist pressure resulting in the inevitable slice.'[32]   Adcock, a keen and very proficient golfer, was among the guests to enjoy the scenic splendour of this Nefyn course.

There were to be plenty of joint Hallward-Macklin family holidays, and it amused Bertrand to recall the effect his dominating personality had on these groups. 'There is no doubt that the over-masterful and perhaps less than tactful Bertrand' (he admitted) 'excited competitive feelings in Hilary and Alice which caused amusing situations of open competition on joint holidays for choice of lunch site or camping ground. But I think in the main it was an undercurrent of subtle stresses and never amounted to anything like a quarrel or open disagreements.'[33] Bertrand's ex-pupil Nick Hammond, by now a Fellow of Clare, visited Tyndon with his new bride, also called Margaret, and encountered the mischievous brand of Hallward enterprise that Bertrand's friends and family knew so well. According to Hammond, 'BLH was in rumbustious form saying "It's Bank Holiday today in the rest of England and they're packed like sardines on the beaches: let's all go and have a naked bathe on the wide sands of Hell's Mouth." I was slightly daunted at the prospect of a *Club Méditerranée* with my wife immediately on arrival. However, Margaret [Hallward] quickly took Margaret [Hammond] to their own room and with much laughter told her "don't listen to a word he says".[34]

To most people who knew him in the 1920's and 1930's Bertrand Hallward seemed a fit, handsome, sporting man with a sharp brain, restless energy, and an interest in everything. Yet Adonis had an Achilles heel. Throughout these years his health was a serious worry to him, largely because of the pain he suffered from duodenitis. This seems to have been a stress-related complaint and emphasizes the extent to which, beneath the dazzling exterior, lay the strains of work, responsibility, and worry. In 1991 he wrote:

> Having arrived at the age of 90 in a fairly good state of general health which I accept with gratitude, it is a little surprising to look back and record my very considerable health problems in my early working career. In my first twelve years of married life I was in hospital twice for a bismuth meal and X-ray examination. I had my appendix out and all my teeth out again in hospital, I had consultations with the Regius Professor of Medicine at Oxford, Professor Ryle, and with Dr Leslie Cole and in 1938 I went into the Windsor Health Clinic for a fortnight. I was in severe pain from duodenitis yet no ulcer was ever diagnosed. I can see now that my trouble was a complex one of psychological work stress, probably excessive exercise and therefore hunger, and eating too quickly, and over-rich food at Peterhouse High Table. Ryle's remembered words 'flop like a sick hen' was the cure which I found it so difficult to adopt. Dieting and 'little and often' were prescribed. At the Windsor Clinic I started with one-hourly feeds and this seemed to work. But through this period I was undoubtedly very anxious about my health, now that I had the responsibility as the bread-winner for Margaret and four daughters. I had watched the Headmaster of Bishop's Stortford College, H.L. Price, a brilliant Oxford athlete and delightful man fail to cure an exactly similar trouble to mine, collapse with duodenal ulcers and die.[35]

While he was being treated in the Windsor Health Clinic in March 1938, Bertrand wrote to Margaret almost every day revealing himself to be, even in pain, a restless patient. However, he was particularly relieved when tests showed that there was no ulcer and that there were no signs of cancer — something that had been at the back of his mind. He had a visit from Margaret's brother George, a master at Eton, nearby: 'George has a story that everyone is furious with the bad manners of Ribbentrop, the recent German ambassador. After his interview with the King he was caught imitating the King's stutter derisively to his friends.'[36] Among those who inspected him was the distin-guished specialist Sir Arthur Hurst, a 'queer small ferret faced man, very deaf and slightly asthmatic. Entered the room without looking at me or saying anything and sat down and started straight away jerking technical questions at me. He impressed me and gave one confidence though he treated me purely as a specimen and not as a human being.'[37] Towards the end of the fortnight he was feeling much better, and after so much inactivity burning to see his wife again. 'In myself I am feeling so strong, vigorous and rampant as I hardly need to tell you perhaps! And I have ceased to have any worries, anxieties or psychological stress but only the longing — wild lawless wanton longing — to see you.'[38]

Soon enough, he was back at Peterhouse and firing on all cylinders again. Since 1934 his position within the College had been an eminent one because in that year Paul Vellacott accepted the headmastership of Harrow, and the chief influence within the College passed to a triumvirate of Fellows: Charles Burkill, Roy Lubbock and Bertrand Hallward. In 1938 Birdwood (who was ennobled in that year) retired as Master and Vellacott eventually returned from Harrow to replace him in 1939. Among the many posts and responsibilities held by Lord Birdwood was the position of President of Clifton College, his old school, where a crisis occurred in November 1938 upon the resignation of the Headmaster, Norman Whatley, after disagreements with the Council. Whatley was due to leave in April 1939, and a successor had to be found. Without hesitation, Birdwood recommended Hallward to the Clifton Council, and urged Bertrand to apply for the post. This he did, and although the Council considered many other people, after interviewing Bertrand in March 1939 they offered him the position, preferably from the summer term of 1939.

As we have seen, Bertrand had set his sights on a headmastership but after the Felsted application he had concentrated on gaining more experience as well as years. As Proctor, and through his many responsibilities in the University and the College, he had now done this. It was clear to him that he was not interested enough in writing and research to gain a Chair at Cambridge, and in any case there was no prospect of an imminent vacancy. Clifton was a major public school with a fine academic record, situated in one of Britain's most attractive cities. It was a top job, and he decided to take it. He wrote his letter of acceptance in March and, characteristically, agreed to start in May. A whirlwind suddenly fell upon the household at Grange Road as everyone packed with all speed for Bristol. In future they would all be very much more in the public gaze: the privacy of a don's life had gone for good.

Part Three

Clifton 1939-1948

A New Headmaster

Clifton College, was, like Haileybury, a comparatively new foundation in 1939: indeed both schools opened in the same year, 1862. But whereas Haileybury had moved into the old classical buildings of the East India College, Clifton was purpose-built on its attractive site in Bristol's most fashionable suburb by Charles Hansom, an architect who specialized in Roman Catholic churches and Anglican boarding-schools. He also designed Malvern College and he used what could be described as a neo-Renaissance Gothic style for both institutions. His original design for Clifton was extremely ambitious and, because of the cost, the school was never built to this plan. In retrospect this seems a major mistake because the first plan contained two very large halls, something that Clifton has always lacked. Only one was built and, as we shall see, it had eventually to serve as both Assembly Hall and Dining Hall. On the other hand this 'Big School' is a very fine and well proportioned building. Next door to it lies School House, originally the Headmaster's house, and on the other side a range of buildings including a handsome tower, reminiscent of Lupton's tower at Eton, or the tower of St John's College, Cambridge. This cluster of buildings is finally united and dominated by the Chapel — Charles Hansom's original, rather mundane structure spectacularly enlarged and transformed by Sir Charles Nicholson for the 1912 Jubilee of the school. Although Hansom did not plan Clifton to look quite as it does, the result of piecemeal building is nevertheless a very happy one and, seen to advantage from 'the Close', the green playing-field that stretches before it, Clifton College is by general consent a fine sight.

There is no doubt that in the quest for the status of a 'major' public school fine buildings play an important part, and in this respect Clifton had been well served by the group of Bristol business and professional men who had bought shares in 'Clifton College Company Ltd'. They had also been extremely lucky in the choice of the Headmaster who actually opened the school, John Percival. Their first choice, Charles Evans, had taken part in the initial planning but, just before the school was due to open, he accepted the headmastership of King

Clifton College seen from the Close.

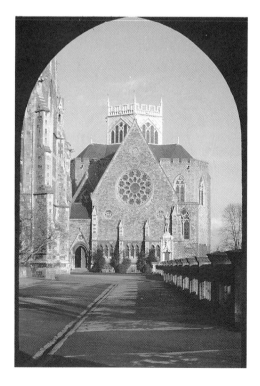

*Clifton Chapel seen from
the War Memorial Arch.*

Edward's, Birmingham, leaving the Clifton College Council in the lurch at the last minute. The Headmaster of Rugby recommended a young man on his staff, John Percival, even though he was only 28 years old. It proved a brilliant appointment and Percival was to become a major figure in late Victorian England. Not only did he build Clifton into a thriving and successful school during his seventeen years as Headmaster; he also revitalized Trinity College at Oxford, where he became President, and founded Somerville College for women. Moving on to tighten up the discipline at Rugby School as Headmaster, he was eventually appointed Bishop of Hereford. Apart from his work at Clifton College he also helped to found Clifton High School for Girls, Redland High School and Bristol University itself.[1]

Although Percival ceased to be Headmaster of Clifton in 1879 he very soon became a member of the Council, and was Chairman of it from 1893 almost to his death in 1918. From this position of power he retained a close control over 'his' school, recommending his immediate successor James Wilson, and actually appointing the next three headmasters, Glazebrook, David and King. He also made sure that the school did not stray from the course he had mapped out for it. He regarded academic results as a high priority, and also 'moral tone'. He considered that day boys should be treated on an equal footing with boarders (which was not the case in most public schools) and he had opened a house for Jewish boys. As Headmaster, he urged his boys to go out into the world and make their mark, and many had done so, in every walk of life. Percival's reward, as a white-haired patriarch, was to hear King George V tell the boys of Clifton at the Jubilee celebrations of 1912 that 'the steady progress of your school since its foundation fifty years ago has earned for you a place among the great public schools of England, of which you may well be proud.'[2]

During the 1914-18 War Cliftonians made a great contribution to the fighting and paid heavily with their lives. Just over 3,000 served and 578 were killed. Douglas Haig, who had been a boy in School! House under Percival, rose to command the largest force Britain had ever sent into the field of war. William Birdwood was an Army Commander, and there were 23 Cliftonian Major-Generals and 52 Brigadier-Generals. Although conditions at Clifton during the war were strained, as they were at Haileybury, the numbers in the school nevertheless rose from 594 in 1914 to 689 in 1918. By 1923 the time had come to appoint a new headmaster, and for the first time the Council were not influenced by the presence of Bishop Percival, for he had died in 1918 and had been buried beneath the altar of Clifton Chapel.

The man who was Headmaster of Clifton during the whole time that Bertrand Hallward was a Fellow of Peterhouse was an ex-Oxford Classics don called Norman Whatley. Anyone more different from John Percival in looks and demeanour it would be hard to imagine. Percival was famous for his commanding presence and handsome profile; Whatley made no pretence to grandeur of this sort and went about his business in a methodical, donnish kind of way. His first ten years were very successful and extremely important for the future development of the school. In 1927 the Prince of Wales opened what was widely regarded, with envy, as one of the most modern and best equipped Science Schools in Britain, boasting superb laboratories and an excellent Science Library. The mastermind behind this new development was Dr E.J. Holmyard, Head of Science from 1919 to 1940, and a major figure in the world of science education in schools.

Whatley then set about an even more important change. Percival's Clifton had been essentially for boys from eleven to eighteen. Taking advantage of the cheapness of property because of the repercussions of the 1929 Wall Street crash, a site was cleared near the main buildings for the construction of a new Preparatory School, opened in 1933. This provided an Assembly Hall and range of classrooms in a modified Gothic style. *The Times* considered it 'a model of practical convenience'.[3] In time the Clifton 'Pre' (pronounced 'Pree') was to grow into a large and influential school in its own right, though Whatley's intention was that it should remain very much under the control of the Headmaster of the 'Upper School', who made all appointments in the Pre. The new school, under its first Headmaster E.G. Sharp, was a great success and provided a steady stream of boys to the Upper School.

In 1931 the Clifton uniform of black jacket and pin-stripe trousers was abandoned for grey flannel trousers and a grey flannel blazer, edged with blue. All boys wore a (rather unpopular) cap, variously coloured depending on the house to which they belonged. During Whatley's time the school averaged nine awards to Oxford and Cambridge, which in those days was regarded as the measure of a school's standing. In 1932 there were fourteen awards and in 1937, seventeen. In 1930 the *Morning Post* wrote a series of articles on leading schools which prompted the Editor of *The Cliftonian* to write: 'We had always suspected the fact, but now it lies before us in clear black and white where every Tory in the land may read: "Our Greater Public Schools. No 9: Clifton College, Bristol."'[4] In many respects, Whatley had done a fine job.

Unfortunately, everything went wrong for him as the 1930's wore on. First of all he had a serious bout of double pneumonia from which, according to some observers, he never really recovered in temper or in spirit. Then he had a most unfortunate row with Robert St John Reade, a member of the Clifton staff who wished to stand as a Labour candidate for local elections. Whatley would not allow this and eventually sacked him. Reade went on to be a most influential local politician in Bristol and a bitter enemy of Whatley and all that Clifton stood for. Then Whatley began to have problems with the man who had been appointed first official Bursar of the school in 1930. Whatley decided he was incompetent and eventually persuaded the Council to dismiss him in 1936. However, within months of the appointment of a new Bursar, Colonel Badcock, Whatley was denouncing his incompetence too. All this took place against a background of economic problems in the nation as a whole which affected the ability of parents to pay fees, so numbers at Clifton, as at other schools, went into decline. From a high point of 792 in 1924 they had slumped to 630 by 1939, both Upper School and Pre included.

The position of Headmaster is more vulnerable than it seems, and never more so than in a fee-paying school where numbers are falling. In retrospect it is clear that the decline was a widespread phenomenon but it was difficult to gauge this at the time; and in any case, it could be argued that if times *were* hard, it was all the more important that the Headmaster should be vigorous and dynamic. This was certainly the line taken by two of Whatley's sternest and most influential critics on the Council, Sir Robert Waley-Cohen and Sir Robert Witt. Waley-Cohen suspected Whatley of being anti-semitic while Witt, the Chairman of Council and a man capable of losing his temper, had even resorted to shouting at the Headmaster while a guest in his house.[5] By November 1938 Whatley had had enough and he resigned, giving one term's notice. He was only 54 and had no other job to go to, though to be fair to the Council they made provision for a pension and spoke publicly in glowing terms about his services to the school. 'Governors' Tribute to Great Services' ran a headline in the *Bristol Mirror* which went on to refer to Whatley's achievements in maintaining a high academic standard and in building the Science School and the Preparatory School. His knowledge of business and affairs was considered 'unrivalled and outstanding', while 'his staff supported whole-heartedly and with a loyalty which he himself was always the first to acknowledge. By the boys he was regarded with equal respect and affection.' The article ended in a quotation from Sir Robert Witt: 'I am sure', he said, 'that I am voicing the wishes of all here that he may enjoy a long and happy life after his retirement.'[6] Whatley lived to be eighty and was for a time Mayor of Oxford. Looking back from old age he regarded it as a blessing in disguise that he had not been called upon to steer Clifton through the War.

To entrepreneurs of the stamp of Waley-Cohen and Witt, Bertrand Hallward seemed an obvious, indeed heaven-sent, choice to succeed Whatley. No less an academic than Whatley (who had been a Fellow of Hertford College Oxford), Hallward's reputation as a charismatic leader, and the fact that he also *looked* like one, recommended him as the man to attract more parents and pupils to Clifton.

A formal photograph of Hallward taken soon after his appointment to Clifton.
He is wearing his Old Haileyburian tie.

For these reasons the Council offered him the position of seventh Headmaster of Clifton, and very much hoped he would accept it.

The only matter which gave Hallward serious pause for thought was the conflict between Whatley and the Bursar, Colonel Badcock. For advice he turned to F.B. Malim, his Haileybury Headmaster who had moved from there to be Master of Wellington College. Malim, who had been Head of three public schools, replied categorically that in his view bursars should be subordinate to headmasters.[7] Hallward accordingly accepted the post on two conditions: first that the appointment should be for twenty rather than fifteen years, and second that (in the words of Sir Robert Witt's telegram to the Council) 'as regards Bursar, if after reasonable time trial HM reports that Bursar is unable to carry out duties of office satisfactorily as he the HM envisages then Council will support him by making necessary change and that Council will give fullest consideration to views of HM in event of such change.'[8] These conditions were agreed, and the appointment was accepted on March 14th 1939.

An article in the *Daily Mail* by John Rickman, the newspaper's educational expert, gave in January 1939 a very shrewd summing-up of the pressures that by then the public schools and their headmasters were facing.

> Nowadays, changes in headmasterships among the 250 public schools in these islands pass for the most part unnoticed, but when the governing bodies of such famous schools as Clifton and Marlborough set themselves to find new leaders the interest in their choice is not confined to within the walls of their colleges. These jobs are the fat plums of the educational harvest, but they carry with them great responsibilities which seem to increase every year.
>
> There are more public schools today than ever. Competition for boys is therefore keener. When a school's governing body prepares to choose a new headmaster in most cases it seeks a man who possesses not only the essential attributes of learning, character, tact, and enthusiasm but one who, to put it simply, will be good with parents.
>
> More is required of a headmaster today — or so it seemed to me after interviewing fifty heads recently. Charm and personality count for much. And a headmaster must be something of a psychologist too. He must be able to convince his governing body when he says: 'I think we ought to build so and so, install that, or feed the boys on this.'
>
> He may have an intuition that before very long nearly every mother who comes to look at his school will be asking about these things. A satisfactory answer — and the boy is as good as entered. Mothers are like that.

Schools may not advertise. Some years ago they would not have advertised even if they could. They had waiting-lists. There were boys in plenty. There are still waiting-lists, but at a few schools only. The rest are glad to take boys at short notice.

A school soon gets known if it is a good one. So it does if it is bad. If a school has won a name it is the headmaster's business to see that the name is preserved; if it has a doubtful reputation his task is to wipe it out. Each is difficult. He must be something of a diplomat, a salesman, and a dictator to succeed.[9]

When the news of Bertrand Hallward's appointment was released to the Press, the *Sunday Times* described him as 'one of the most handsome of the younger generation of Cambridge dons. Tall, athletic, with a head of corn-coloured hair, he would seem in appearance, though not in experience, to be nearer twenty than forty.' 'Mr Hallward is a fine teacher', the article went on. 'At Cambridge he has long been regarded as one of the best all-round classical tutors. He is also an able administrator. He is married, and according to the best headmaster tradition, is the father of four young daughters. Outside his study Mr Hallward is an accomplished games player, an engaging talker, and a keen amateur gardener.'[10] On whether he was also a diplomat, salesman and dictator the newspaper did not commit itself. Time would, presumably, tell.

The Bombing of Bristol

The Hallwards had less than two months to leave Grange Road and settle into the house provided for the Headmaster of Clifton. This was Number 24, College Road, a large Victorian house on three floors with bay windows in the main rooms giving a good view of the school buildings and the Close. On the other hand, there were roads on two sides of the house, it was very much in the centre of the school, and the garden was rather small. Hallward was not very impressed with it, and made his views known to the Council. Nevertheless, when term began in May the new Headmaster, his wife and four daughters, and his mother were all duly installed there.

Although there are obvious points of contact between a fellow of a Cambridge college and the headmaster of a major school, they are in reality completely different jobs. No longer would Hallward be lecturing to undergraduates and supervising College classicists; nor would he be keeping abreast of the latest scholarly developments in his subject. He would teach several lessons, usually about eighteen a week. The Royal Charter granted to the school in 1877 gave the headmaster sole responsibility for the appointment and dismissal of staff and boys, the administration of academic affairs, and the maintenance of discipline. Hence Hallward's main duties were administrative. He had to make sure that the staff taught properly, that the boys behaved properly, and that the school gave a good account of itself. Above the headmaster the Royal Charter placed a Council of about fifteen members, who elected a Chairman. The headmaster was not a member of this Council by right and was accountable to it in all respects. He was appointed by the Council and could be dismissed by it if a two-thirds majority voted in favour. Hence the Council was in theory all-powerful. On the other hand members of Council were often distinguished Old Cliftonians holding down busy jobs elsewhere and Council meetings took place only once or twice a term. A successful and forceful headmaster could probably carry a Council willingly with him.

The Chairman of Council since 1934, Sir Robert Witt, was to hold office during the key years of Hallward's headmastership. He had left Clifton in 1890 and prospered as a London solicitor with an excellent reputation. His main interest in life, however, was art and art history, and his vast private collection of reproductions of paintings and drawings eventually became part of the Courtauld Institute. Witt himself was a Trustee of the Tate Gallery and Chairman of the National Gallery. Unfortunately he suffered from severe arthritis and was often in considerable pain. He was an able and a formidable man, but he needed careful handling. Sir Robert Waley-Cohen had left Clifton's Jewish House (Polack's) in 1896 and was knighted for his achievements as Managing Director of Shell and Chairman of Anglo-Egyptian Oil. Whatley had found that 'as long as one agreed with him he was charming, but he could not tolerate opposition'.[1] Here was another Council member to be treated with care. Fortunately Hallward had a strong ally in Lord Birdwood who was a Council member and also President of the College, an honorific position which gave him considerable influence. In any case, Hallward started off in a strong position because having had a row with their former Headmaster, the Council members would be anxious to co-operate with their new one.

Next came the academic staff, of whom there were about fifty in the Upper School. These were led by the Second Master, Cecil Taylor, whom Hallward knew already through Cambridge connections. Indeed, he had consulted Taylor about the situation at Clifton before accepting the post. Taylor had a similar background to Hallward and was a man after his own heart. Educated at Charterhouse and Emmanuel, Cambridge, Taylor had also gained first classes in both parts of the Classics Tripos, had been a member of the élite group of intellectuals known as 'The Apostles', and was a fringe member of the Bloomsbury Group. Over the years he acquired a notable collection of paintings by Vanessa Bell and Duncan Grant, including a portrait of himself as a handsome young undergraduate by Grant. Apparently refusing a Fellowship he came to Clifton in 1912, becoming classical sixth form master in 1920. There is no doubt that he was a brilliant teacher: inventive, witty, never dull. In 1926 Whatley appointed him housemaster of School House where, as a bachelor, he lived in great state in what had been the apartments of Clifton's headmasters (Whatley had refused to be both headmaster and housemaster). Taylor was not at his best, however, controlling a house of eighty boarding boys which became unruly during his time. He was much more effective as Second Master and was ideally suited for working in close harmony with Clifton's dashing new Headmaster.[2]

Then there were nine housemasters, seven of boarding and two of day houses, and eight heads of academic departments. Many of these were highly qualified men, distinguished in their own fields, such as the Head of Science,

Dr E.J. Holmyard, the Head of Maths, P.C. Unwin (a Cambridge Wrangler) and the remarkable Head of Music, Dr Douglas Fox, a legend in the profession. A brilliant young pianist and organist, his career seemed to have ended in 1917 when most of his right arm was amputated on the Western Front. However he developed an outstandingly skilful use of his left hand and was subsequently able to perform on the organ and piano up to concert standard, which made him something of a celebrity. He was Director of Music from 1931 to 1957, during which time he secured for Clifton's music, and for himself, a national reputation.[3]

And then there were the boys, about 500 of them. The boys of North Town and South Town, the two dayboy houses, lived in or close to Bristol. It had always been one of Percival's precepts that the ideal in education was the combination of a good home with a good school and he gave the dayboys high status at Clifton; indeed it is significant that one of the most archetypal of late Victorian schoolboys, Henry Newbolt, was a member of North Town and lived only five minutes' walk from the school.[4]

There was Polack's House, for Jewish boys, already a feature unique in the English public schools. Percival had opened this house in 1878 and it took its name from Joseph Polack, who became housemaster in 1890; the current housemaster was his son Albert, which was another unusual feature. Finally, there were six boarding houses, the grandest of which was School House. The other five were named after distinguished early housemasters (Brown's, Dakyns', Oakeley's, Wiseman's, Watson's). Vast and rather ugly structures of the late nineteenth century, they stood close together along College Road.

Within the little fiefdoms of the boarding houses, the elaborate pantomime of public school life was played out. The housemaster and his family (if he had one) lived on the 'private side' in spacious, even grandiose, accommodation. The boys were crammed less luxuriously into their quarters: large dormitories for sleeping, and studies shared with two or three others for working. Most boys spent four or five years at school and started at the bottom as a 'fag', at the beck-and-call of the sixth form. Each year in the House thought itself superior to the following year's intake, and the rulers of the House were those in their last year. Some were what Clifton called 'Praepostors' (School Prefects), some were 'House Sixths' (House Prefects). They had the power to cane junior boys, with the housemaster's permission, for breaches of discipline.

Some of the senior boys did not take kindly to the sudden disappearance of a dignified, elderly Headmaster whom they had in general liked, and to the arrival of someone who looked and behaved so differently. 'Whatley was, I suppose, on the austere side and his want of charisma was reflected by his nickname *The Cod*', a pupil of that time has written. 'But he was a good classicist and a solid character who chose his teaching staff well and when he was eased out after a row with the governors ... many of us were shocked.'[5] 'I was in the last of my fifteen terms at Clifton,' another has written, 'when Mr Hallward was appointed, to everyone's surprise. We had been told about it only at the end of the previous term, and as far as we were concerned the school was prospering both in work and games. The masters seemed as much taken aback as the boys. Certainly in that first term our new Headmaster was not highly regarded: we were unused to anyone who paraded his youth and good looks, and of course the school continued on Mr Whatley's lines while Mr Hallward, correctly, took stock of the position. We widely approved of Mrs Hallward, who was regarded as being a lady.'[6]

According to the Editor of *The Cliftonian*, who jovially bracketed together the arrival of a new headmaster and the installation of a new school clock, Hallward made several popular innovations in his first few weeks. These included expeditions into the country by bus and the opening of Beggar's Bush (the school's extensive playing fields on the other side of Clifton Gorge) to the sixth form. On the other hand, only three weeks into the term someone wrote HEIL HITLER in large yellow-painted letters on the roof of the Percival Library. Whether this was a reference to international politics or the Aryan looks and Führer-like behaviour of the new Headmaster was not explained. Fortunately for Hallward's credibility the culprits were discovered by the School Marshal, A.G. Moss. The public nature of Hallwood's new job is underlined by some of the events that took place in June and July, 1939. On June 21st H.C. Beaven, who had been a Clifton master for thirty-eight years, died in harness quite suddenly, and Hallward was called upon to give the funeral oration of a man he hardly knew. Carefully primed by Cecil Taylor, Hallward's lengthy speech, described as an 'Eloquent Testimony' was printed in the local papers.[7] Almost simultaneously the School Orchestra, under the bâton of Douglas Fox, was broadcasting for the BBC.

Then at the end of June Hallward presided over his first 'Commemoration', a mid-term speech day, prize-giving and garden party, potentially every headmaster's nightmare. The Chief Guest was Sir Thomas Inskip, an Old Cliftonian who was then Secretary for the Dominions. Hallward, in his speech of welcome, decided to read out some of Inskip's old school reports such as 'no sense of responsibility in the house', 'still takes things too easily', and 'might do better yet'. This, we are told, was received with 'roars of delight' by the boys. Inskip, in revenge, accused the Headmaster of breaking the Official Secrets Act. In his own formal speech Hallward tactfully referred to his predecessor as 'a great Headmaster' and went on to welcome the recent Bill introducing six months conscription in the forces. He saw it as a good way of integrating young men of all backgrounds, especially Cliftonians, for 'the charge is often levelled at our public schools that they foster and develop class prejudice', he pointed out.[8] The Commemoration celebrations passed off well and Hallward found that, as he had suspected, he enjoyed the rôle of Master of Ceremonies. It was perhaps no accident that one of his guests on this occasion was John Sheppard, now Provost of King's, who had directed him twenty years earlier in a Greek Play and could look on with some amusement as his Apollo took centre stage again.

Towards the end of July Hallward was asked to give away the prizes at the Royal West of England Academy School of Architecture in Bristol. He was welcomed as 'a newcomer to Bristol and as the distinguished Headmaster of Clifton College' and then gave his audience the benefit of his views on architecture. 'We have seen many of our finest roads ruined by hundreds of bungaloid growths', he complained. 'The desecration of this land by foul architecture is one of the most terrible things in our generation. We have seen commercialism rampant wherein ideals of art and the purposes of art cease to have any play at all. It is up to all of us, and particularly anyone interested in education, to take part in the stand against this monstrous growth of evil building.' Presumably he had worked out that very few Clifton parents lived in bungalows. Finally, he explained 'that his own interest in the subject of architecture sprang up as a result of his first visit to Greece.'[9]

So passed Hallward's initial term at Clifton, and with it about a hundred of the influential senior boys who might have felt more loyalty to Whatley. On the whole things had gone well. During the summer holidays he and the family moved from Number 24 College Road to a truly palatial house overlooking Clifton's celebrated Downs. This was *Glenavon*, half of a huge building not unlike Queen Victoria's Osborne House in its architectural features. It belonged to the Trustees of Clifton Zoo who were prepared to lease it to the College on favourable terms. Standing in his colossal new drawing-room and contemplating the ten or so bedrooms above, Hallward could feel well provided for and begin to form his plans for Clifton's future over the summer holidays. However, those holidays were, for him, much shorter than expected.

Hallward's decision to move from Cambridge to Bristol had been taken against a background of international crisis. Hitler came to power in Germany in 1933 and his Nazi Party rapidly dismantled the democratic Weimar Republic and set up a dictatorship which aspired to dominate Europe. The bombing of Guernica in the Spanish Civil War in 1937 demonstrated the effectiveness of air strikes, and a series of aggressive moves by Hitler in 1938, in defiance of international law, made war seem a real possibility. The Prime Minister, Neville Chamberlain, postponed the crisis by conceding Hitler's demands at the Munich Conference that year. 'Only a month ago it was hardly credible that war had been avoided', *The Cliftonian* reported in October 1938. 'There was no other topic of conversation: even the weather had to take a back seat for a while.'[10] When Hallward applied for the post at Clifton he knew that war was a possibility in the near future but in the early summer of 1939 the crisis seemed to have passed. However, in August came the news of the alliance between Nazi Germany and Soviet Russia, a pact between two dictators, Hitler and Stalin, safeguarding Germany's eastern frontier so that Hitler could strike at Poland. War now seemed imminent and, breaking his holiday, Hallward called together the Clifton housemasters and a few others to consider safety measures at the school. Hitler invaded Poland on September 2nd, ignoring his promises at Munich, and the British people listened to the doleful voice of Neville Chamberlain on the wireless informing them that from 11 o'clock on Sunday, 3rd September, 'this nation is at war with Germany.'

The boys were not due back at Clifton for another three weeks, so it was left to Hallward and the housemasters to take some steps which might protect the school from possible air-raids, even though Bristol was generally thought to be beyond the range of bombers flying from German airfields. Dayboys were encouraged to volunteer to fill sandbags which were used to strengthen basement rooms in the houses and elsewhere round the school. Masters' wives worked hard to make curtains for the blackout. By the time the boys came back on September 22nd a good deal had been done, but it proved impossible to black out the huge Gothic windows of Big School, the Chapel, and several classrooms. So Hallward had to reorganize the school timetable in order that no lessons should be taught after dark. He also abandoned the second compulsory service (Evensong) on Sundays.[11] The newspapers urged people to be scrupulous about the blackout, and to be ready for gas attacks — 'Hitler will send no warning, so always carry your gas mask' the advertisements insisted.[12]

In fact, because Hitler concentrated his campaign on eastern Europe for the first six months of the War, nothing very much happened as far as the people of Britain were concerned, and they began to call this 'the phoney war'. Gas masks were soon abandoned and, apart from the blackout regulations, life at Clifton was fairly normal in the Christmas term of 1939. 'Still,' as the housemaster of Watson's, S.P. Beachcroft, wrote later, 'the slight dislocation of the usual Christmas term routine, the physical gloom of the blackout and the uncomfortable expectancy of something worse to come all went to give a sense of unreality.'[13]

Having dealt for the time being with the problem of security, Hallward's chief concern for the rest of the winter term was finance. In the end he had no serious problem with Colonel Badcock, the Bursar, because with the outbreak of war Badcock volunteered to leave Clifton and return to the forces, a solution that suited both sides. In his place the Council appointed Alan Imlay, an Old Cliftonian and former housemaster, now close to retiring age. Loyal, hard-working and efficient he was the perfect choice to follow Hallward's lead and help to put his plans into operation. When he was appointed Headmaster Hallward had decided not to use the traditional headmaster's study in School House but had instead moved into Number 32 College Road, an administrative building that also housed the Bursar and his staff. He was now able to work closely with Imlay, which, as things turned out, was greatly to the advantage of the school.

Clifton had been losing money for several years because it had no substantial endowments and relied upon fee income to survive; and Whatley had been unable to keep the school full in the 1930's. With the outbreak of war it was very likely that the situation would get worse rather than better so Hallward produced a drastic financial plan. This involved the closing of one boarding house in the Pre (Hartnell's) and one in the Upper School (Watson's). The decision to close Watson's was made easier because the housemaster of another house (Dakyns') was anxious to volunteer for service. This was Major Rodney Gee, who had fought with distinction in the 1914-18 War and won the Military Cross. However, he had a first-class degree in English, he was an experienced schoolmaster, and Hallward was reluctant to let him go. In the end Gee had his way, but was unlucky enough to be made a prisoner-of-war early in 1940. With Gee gone, Hallward might have chosen to close Dakyns' but he closed Watson's and moved its housemaster (S.P. Beachcroft) to Dakyns'. All these complicated manoeuvres had the effect of irritating Gee, Beachcroft, and the boys of both houses.

The housemasters as a body were, however, outraged by the second part of Hallward's plan, which was to reduce their salaries by £450 a year. When he first arrived at Clifton he had been amazed to see how much they earned, compared with his own salary as a Cambridge don. He told the Council that with the maximum teaching salary of £670 plus free living in the House plus £10 for each boy, a housemaster could earn nearly £1,400. A member of Council who was himself a don observed that 'at university no don could hope to receive more than £1,100 per annum.'[14] But the housemasters dug their heels in over this and Hallward had to be satisfied with a cut in the capitation fee from £10 to £5, and a 10% reduction of salary for all staff. These measures were not popular, of course. On the other hand, hard-headed businessmen on the Council were delighted that their new Headmaster was prepared to take the bull by the horns.

The first term of 1940 proceeded normally except for the closing of Watson's and the introduction of food rationing which began in the nation as a whole in January 1940. At this time there was no central feeding system at Clifton; all the boarders ate in their houses where the housemasters were responsible for catering arrangements. Inevitably standards varied and some housemasters were more generous than others. At the beginning of the summer term the War, hitherto rather a remote affair, suddenly came much closer to home when in May Hitler's armies swept into France and within six weeks conquered it. This transformed the situation as far as Bristol was concerned because German bombers could now use French airfields and thus reach Bristol with ease, seeking to destroy its busy industrial port and the aircraft factory at Filton.

Here was a new crisis for Hallward and the Council to deal with. It was now certain that Bristol would, sooner or later, be bombed. Should the school move? If so, where? Early in June Hallward drove with the Bursar round the seaside resorts of North Cornwall and Devon which he thought would be as safe as anywhere. It would probably have been possible to make very suitable arrangements for evacuation and Hallward was in favour of doing so, but he encountered two major problems. One was that the Board of Education was not in favour of a move at this stage; the other, which was the more important, was that the Chairman of the Council, Sir Robert Witt, was totally opposed to evacuation, so nothing was done.[15]

Then, on June 24th, the first bombs fell on Bristol, though not within one and a half miles of the school. The best precautions Hallward could take were to send boys to the makeshift basement shelters for several hours at night. After three nights of this he decided that the boarders should be sent home five weeks before the scheduled end of term. This was a brave decision because he knew that the Chairman was opposed to any sort of capitulation to Hitler. Himself of Jewish ancestry, Witt would, according to Hallward, shake defiance at German bombers with his stick as they flew over his London home. Hallward got round the problem of Witt by securing the approval of some local members of the Council, having failed to reach the Chairman by telephone.[16]

With the school empty of all except a number of day boys, the Headmaster and Council deliberated what to do next. Hallward wanted to move to some large hotels in seaside resorts, and had made provisional arrangements to do so. But Sir Robert Witt, firmly back in the Chair, opposed this scheme and persuaded the Council to spend £5,000 building new air-raid shelters at the school. Work started on these at a frenzied pace so that they should be ready for the September term: they were long, brick structures with three tiers of bunks

A Clifton air-raid shelter.

on each wall and a reinforced ceiling. Meanwhile the Battle of Britain was fought and won in the skies above Southern England and, abandoning his plans for an invasion of Britain, Hitler determined to bomb the population into submission instead.

When term began again in late September, no serious action had yet been taken against Bristol, though Clifton boys were required to sleep in their new shelters, listening out for air-raid warnings. Then, early on the night of Sunday, November 24th, the blow fell. According to local historians:

> The first big attack on Bristol came on the evening of Sunday 24th November 1940. The sirens sounded at about 6 pm and almost at once German planes began to drop flares. Although only about sixty planes took part in the attack, they dropped hundreds of incendiary bombs on a deserted town centre. As most people were sitting at home, it took a short time for people to realize what was happening. By that time large parts of the central area in the city, Clifton, Bedminster, Knowle and St George were well alight. There were so many fires that the Fire Brigade and the Auxiliary Fire Service were unable to cope. The water pressure fell so that there was not enough water to fight the fires. Miles of hose had to be laid to pump water from the quays in the harbour to parts of the city.

After the incendiary bombs, a number of high explosive bombs were dropped which made it more difficult to fight the fire. The raid lasted for about three hours and by 10 pm a great wall of fire spread across the city and people on the Welsh bank of the Severn could see the glare in the sky as the city burnt. The All Clear sounded just after 11 pm but it took until dawn to put most of the fires out. As people struggled through the dirty streets, littered with glass and fire hoses, they could see what had happened to Bristol overnight.

Most of the main shopping area, centred on Castle Street and Wine Street, had been destroyed by fire. Another area round Park Street and Queen's Road had also suffered. The Great Hall of the University, the City Museum and the Prince's Theatre had been burnt down. Many shops had been destroyed and part of the Grammar School had been seriously damaged. The most tragic losses were the Dutch House which had stood on the corner of High Street and Wine Street for 350 years, St Peter's Hospital which was even older and the Temple Church with its famous leaning tower.[17]

Two letters which came to light in the Clifton College Archives in 1994 give a pupil's eye-witness account of these events. They are both signed 'Tim' of Brown's House and are addressed to 'Dear Mum and Dad'. The first (not dated) appears to have been written on Sunday 31st November.

I will tell you first about last Sunday's blitz. We were all in the Pre Hall watching a flick when the sirens went, but we disregarded them as usual. But then the guns began to fire so we couldn't go back to the houses. When the film ended we remained in the Pre School. While we were there we noticed a glow in the sky and saw that there must be a fire. Guns, bombs, planes and searchlights were all going at once, and this fire got bigger and bigger until half the sky was lit up. The time was now about 7.30 and during a lull we were allowed to race back to our house shelters. Coming back we noticed that another fire had started. Once in our shelters, we remained there, and the noise outside still continued. We were only allowed out of the shelter two at a time. Suddenly there were three terrific concussions and the doors opened and shut. After that it quietened down, and later we were allowed to undress in the dorms with all the windows open (shivers!). Coming back to the shelter, I noticed more fires.

On Monday I went down to look at the damage. Clifton Parish Church is gutted with only the shell standing and the clock stopped at ten to ten. Numerous houses were burnt in big Georgian blocks, the ones on either side being intact. High explosive bombs were in evidence at scattered points, but the main street of Clifton itself is quite undamaged. The three terrific explosions we heard were about 500 yards away, near Polack's, in Camp Road. There were two small and one big H.E. bomb craters. Of the houses [in Camp Road] there was quite a lot left except where the big bomb had landed, where there was hardly any house at all. All the tiles of the houses were off and all windows were blown in and glassless. As we walked through Clifton that morning we heard everywhere the tinkle of broken glass being swept up — it was very peculiar.

On Wednesday I went down to Park Street. I have never seen such a mess in my life! There are about three shops left glassless, but intact, in the whole street. All the rest are burnt out or bombed to pieces. Even on Wednesday cars could not get up the road and firemen still plied hoses. Imagine a street of shops, exclusive shops, all burnt out and destroyed — that's what it looked like. We had to walk up by side streets to Whiteladies Road at the top. All the way we could see burnt-out houses and garages near us, and leaping flames. Lots of burnt-out cars look very strange.

We could not get along Whiteladies Road either, as it is burnt out too. The R.E.'s were still blowing up tottering buildings when we came. The museum is a shell, as is also most of the University. However, the tower still stood, although threatened by a time-bomb. It was all very dreadful and they say it is worse in Bristol Central. I think all Germans ought always to be shot on sight. It was a so-called reprisal raid, and no effort at all was made to hit military objectives, Lord Haw Haw [the traitor William Joyce who broadcast on British airwaves] told the citizens of Bristol that it was very hygienic as they would be able to widen Castle Street. He ought to be stewed in boiling oil!!

After a few references to his School Certificate exam which he had recently taken, Tim ended with a weather report. 'Had our first heavy frost on Friday night, and there was ice on the puddles. There was a fog this morning — ash from the fire I suppose. Very cold in the shelter, but I am warm enough.'[18]

To anyone who knows the Clifton area well, it will be clear from this letter that Clifton College had so far enjoyed a lucky escape. Most of these bombs fell within half a mile of the main school buildings, while Camp Road was no distance at all from several boarding houses. The lack of damage to the school was some consolation to Clifton's Headmaster, but Hallward was naturally very anxious about the possibility of further raids, and the cold conditions in the air-raid shelters were also a cause for worry.

Then, on the night of Monday, December 2nd, the school buildings were hit. 'Tim' wrote a few days later to tell his parents all about it.

Bomb damage at Clifton College.

We went down to the shelter as the Jerries seemed to be near, and after a short time there were some VERY LOUD concussions and we heard some more, not so loud. All Saints Church, the one with a queer lead tower, we saw burning with a bright flame, about 500 yards away.

They scattered incendiaries very freely. Two incendiaries landed in the Masters' Common Room and were put out. The School Cert. papers were only 10 feet from one, but were saved!!! One incendiary landed only 10 yards from the Chapel. There were several on the Close and many on the New Field. A 1,000 lb bomb landed between the Wiseman's and Polack's shelters whose doors were smashed by it, demolishing completely the fives courts and two squash courts. The other squash courts were left in a wrecked condition. Polack's House has no windows and hardly any tiles, all furniture and curtains being smashed. Two little bombs landed very near Wiseman's smashing walls, tiles and windows in the vicinity. Many roofs in the locality, including ours, have been broken by the same.

Two 500 lb H.E. bombs landed on the Pre Close between Emmanuel Church and the Science School, not doing much damage, only about seven small panes of glass being broken in the Science School. One of the big limes was entirely uprooted and its top now lies near where its roots were. An incendiary landed on the Pre Hall roof and burnt a large hole through. Many here have got incendiary bomb fins, and some have undetonated ones (bombs, I mean).

On Monday night we didn't undress until 11 o'clock and even then only in dorms with windows open, hence I have a streaming cold which is very upsetting. Life is very trying. I can't help thinking what silly mugs we were to get into war again. P.S. Haw Haw says there is going to be another raid on Clifton on Saturday!!![19]

The heavy bomb that had fallen on the New Field missed one air-raid shelter full of boys from Wiseman's House by 30 feet and another full of Polack's boys by 60 feet. As both houses had been rendered uninhabitable, Hallward sent the boys of these two houses home the next day (December 3rd), and the rest of the boarders shortly afterwards, though lessons continued for day boys. On Saturday December 7th an emergency meeting of the Council took place at Clifton under the chairmanship of Lord Birdwood, as Sir Robert Witt was unable to attend on that day. This placed Hallward in a strong position to argue the case for evacuation again, and in this he was backed up by the Regional Commissioner, Sir Hugh Elles, who happened to be an Old Cliftonian. After a long discussion the Council voted for evacuation on the grounds that many parents had already withdrawn their sons from the school and a safer site was now essential.[20] This did not please Sir Robert Witt who sent a telegram deploring the

Damage done by the bomb that fell between Polack's House and Wiseman's House.

decision and also complaining that the Council had not held their meeting on either the Thursday or Friday when he was free to come.[21]

The decision to move Clifton College from Bristol, though not his alone to take, was certainly one of which Hallward fully approved, and which, indeed, he had urged for some time. It was without question the most important decision made in his professional life so far. Was it a thoroughly wise move, or a rash adventure which might have ruined the school? Sir Robert Witt considered it a panic measure and up to a point events proved him right because the school buildings were not in fact damaged any more, the raids on Bristol petered out and the flying bombs of 1944 plagued only the south east. Indeed, as we shall see, while Clifton was in exile the school buildings were thought safe enough to become the headquarters of U.S. General Omar Bradley and the centre of a highly secret network involved in the planning of the D Day landings. If a bomb had dropped on the central school buildings in the early months of 1944, full as they were of U.S. Army personnel and detailed plans, maps and codes being made ready for D Day, a great deal more than the future of Clifton College might have been at stake. It can certainly be argued, with the advantage of hindsight, that Clifton should have stayed put in 1940. After a few quiet months with no further damage to the school, confidence, and pupils, might well have returned. But Hallward did not have the advantage of hindsight. He felt the risks were so great that Clifton must go — but he knew that he had to make the evacuation work, and that his reputation depended on it.

As they emerged from the Council meeting on that Saturday, all concerned were well aware that, having taken the decision to evacuate, they now had to find, with all speed, somewhere to go. Sir Robert Waley-Cohen gave his full support to the Headmaster and rang round all the government departments from his home on Exmoor, only to meet with refusals. 'This is a national scandal', he said to onlookers. 'I shall speak to Winston about it.'[22] For a time it seemed as though Malvern College could provide a home but this scheme fell through when Malvern in turn was required (ironically enough) to evacuate to Harrow to make room for a government department. Eventually it was yet another Old Cliftonian who came to the rescue of his old school. As Quartermaster-General, Sir Walter Venning was well placed to make the following arrangements, which suited all parties. A number of small hotels in Bude, currently occupied by the Army, would be released for use by Clifton College. In return the buildings at Clifton would be used by the Army, who would pay rent for them to the school. The Preparatory School would move to a small manor house, Butcombe Court, about ten miles south of Bristol. These plans were finalized by the beginning of January 1941, and the Council now looked to their Headmaster to set the great wheels of evacuation in motion.

Evacuation to Bude

In a way, Bude was the perfect place for someone with Hallward's love of fresh air and exercise. It was remote and wild; there were awesome black cliffs and jagged rocks, and huge Atlantic rollers crashed on to the sandy beach. The small town could be reached only by twisting roads and a one-track railway: it was a world on its own dominated by the sea, the sky, and the wind. The school had been given two medium-sized hotels and four boarding-houses on Summerleaze Terrace, facing Bude Haven, and a café on the headland. That was all. Somehow 310 boys and about thirty masters with their families had to be accommodated, lessons had to be taught, games played, public school life lived. Space was at a premium. Housemasters were limited to furniture for two rooms only; other masters were allowed only a margarine box full of books. The move from Clifton began on January 30th 1941 and was made no easier by very cold weather and snow. Hallward and his family crammed themselves into a few rooms of a small hotel while most of the Clifton boys' houses had a floor each of the larger hotels. All boys ate centrally in what had once been the Headland Café, all staff and their families (including the Hallwards) dined in a Staff 'Refectory' in the Westcliff Hotel. On Sundays the school trooped out to the charming little church of St Olaf's, Poughill, for a weekly service. Games were played on some very makeshift rugby and (later) cricket pitches. Science was taught in the laboratories of Bude County School and another school at Stratton, a few miles away — but these facilities could only be used when the local pupils had gone home after 4.00 pm.

Hallward had to take all the decisions concerning these arrangements and to delegate the details to members of staff, some of whom, such as bachelor Martin Hardcastle, enjoyed the adventure. But for housemasters with families the necessity of living in very cramped conditions cheek-by-jowl with their boys was in many ways a most unwelcome hardship. The entire experience of boarding was a novelty to some of the pupils because the day boys had been

The coastline at Bude.

given the option of going to Bude as boarders, and most of them did. So for four years and one term Clifton made a new life for itself in the far from ideal conditions at Bude. How did it fare?

The answer is: amazingly well. Perhaps the most obvious confirmation of this is the fact that numbers remained very steady: 310 boys went down to Bude in 1941 and 295 returned in 1945. Given the accommodation available, this was about as many as could be coped with. Hallward was well aware of the need to reassure parents that the move to Bude had been a success and in March 1942 he spoke to a large gathering of Clifton parents in Emmanuel Parish Hall, Clifton. According to the report in the *Bristol Evening Post*, he said 'what had astonished him was the way one could take a school out of its original buildings and transfer it to another place. It had shown him there was a soul, a spirit, inside a school that was much stronger than the buildings, and he had been amazed at the way the school had flourished, and flourished exceedingly. They had been at Bude four terms, and this last term had been extraordinarily successful. He would welcome discussions with parents who were separated from their boys and who did not have the opportunity of going to Bude'. Finally, 'he asked for frank, constructive criticism: "I want to make Clifton better, if possible," he said.' Following this E.G. Sharp, the Headmaster of The Pre, took the opportunity to point out that 'the arrangements at Butcombe were especially good'.[1]

Unloading at Bude.

Commemoration was celebrated at Bude in June 1942, and Hallward had invited Paul Vellacott (now Master of Peterhouse) to be the Chief Guest. At the last minute Vellacott was prevented by his War Office responsibilities from attending and, in a friendly gesture, Hallward invited Norman Whatley to take his place. In his speech, reported in the Bristol papers, Hallward emphasized that numbers had been well maintained and that 'the entry for next term was larger than the number of boys expected to leave in July, which meant that nearly all the boarding-houses would have as many boys as they could take in their present quarters, while in the Preparatory School also the numbers would be up next term.'[2] So the word went round that all was well with Clifton at Bude and that it was a safe, healthy and successful school.

To judge by the yardstick which at that time was everywhere recognized as the indicator of quality — scholarships to Oxford and Cambridge — the early years at Bude were astonishingly successful. In 1941 twelve awards were won, in 1942 sixteen, and in 1943 a record twenty-one. These results took Clifton to the top of the public-school league tables, a position that it had never reached before. In 1942 *The Spectator*, taking into account the fact that the numbers at Bude were much smaller than academic rivals like St Paul's, Eton and Manchester Grammar School, placed Clifton first on average. In 1943 Clifton's twenty-one awards won outright, forcing M.G.S. into second place (20) with Eton and St Paul's equal third (18).[3] What were the reasons for this success?

First place must be given to the fact that the intellectual quality of the boys admitted to Clifton in Whatley's last years was definitely high. By the time they had reached the sixth form many of these boys found themselves transported to Bude where there was little to distract them from their academic studies. Moreover, there was a consciousness that in the world outside Clifton everyone was 'doing their bit' for the war effort, and it seemed right and proper to work hard to achieve good results. The third factor is that of the 37 awards gained in 1942 and 1943 no less than sixteen were won in History and those concerned are unanimous in giving the credit for this to a very young man called Denis Mack Smith. Hallward had been having difficulties with one of the older History teachers who seemed on the edge of a breakdown. 'Next time you come across a good history man, don't hesitate to chuck out P.H.B' a pupil had recently written in a confidential letter to the Headmaster, and by the end of the summer term Hallward had acted on this precocious advice.[4] Mack Smith had been Head of School at Haileybury and his scholarship papers for entry to Peterhouse had been so good that they had been sent round the other Colleges for comparison.[5] By the summer of 1941 he had gained a first class in Part One of the History Tripos, though he had not yet taken Part Two and was not, therefore, a graduate. However, with a Haileybury and Peterhouse pedigree and such brilliant

The Clifton staff at Bude.

academic credentials, he was not to be missed. From Mack Smith's point of view he had been declared medically unfit for military service, and to help with the task of educating historians at Clifton when the History department was in something of a crisis seemed an appropriate contribution to make, so he duly arrived at Bude for the beginning of the September term of 1941.

It must be remembered that most of the younger Clifton staff had already gone to fight in the War, and the teachers at Bude were nearly all middle-aged and over. Denis Mack Smith was barely twenty-one and still in the exuberant mood of an undergraduate: his appeal to members of the sixth form was irresistible. Moreover, as only a few years before he had written some of the best History scholarship papers seen at Cambridge, he was in a good position to pass on the knack to his attentive Clifton pupils. He stayed only two years and this was partly because Hallward, anxious to make him into a 'good schoolmaster' was keen that he should teach lower forms and uncongenial subjects. Neverthe-less the two men shared a great deal of common interests and, looking closer in age than they actually were, gave a youthful and strongly intellectual thrust to life at Bude in the middle years. Mack Smith left in 1943 to work for the War Cabinet Office before returning to Cambridge to finish his degree, and become successively a Fellow of Peterhouse, a Fellow of All Souls, Oxford, a Fellow of the British Academy, and a world authority on Italian History.

But it would not be true to say that academic work was the only option available to Bude Cliftonians. Hallward strove to maintain the full range of activities that are the hallmarks of the public school, and in games a high standard was maintained. The rugby 1st XV lost only seven of its twenty-three matches during the Bude years, and the cricket XI did even better, losing only three out of seventeen games and maintaining the Lord's fixture with Tonbridge. Hockey was played in the Lent term and there were endless opportunities for cross-country runs, and swimming in the open-air pool down at the beach. Douglas Fox worked hard to keep the music alive at Bude and Cecil Taylor produced an annual school play. In 1942 each house was for the first time required to put on a short play as part of a House Competition, and this was the beginning of what became, and still remains, an important feature of Clifton life. Hallward tried to keep the school in touch with the outside world by inviting down celebrities to lecture and adjudicate — people like the musicians Sir Hugh Allen and Leon Goossens, artist John Piper and poet John Betjeman.

There can be little doubt that the remarkably buoyant mood of Clifton at Bude owed a great deal to Hallward's example. A former pupil wrote to him after a reunion in 1991: 'We were thinking a great deal about you, and of your inspiration and energy. It was more than just the success of survival in war-time; I think that most of those who, like me, spent part of their schooldays at Bude and part at Clifton enjoyed the Bude years most. There was a sense of freedom and community: I still don't know how you managed to keep so many activities — cultural, athletic, musical — going in such a remote spot.'[6] Another former pupil, writing in 1994, pointed out that Hallward 'had the highest expectations of those he encountered. Doing well was insufficient. It had to be doing one's best. And of course we all remember him at Bude as we cowered against the Atlantic gales "Vigour, vigour, vigour!", he would exclaim, gown flying behind him, as he strode unsweatered along the hotel fronts. We laughed at this, but admiringly.'[7]

No headmaster is universally admired, however, and many of the senior staff at Clifton and at Bude found Hallward difficult to take. They had been affronted by his attempts to reduce their salaries and they were not entirely happy about having been decanted from Clifton into such very cramped quarters in Bude. Sound and solid schoolmasters, they were in general no match for Hallward's intellect and found his bumptious confidence irritating. In particular they disliked his methods of gleaning information about the school from pupils, whom he encouraged to write to him in confidence. This is always a risky strategy because certain pupils take advantage of the opportunity to release their frustrations, and an atmosphere of suspicion can be created. A number of letters to Hallward from pupils have survived, and in them words are not minced. One which arrived just before the move to Bude insists: 'I do not think it an exaggeration to say that the staff is honeycombed with sedition. I have heard mutterings and grumblings about you and each other which seem to denote an approaching crisis. The salary cuts have of course annoyed them.' Clearly an historian, this informant went on to liken the situation to that of 'A Liberal Prime Minister and a Tory Cabinet'.[8]

With the move to Bude this 'crisis' — if indeed there really was one — blew over in the face of the immense task ahead. But that Hallward had influential critics on the staff there is no doubt, and chief among them was Forbes Mackintosh, the housemaster of School House. Educated at Merchiston and Oriel College, Oxford, Mackintosh had been a housemaster in the Pre until 1938 when Whatley had moved him to take over School House, which needed tightening up after the *laissez-faire* reign of Cecil Taylor. His reputation as a hard man was by no means undeserved and pupils everywhere ran for cover when he was in one of his bad moods. 'Sir, I have been having difficulties with my housemaster', a School House boy explained to Hallward. 'So have I, so have I' came the retort.[9] Tall, vigorous, athletic and, in his own way, dynamic, Forbes Mackintosh was something of a match for his Headmaster.

On the July 10th 1943, towards the end of the summer term, a short note, written in block capitals and unsigned, reached Hallward. 'Dear Headmaster,' it began, 'The school is becoming very immoral. Why can't we have strong housemasters? The Town Houses will go to the dogs completely after this term. Mr [X,Y and Z] know nothing that goes on. They are afraid to find out. This is only written because I love Clifton and hate what is happening in the lower part of the school. It really is becoming pretty serious only naturally no-one will come and tell you.'[10] No headmaster could ignore such a plea, though many would have proceeded cautiously. But in matters of sex and morals Hallward was as breezily frank and forthright as in anything else and he took vigorous action to find out what was going on. This resulted in a typed letter, signed by all eight housemasters, which reached him on 25th July. It complained that in recent terms Hallward had by-passed housemasters and listened too much to the critical opinion of pupils. 'We are all fully aware of our responsibility for the welfare of the boys in our charge. We have reason to think that our awareness could be more openly recognized, and to wish that your confidence in us were more plainly demonstrated. We share your anxiety about the moral condition of the school and will do all that lies in our power to improve it. But we would ask you to consider whether this aim would not best be achieved if discussion of individual boys were with their housemasters and not with their contemporaries.'[11]

The first signature was that of Mackintosh, but for a headmaster to receive such a letter from *all* his housemasters was indeed a dangerous sign, and Hallward began to suffer again from the duodenitis problems that had affected him in times of stress at Cambridge. The Council agreed to allow him leave of absence for the following term, during which Cecil Taylor filled the role of Acting Headmaster. The Hallwards moved from the small pink-washed house next to the Hartland Hotel which had been their home for the last couple of years and took up residence in a bungalow near Tintagel which was the holiday home of Margaret's brother George Tait, the Eton housemaster. Meanwhile Forbes Mackintosh penned a doggerel poem which, though doubtless passed privately to his friends for their amusement, did not see the official light of day for over forty years.

Alice in Wonderland (Cornish Edition)

'You are young, Brother Bertrand', the House Sixth said
'And so painfully breezy and bright:
Yet your policy frequently stands on its head —
Do you think, in your job, that is right?'

'In my youth', said his Master, 'I studied too much
To admit of its mental digestion.
So now I rely on the personal touch,
Which "my parents" accept without question.'

'You are young' said the lad, 'as I mentioned before,
And your hair has remained very yellow.
But your voice and your laugh I can only deplore —
What gave you that thunderous bellow?'

'As a Don', replied Bertrand, 'I found, when I spoke,
Undergraduates left in a hurry.
But, now I have schoolboys to laugh at each joke,
There's no great occasion to worry.'

'You are young', said the boy, 'and the juvenile soul
Is eager, impetuous, quick.
Yet you talked to the Sixth about natal control —
Wasn't *that* just a little too thick?'

'When I came', said the Head, 'I did not know enough
To make my position quite plain:
But, now that I've skimmed through that Freudian stuff,
I shall do it again & again.'

'You are young,' said the Sixth, 'and your taste for intrigue
(Which, as all must admit, is enormous)
Has made this School top of the Backbiters League —
Why *are* you so keen on informers?'

'I have answered three questions', said Bert, with a laugh
That echoed from Widemouth to Scadgehill:
'You can put any more that you have to my staff —
I am off for the term to Tintagel!'[12]

It is possible that Hallward's absence for a whole term induced a sense of remorse among the housemasters who were, after all, a very decent group of men, and that by the end of it they realized how much the school's success at Bude depended upon the dynamism in their Headmaster that they found, on occasion, so irritating. At all events Hallward was back in harness for the January term of 1944 and the matter had seemingly blown over. All the same the affair would have raised question marks in the minds of the members of the Council, and this must have been, for Hallward, the low point of his career as a headmaster.

After the War

As we have seen, Clifton had been allowed a move to the Bude hotels in return for releasing the College buildings to the Army. At first they were used as an Officer Cadet Training Unit, but in November 1942 'Old Glory' and the men of the U.S. Army V Corps came marching in, and Clifton's hallowed Close — the scene of many a century by W.G. Grace as well as the world record for a batsman (628 not out) made by a Clifton schoolboy Arthur Collins — became a baseball ground. In October 1943 General Omar Bradley arrived at Clifton, establishing the school as the headquarters of the U.S. First Army and working on detailed planning of an invasion of the Normandy beaches — a location chosen by an Old

U.S. soldiers on the Close at Clifton.

Cliftonian, General Sir Frederick Morgan. By the summer of 1944 Bradley had gone and the D Day invasion had been successfully launched, though U.S. Army units remained at Clifton until September. In November the school was notified that the buildings were not required for further use by any military or government department, and Hallward was able to start discussing with the Council a date for Clifton's return to Bristol.[1]

The War was by no means over yet, and flying-bombs, Hitler's 'secret weapon', were causing havoc in the south-east. On the other hand all the signs were that Germany would soon collapse, and with the capture of the Peenemunde rocket sites the threat from the air was over. The Bursar, Alan Imlay, took stock of the damage that had been done to the school buildings by their various occupants during the evacuation years and came to the conclusion that with £47,000 of compensation from the government and the hard work of eighty men, the school could re-open at Clifton for the summer term of 1945; and indeed it did.

If the move to Bude had been a formidable administrative task, the re-establishment of the school at Bristol was, in a way, equally problematic. The buildings were now far too big for the 294 boys, so a rapid expansion in numbers was necessary. Moreover, the U.S. Army had converted 'Big School' into a Dining Hall, complete with fully equipped kitchens, so the decision was taken to abandon catering by houses and feed centrally. As the school had done this at Bude, it seemed a perfectly natural step to take. Commemoration was held on June 30th, shortly after the war with Germany had ended. The Guest of Honour was Commander Herbert Agar, representing the U.S. Ambassador, and he presented Lord Birdwood (still President of the College) with a Stars and Stripes flag to mark Clifton's special place in the affection of the U.S. Army. In his official Headmaster's address Hallward spoke of 'a new era of Clifton history'. He emphasized that under John Percival Clifton had been a reforming, liberal school and he pledged himself to continue that tradition, chiefly by extending schemes for taking 'bursary boys' as recommended by the Fleming Report of 1942.[2] Like a lot of liberal-minded people working in Britain's public schools, Hallward approved of the education they provided but regretted that it was, in general, available only to those who could pay — and pay handsomely.

The years immediately following the return to Bristol saw many staff changes. Forbes Mackintosh left in July 1945, having secured (without a testimonial from Hallward) the headmastership of Loretto School near Edinburgh. To replace him in School House Hallward chose Martin Hardcastle, whom he perceived to be a 'great schoolmaster'. A Wykehamist with aristocratic connections, a handsome bearing, and a dusty degree, Hardcastle followed the Pigou tradition of educating boys by adventure, first in the Rover Scouts and then in an organization called 'Terriers' which he had perfected at Bude. Hallward truly admired Martin Hardcastle: academics aside, he was a man after his own heart. Another non-academic whom Hallward advanced to a housemastership was the Revd. Peter Brook, a former England rugby international and all-round sportsman who was also School Chaplain. When Major Rodney Gee was released from his prisoner-of-war camp he returned to Clifton and was given the task of re-opening the closed Watson's House. Indeed, during this period there were changes of housemaster in seven of the eight houses, and in making these important internal appointments Hallward shaped the course of Clifton's development for the next twenty years and more.

Circumstances up to 1945 had meant that there were very few opportunities to make new additions to the Clifton staff, but in his last three years as Headmaster Hallward was able to make up for this by appointing twelve new men to the Upper School Common Room. In many cases he asked contacts of his to recommend suitable people and then suggested to them that they might like to apply for a post at Clifton. 'I am afraid that you have not got the qualifications that I need for the post for which I was considering you, namely a first class degree,' he wrote to one candidate, and indeed of his twelve appointments eight did have first class degrees (one of them from Peterhouse).[3] Five of Hallward's new staff subsequently became headmasters (Arthur Bell at Cheltenham Grammar School, John Thompson at Keswick School, David Baggley at Bolton School where he was Chairman of HMC, Harry Edwards at Queen Elizabeth's Hospital, Bristol, and Robin Hone at Exeter School), and three, after distinguished careers at Clifton, were appointed Senior Lecturers at Bristol University (David Gaunt, Philip Polack, Evan Prentice). Others, like Michael Lane, Hillary Crauford and 'Bill' Leadbetter, became legendary Clifton figures with characters much larger than life. In addition, two of Hallward's appointments to the Pre Staff became Senior School headmasters in due course (Tom Brown at the King's School, Gloucester and Nigel Gibbs at Colston's School, Bristol). Considering that Hallward made all these appointments between May 1945 and his departure in the summer of 1948, it is a very distinguished list.

Hallward also had to find a new headmaster for the Preparatory School in 1946. A new Bursar had been appointed by the Council in 1945, but this, their third attempt to appoint a satisfactory Bursar, proved as fruitless as the first two and the man concerned resigned after a few months. This may have led a few long-standing members of Council to wonder if Whatley had not been right about his Bursars all along. A solution to this dilemma was found by appointing E.G. Sharp, the Headmaster of the Pre, to the position of Bursar. He knew the school well, was efficient and well respected, and was used to working with the Headmaster. After quite a long search, and again using his network of contacts,

Hallward found L.H.A. Hankey, a thirty-seven year old housemaster at Giggleswick School. 'Hank's' appointment to the Pre set it on a course of expansion and development which was to make it one of the leading Preparatory Schools in the next decades.

When Hallward arrived at Clifton in 1939 the school, as has been explained, had been running at a loss. One of the unexpected though very welcome side effects of evacuation to Bude was a marked improvement in Clifton's finances. This occurred because the cost of running the school at Bude was a fraction of what it had been in Bristol, and considerable rents were paid to the Council by the Army, and by other organizations that had hired some of the school buildings — such as the BBC and Imperial Airways. Also, two legacies totalling £80,000 had been left to the school by Old Cliftonians during the War years.[4] With the money granted to the school as compensation, and a dramatic increase in the number of pupils, which had risen to 781 in both schools by the time Hallward left, Clifton was placed on a strong financial footing, much to the satisfaction of the Council. Sir Robert Witt, who had loyally supported Hallward at Bude despite his initial opposition to the evacuation, retired as Chairman of Council in 1946 and his place was taken by Raymond (Lord) Evershed, a High Court Judge who later became Master of the Rolls, and who proved to be not only a widely experienced, but a very congenial Chairman.

In the summer term of 1946 Winston Churchill, who was Chancellor of Bristol University, made a brief visit to Clifton College, driving through the school in an open car and being greeted by Hallward and the Head of School. 'So you're Head of School are you?' he enquired of R.B. Gorrie in a famous put-down. 'Congratulations. I was always bottom of mine.'[5] He was no longer Prime Minister, of course, because the Labour Party had swept to victory at the polls in 1945 and its plans for a New Britain included schemes for the modification — even abolition — of the public schools, which they considered socially divisive. Despite his own traditional 'upper-middle-class' background, Hallward was not a hidebound Conservative and had a good deal of sympathy with those who sought to break down the barriers of class. 'There is very little doubt that bringing to the school each year a number of really able boys from elementary schools is a practical means of carrying out the policy of opening the door of Clifton to the ablest and most suitable boys, irrespective of birth or wealth, who will profit by the education we offer', he had told the Council in 1943, arguing in favour of the extension of bursaries.[6]

Meanwhile Hallward was able to entertain the citizens of Bristol with his views on a variety of other subjects. Early in 1946 he was urging members of Bristol Round Table not to be satisfied with less than three children in their families, lest the population of Britain should dwindle away. He followed this

Hallward greeting Winston Churchill at Clifton in 1946.

with the view that 'the problem child was in seven cases out of ten the only child in a family'. Not surprisingly, 'a lively discussion followed Mr Hallward's talk', as the *Western Daily Press* reported.[7] Later he is found encouraging the Bristol Naturalist Society, at their annual dinner, to think big and establish a rival to Kew Gardens in Bristol, or 'a Whipsnade of the West, with the Zoological Gardens on the other side of the Suspension Bridge'.[8] Perhaps he had visions of Clifton College taking over the Zoo's present site across Guthrie Road from the school. 'Head warns "pagan" parents' ran a headline in the *Daily Mail*, reporting Hallward's Commemoration speech of 1947. 'The educational responsibility of parents in this country has not been fully maintained during the War', he told his audience. 'The old English standards of honesty and right dealing have been allowed to go by the board. Transactions under the counter, or in the Black and Grey Markets are referred to in the home by parents in front of their boys', he complained. And he regretted that so many boys did not attend church during the holidays. These 'pagan homes' were frustrating the school's attempt to produce God-fearing gentlemen.[9] Here was Lord Chalmers' 'flying-buttress of the Anglican Church' doing a bit of public buttressing.

Given that his views on religion were by no means orthodox, Hallward nevertheless understood the importance of presenting a strong moral lead without stepping across the line of hypocrisy. At Bude, where the vast bulk of Clifton Chapel did not dominate the scene, he would usually read to the school at morning assemblies held in the Headland Café. The *Book of Wisdom* was a favourite of his but his audience could sometimes be restless. 'BLH dealt with this by sheer force of personality,' a Bude pupil remembered. 'He simply stood there, chin held high, in characteristic pose, and said "Quiet" very loudly, once or twice. It worked — and the readings from *Wisdom* continued, for a time at any rate. He read aloud extremely well. In particular, I remember he used to raise his voice at the end of a sentence, instead of dropping it, as is more usual.'[10] Hallward's distinctly 'pukka' voice was always a source of entertainment to some of Clifton's less 'pukka' pupils, who enjoyed imitating it as long as he was not within earshot.

Back at Clifton these morning readings continued. 'The one time of day we usually saw BLH was in Chapel, where on weekdays either he or C.F. Taylor read to us either from the Bible or, as in one term, from *Pilgrim's Progress*', recalled a boy who was later ordained. 'On Saturday mornings he often conducted the worship putting on a rather unusual-looking surplice — could it have been his Scholar's Surplice from King's? — and sitting not in his own stall but that of the Chaplain.'[11] The *Pilgrim's Progress* readings were singled out by a member of staff in 1994 as one of his chief memories: 'BLH continued these for a term or two, and I personally would not have missed them,' he wrote.[12]

Among the boys Hallward had the reputation of being a strict disciplinarian. 'I remember that during the first term back at Clifton the Head of a certain House was caught by the Marshal leaving a cinema in the centre of Bristol. He was immediately stripped of his responsibilities both as Head of House and Praepostor. This had the desired effect of making us younger boys realize that we had to obey the school rules,' another pupil recalled.[13] Although both at Bude and at Clifton housemasters and prefects made free use of the cane, Hallward claimed never to have used corporal punishment himself.[14] He achieved the results he wanted by natural presence and a well-judged sense of theatre. Some pupils and parents found him unreasonable in refusing comparatively minor requests, such as to miss school for family occasions, and he was never predictable, or a 'soft touch'. This advanced his reputation for discipline, but lost him a few friends. So, sometimes, did his affable, *bravura* manner, which could be misinterpreted. 'Leaving this term are you, Bloggs? Good! Good!'[15]

Although he taught quite a lot of lessons, Hallward left the main Classics teaching to C.F. Taylor. Hallwood's ability to translate was sometimes a bit rusty but as a Classics pupil recalled, 'I enjoyed his Ancient History lessons. He did

Roman Britain with us as a special subject and brought it to life very well.'[16] A Polack's boy remembered that 'when I was in the History sixth at Bude, I attended a series of lectures he gave on one of his many great enthusiasms, to wit Dante, whose name he pronounced as *Dunnteh*. In the course of one of these, he asked us for a list of the ten greatest novels in world literature. I don't remember his full list but it certainly included Flaubert, Tolstoy and Dostoievsky, and to our amazement, *The Picture of Dorian Gray*'.[17] Another pupil thought that 'BLH was a good, stimulating teacher of English Literature to the VIth. He used to bring in a great pile of books to his lessons, each marked with slips of paper in appropriate places. These he used to illustrate points. He could also well convey a point by physical movement: I recall him standing four-square, legs apart slightly, to illustrate the essential character of Samuel Johnson, saying at the same time "Johnson was *plantez-là*", and suiting his action to the word.'[18]

In a school of several hundred boys, the fact that the Headmaster's family consisted of four daughters did not escape notice. As the three eldest girls had been born between 1927 and 1930 they reached adolescence during the Bude years, though in term time they were generally away themselves at boarding-schools. However, a Bude pupil clearly remembered 'Sunday night suppers for the sixth form in the Headmaster's house. This was an enormously important civilizing influence with Mrs Hallward and the four girls. The weekend speakers would be there and we learnt to improve our social graces. He had a radiogram and the classical Red Label HMVs in the days when they were a rarity and a treasure.'[19] From the family point of view, Bude was a splendid place for the Hallwards to spend the summer holidays, with the school closed and plenty of time for the beach and bathing, and the opportunity of friendships with the children of several members of staff. Nevertheless, it was rather a disrupted nine years, with homes at 24 College Road, then *Glenavon*, then the Hartland Hotel, then the Pink House, and back to *Glenavon* again.

By 1947 Hallward was giving careful thought to the future. He was approaching the age of fifty, after which it would be difficult to make a career move within education. His work at Clifton had won him a notable reputation, and he was approached as a candidate for the headmastership of Charterhouse to succeed Robert Birley.[20] But another public school did not attract him as much as the expanding world of the universities where, as he perceived, exciting opportunities lay. He let the Cambridge Appointments Board know of his ambitions and when the post of Principal of the University College at Nottingham was advertised late in 1947, he applied for it. So did many distinguished candidates, including two other headmasters — Hugh Lyon of Harrow and Charles Morris of King Edward's, Birmingham. Hallward's cause was helped considerably by Rutherford Ikin, a King's contemporary who was Headmaster of Trent College, near Nottingham, and who spoke warmly of Hallward to many members of the University College Council. Another chance that helped Hallward was the fact that Charles Morris withdrew from the Nottingham race on his appointment as Vice-Chancellor of Leeds University.[21]

'On the first day of the January term 1948', a Clifton boy remembered, 'BLH was conspicuous by his absence and most of us were surprised that he was not there, and wondered why. We did not have long to wait because during the day the Marshal came round with a notice summoning the whole school to assemble after afternoon school in Big School for the second time that day. When we assembled, C.F. Taylor read out an announcement from BLH informing us of his appointment to Nottingham as Principal of the University College, which is where he was that day. The appointment was to take effect in September, and the notice went on to say that he would therefore be leaving Clifton at the end of the summer term'.[22] 'I remember him returning from Nottingham in January immediately after his appointment as Principal', another boy recalled, 'and declaring in strident tones that his priority was to develop microbiology and biochemistry. We thought this terribly funny because the terms were unfamiliar and sounded ridiculous. The point of the reminiscence is that it was typical of

Four headmasters of Clifton. Left to right: Hallward, Whatley, Hammond and Lee.

him to have embraced with enthusiasm genuine possibilities which were probably little less strange to him than they were to us.'[23]

With the Nottingham appointment confirmed, the Clifton Council had to move swiftly to find a suitable successor as headmaster and appointed a Selection Committee on 29th January, headed by the Chairman, Lord Justice Evershed. They received thirty-seven applications and interviewed seven candidates but, as Evershed explained in a letter to the whole Council, 'it was felt that none of them was quite in the first rank. The standard we set for ourselves was no doubt high, but we felt that the position demanded it'. In short, Hallward was a hard act to follow. In the end, he himself urged the Council to approach his former pupil Desmond Lee, then a Fellow of Corpus Christi College, Cambridge. Lee had not thought of applying for Clifton, or of being a headmaster, but he attended an interview where 'every member of the Committee was as greatly impressed with him as I had been', Evershed explained, 'and everyone felt that he was in a class by himself compared with all the other possible candidates.'[24] So the pupil followed his teacher and Hallward proved again his flair for choosing the right man for the right job, because at Clifton and later at Winchester, Sir Desmond Lee was recognized as a paragon among headmasters. Nor did the Hallward link at Clifton end here for when Lee moved on in 1954 he was succeeded by Nick Hammond, another of Hallward's former pupils, and a close family friend.

When Clifton celebrated its Centenary in 1962, a volume of essays about the school's history was published and S.P. Beachcroft, who had been a housemaster at Bude, wrote a piece about the evacuation which emphasized the success of the move and the very special atmosphere that had been created in Cornwall among a generation of boys who were already achieving distinction in many walks of life. 'It would be less than generous', Beachcroft concluded 'to fail to say categorically that the success of Clifton at Bude was due basically to the inspiration, resolution and energy of one man, the Headmaster. It is true enough that there were many at hand to help, to advise and to undertake some of the detailed planning but on him throughout fell the full burden of responsibility and decision in the face of very many awkward situations. There are not many men who could have withstood such a strain. At the same time much of the intellectual vigour and the enterprise which were characteristic of the school at this period found its origin in him.'[25]

At Commemoration in 1948 there were warm words of thanks from the Council, and Sir Robert Witt produced a sepia drawing of the Acropolis at Athens, reputedly by Turner, as a leaving present. Perhaps the most telling tribute came from the boy Editor of The Cliftonian who wrote: 'To those who might have been pardoned for despondency as they regretfully compared

Summerleaze Terrace with College Road, the Headland Pavilion with Big
School, the Headmaster never failed to set a magnificent example of cheerful
courage. It was his finest service to Clifton. In March 1945 the discomforts and
hardships of Bude came to an end, but there were many difficulties awaiting the
school at Clifton. Again the Headmaster's optimism has been justified by the
bewilderingly rapid rise in the school's numbers, by the gradual approach to
pre-war standards in athletics and the successful continuation of central feeding
which has involved a major alteration to Big School.'

'Energy, interest and charm', the Editor continued, 'are the qualities for
which Mr Hallward will be longest remembered at Clifton. Duties and inevitable anxieties have never prevented him from joining with immense vigour and
enthusiasm into all school games and cultural activities. Although overstrain
forced him to rest for a single term in 1943, he has never seemed tired or bored.
He has poured out a constant stream of original ideas on every subject, and so
varied are his interests that he can completely captivate those who lack his own
clear mind and broad outlook. Those who have had contact with him in school
acknowledge his vitality as a teacher. Even the most apathetic are infected by
his enthusiasm, whether it be for Homer, or Dante, or Population Problems or
Mountaineering. Scholarship successes since 1939 prove increased intellectual
enterprise and a new spirit of enquiry and research. Current Affairs periods,
wide reading and increased interest in dramatics, are the results of Mr Hallward's
impetuous example. The Headmaster's personality and charm have won him
the affection of boys and a parental admiration bordering on idolatry. And those
who have been privileged to meet Mrs Hallward will never forget her gracious
manner, and her startling knowledge of and deep interest in every member of
the school.'[26] Few lines in the whole history of *The Cliftonian* magazine have been
so shrewdly written by a member of the school (N.T. Hardyman). No wonder
that he became a distinguished Civil Servant.

Back in 1939 the *Daily Mail* had said that a good headmaster 'must be
something of a diplomat, a salesman, and a dictator to succeed'. That Hallward
was a natural salesman and capable of being dictatorial was quite clear.
Diplomacy was an art he was still learning, though his own charm and his wife's
tact usually got him out of tight corners. On a personal level he certainly ruffled
a few feathers, but that he served Clifton magnificently as Headmaster there can
be no doubt now, and few doubted it then. Yet it was all, in a sense, just a
rehearsal; for at Nottingham he would encounter challenges and opportunities
to test him far more than even the bombs of Bristol and the biting winds of Bude.
Clifton's first Headmaster, Bishop John Percival, had been one of the great
school builders of the nineteenth century: during his seventeen years as the first
Vice-Chancellor of Nottingham, Clifton's seventh Headmaster would show
himself to be one of the great university builders of the twentieth century.

Part Four

Nottingham 1948-1957

A New University

The Hallwards' new home at Nottingham, Highfield House, was something of an architectural gem. Built about 1799 in a restrained Georgian style, it had been the centre of a small country estate lying within sight of the ancient City of Nottingham three miles away.[1] Joseph Lowe, the first owner of the house, had an ornamental pond dug at the bottom of a slope in front of the building, and by 1948 this had been developed into a formal lake of considerable size. The rooms on the ground floor included a study, a long drawing room with two fireplaces, and a large dining room, so large that the dining-table was in fact a converted billiard table, slightly too wide for conversation at dinner parties,

Highfield House.

Margaret always thought. Two Brueghel prints hung in the room, one (*The Wedding Feast*) nicknamed 'Central Feeding' in honour of Bude and Clifton.[2] A most elegant slender staircase led to the first floor where there was a large number of smallish bedrooms, ideal for a household which included four daughters and the Vice-Chancellor's mother, still in fine fettle. During the nineteenth century the Lowes of Highfield had gazed through their floor-length sash windows at rolling acres of parkland but for the last thirty years, thanks to the generosity of Nottingham's remarkable Jesse Boot, a University College had been built on their former estate.

As early as 1798 an Adult School had been established in Nottingham and in 1873 the University of Cambridge had organized Extension Lectures in the city. These proved so successful that, spurred on by an anonymous donation of £10,000, the City Council agreed to pay for a handsome University College building in Shakespeare Street, designed, inevitably, in the scholastic Gothic style and opened in 1881. From comparatively humble beginnings, and educating along the way D.H. Lawrence, the College grew in size and ambition so that by 1920 the original building was far too small and the site too restrictive. At this point Sir Jesse Boot stepped in and made what was then a mind-boggling offer to finance a new University College building on the Highfield Estate, which he had bought in 1919.

The story of Jesse Boot and his achievements is truly amazing. He was born in 1850 the son of John and Mary Boot, both ardent Methodists who were inspired by John Wesley's book *Primitive Physic* to sell herbal remedies in a tiny shop in Nottingham's Goosegate, the poorest and most crowded area of the town. Jesse's father died in 1860 and at the age of thirteen Jesse abandoned school to help his mother who was struggling to run the family shop. He gradually realized the importance of bulk-buying, price-cutting and advertising and became, in his late twenties, the busiest shopkeeper in Nottingham. In 1883 he opened a completely new chemist's store on Goosegate and specialized in attractive displays to draw in customers. Soon he had bought other shops in Nottingham, and then shops in other cities of the Midlands and the North. At the age of 35 he suffered a breakdown from over-work and, on a rest-cure in Jersey, met the 23 year-old Florence Rowe. They married in 1886 and Florence proved herself a keen businesswoman, particularly interested in the design and décor of the Boots shops, which by 1900 had grown to 250 and in 1913 reached a total of 560 branches. The company survived the War and provided the government with more than 5 million anti-gas respirators, as well as vast quantities of medical supplies, but the strain of over-work again afflicted Jesse who was also suffering badly from arthritis. Indeed it is one of the great ironies that this mass provider of medical relief spent the last fifteen years of his life in

Jesse Boot's new University College, opened in 1928.

a wheelchair. In 1920 he sold his company to an American conglomerate for an estimated £2.5 million and from then until his death in 1931 he concentrated on spending this vast sum (for those days) on spectacular acts of philanthropy, among which his vision for a university campus at Highfields ranked foremost.[3]

Working closely with Alderman Edmund Huntsman who had in the past acted as his solicitor and was both a member of the City Council and the Council of the University College, Jesse Boot planned a new road, University Boulevard, which would lead past his grand new College. He gave the task of building the main structure to the architect Morley Horder, who had been involved in the design of many of the Boots' stores. Horder produced a very well-mannered and dignified creation in a neo-classical style reminiscent of Aston Webb's 1913 front for Buckingham Palace, and built in similar Portland stone. Critics have suggested that the portico and pediment should have been wider and that the campanile is also slightly out of proportion. On the other hand, seen on its hill from University Boulevard, looking across the lake, it made an imposing sight on the day of its formal opening by George V and Queen Mary in the summer of 1928. The King and Queen took tea with Sir Jesse Boot on that occasion in a private room to which he had been confined because of his wheelchair: the next year he was raised to the peerage as Baron Trent.

Principal Heaton supervised the College's move from Shakespeare Street to Highfields in 1928 but he retired the following year to be replaced by Hugh Stewart, a much-decorated soldier as well as a classical scholar who had been Professor of Latin at Leeds University. He proved a vigorous and dynamic leader whose ambitions included a rise in the number of students and the winning of full university status. As a University College, Nottingham was not an independent institution; the City Council was responsible for finance and overall policy, while academically it was under the control of London University which monitored its courses and examinations, and awarded Nottingham students external London degrees. Full university status was an obvious goal but the main problem was one of finance: an autonomous institution had to be financially independent and Nottingham as yet lacked sufficient endowments. Hugh Stewart made a good deal of progress but he died suddenly at sea in 1934, returning from a holiday in New Zealand. To his successor, Professor H.A.S. Wortley, he left a student body of about 500, a staff of 92 and the unsatisfied quest for full university status.

Harry Wortley had been Professor of Education at the Nottingham College since 1923. According to one of his colleagues, he 'could display a bonhomie, a zest for the ordinary recreations of life, like golf and bridge and physical good cheer, a ready flow of talk, never superior or highly intellectual, and behind it all a shrewd practical business sense, which made it quickly possible for the non-academic to get on terms of comfort, even of intimacy, with him. For public and formal occasions he had the advantage of a "presence". On the platform, his large frame and impressive countenance riveted attention, while his utterances had the fluency and emphasis needed to convince the audience that a real contribution was being made to the matter in hand'.[4] As Professor of Education he had made important contacts on a local and national scale and he continued to press for university status. In 1938 the College was granted a Supplemental Charter which, by providing for a much wider representation on the Governing Body, loosened its ties to the City Council. Unfortunately the outbreak of war in 1939 prevented any further progress, and also imposed upon Wortley the extra burden of being Deputy Regional Commissioner for the North Midlands as well as providing facilities for Goldsmith's College and the London Institute of Education which had been evacuated from the capital.

When the War ended in 1945 and a Labour Government took office, the lack of enthusiasm for expenditure on a new university that had characterized the depressed years of the 1930's was a thing of the past. It was hoped locally that the new 'Land of Opportunity' would include a new university for Nottingham, where local men and women could study to improve their own fortunes and those of the nation. With the obstacles to university status thus removed, Wortley began to concentrate on the complex issues concerned with creating a Royal Charter. Unfortunately he fell seriously ill in the years after the War and died suddenly in 1947 as a result, many thought, of strain and over-work. 'Even when he was unable to leave his house', declared an obituary in *The Gong*, the College Literary Magazine, 'and indeed up to the very day of his death, he continued to direct the great work of College development and reconstruction. It was his tragedy that he died at the moment when his plans were about to bear fruit, and when the College was on the very threshold of university status.'[5]

Wortley's death in harness led to the appointment of his deputy, Professor Robert Peers, as Acting Principal, and he immediately devoted himself to the task of completing the draft of the Royal Charter for the new university, which was presented to the Privy Council in June 1947. The Council of the College had, meanwhile, to consider the appointment of a new Principal who would, it now seemed, be the University's first Vice-Chancellor. Wortley had been appointed from the ranks, and the claim of Peers for the post was obviously a strong one. In considering alternative candidates, however, and in appointing a public school headmaster with a national reputation as a dynamic administrator, the Council acknowledged the need to make a decisive break with the past. As it happened the Privy Council, having insisted on one major amendment, swiftly authorized the granting of the Charter, which was dated August 20th 1948. One of the many provisions of this majestic document appointed Bertrand Leslie Hallward first Vice-Chancellor of the new University of Nottingham, and term began in October 1948 in an atmosphere of high excitement prompted by this double novelty.

The title Vice-Chancellor is a misleading one which has its origins, *via* the Universities of Oxford and Cambridge, deep in the Middle Ages. It suggests that the holder is merely a deputy, whereas he is in fact the executive head of the University. The Royal Charter provided for a Chancellor (Jesse Boot's son, the second Lord Trent) but, rather like a constitutional monarch, his powers were limited and his role largely ceremonial. The Chancellor was President of the Court, described as 'The Supreme Governing Body of the University', with absolute power within it, subject to the Royal Charter and the Law of the Land. The Court consisted of about 250 people who were representatives of many institutions in local and national life, and because of its size and diversity it met infrequently. The effective Governing Body was therefore the Council, a much smaller group of men and women, again representing a wide range of (usually) local interests. It was they who appointed the Vice-Chancellor 'who shall be the principal Academic and Administrative Officer of the University and *ex-officio*

Chairman of the Senate and who shall in the absence of the Chancellor confer Degrees.' The Senate was a body representing the academic staff and composed at first of professors, whose task was 'to regulate and superintend the education and discipline of students.' The Charter additionally stated that 'there shall also be a Union of Students.'[6]

Nowadays, there is such a vast difference between a fully-developed university and even a large and famous school that few school heads would contemplate becoming Vice-Chancellors. Even in 1950 Hallward was one of only three Vice-Chancellors who had been headmasters. The other two were Charles Morris at Leeds and John Wolfenden who had just moved to Reading University from Shrewsbury School: both had previously been Oxford dons. During Hallward's time at Nottingham only one former headmaster joined the circle of provincial Vice-Chancellors, and that was Eric James who moved from Manchester Grammar School to the new University of York in 1962. Most Vice-Chancellors were professional academics with experience of running a university department; on the other hand, few university professors could have shouldered as much responsibility as Hallward had by 1948.

One of his first acts at Nottingham was to commission an official history of the University College from Professor A.C. Wood, Head of the History department. It was published in 1953 and provided an elegant and concise account of the years up to 1948, spiced with several lively passages where the author allowed himself personal comment on such topics as the state of the nation, education, the morality of youth, and the character of his colleagues. Of professors in general, he had this to say:

> Professors are a clan of infinite variegations; but, allowing for the innumerable combinations and gradations of gifts, qualities and temperaments which must always exist in any group of human beings, it is possible to discern several well-defined types — and Nottingham has had examples of all of them on its Senate. First, there are the 'born' scholars, who live for the lamp and the midnight hour. A comparatively small minority, this group, they research and write because by some mystery of their mechanism they can do no other. Occasionally (but by no means always) poor in classroom technique, and ineffective in the wider affairs of life, it is none the less they who push forward the frontiers of knowledge and add lustre to the university they serve. Those with a 'business' mentality are a very different lot. Their delight is in the *minutiae* of departmental administration, in bulging filing cabinets and foolproof time-tables. They demonstrate an uncanny — and uncomfortable — intimacy with statutes, regulations, and half-defunct resolutions, they are skilled in all the strategy of internal politics, above all they thrive on the

jading atmosphere of Senates, Faculties, committees of every kind. How-ever prolonged, dizzy or exhausting the discussion, they emerge fresh and alert, full of new points with which to keep more weary, pallid colleagues on the rack. Then there are the showmen or 'blowhards' as the Americans would call them. These progress by the tricks of salesmanship rather than by the toils of scholarship. Not for them the tedious and often unrewarding labours of research. A fluent and persuasive tongue, a good platform manner, a ready flow of arresting, if rather nebulous, projects, an instinct for the spot-light, the capacity to get the last ounce out of their scholastic attainments — such are their chief stock-in-trade. Successful academic careers have been founded, and new departments conjured into being in this way. Finally, in Bismarckian phrase, there are the 'satiated'. For them the professorial chair has meant ambitions satisfied — and satiation is only one remove from somnolence. After all, chairs do some-times induce slumber! These men of low blood-pressure find diligence exhausted by the routine running of their departments, and, when their inglorious tenures end, leave not a trace behind in the files of the library catalogue. A dwindling minority, no doubt, they die stubbornly; most universities can tell of some example who has found a drowsy nook in which to dream the years away.[7]

The University Senate in 1953.

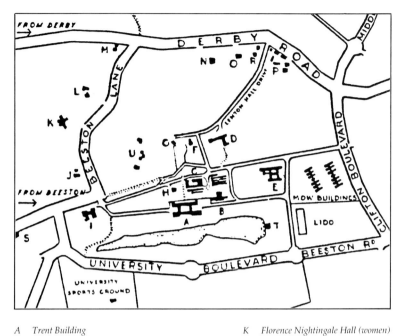

A	Trent Building	K	Florence Nightingale Hall (women)
B	Portland Building	L	Lenton Fields (women)
C	Engineering Dept.	M	Lenton Eaves (women)
D	Hugh Stewart Hall (men)	N	Lenton Hurst (Adult Education)
E	Botany & Zoology Depts.	O	Redcourt (Institute of Education)
F	Lenton Mount (University Club)	P	Wortley Hall (men)
G	The Orchards (Law & Slavonic Studies)	R	Paton Congregational College
H	Highfield House (Vice-Chancellor's Residence)	S	Broadgate House (Univ. Air Squad)
I	Florence Boot Hall (women)	T	Lakeside Pavilion
J	Lenton Grove	U	Boots Experimental Station

The University of Nottingham campus and buildings in 1955.

When the University College had opened in 1881 there had been four professors — of Literature, Physics, Chemistry and Natural Science. Another sixteen were added in the years up to 1933 as the College grew in numbers and scope. In 1947 there was a further burst of expansion with the creation of five more chairs, the opening of an Institute of Education, and the incorporation of the School of Agriculture at Sutton Bonington, a village several miles south of Nottingham. So the new University began in 1948 with about thirty professors and 185 other academic staff. By the time Hallward left in 1965 the figures were fifty-three and 363. Throughout his time as Vice-Chancellor he gave the highest priority to seeking out the best available academic brains and though all appointments were made by committees which included representatives of the Council and the Senate, his own personal influence, exerted by a mixture of force of character and political manoeuvring, was usually decisive. There is no doubt that his clear objective from the first day in office was to encourage and pursue academic excellence.

The University Council of 1952-1953. Hallward stands on the right
of the President of Council (Sir Francis Hill)

This is in itself perhaps unremarkable: most vice-chancellors would have done the same, but few have enjoyed the opportunities for expansion and development which opened up before Hallward in 1948. At that date the University stood in 122 acres of land and was dominated by the main College building. In addition a hall of residence for women had been built in a simple classical style in 1929 and named after Jesse Boot's wife Florence, who provided the money for it. In 1930 a hall of residence for men, later named after Principal Hugh Stewart, was opened in Lenton Hall, a country house complete with gothic windows and crenellated towers. In 1945 a range of semi-permanent offices had been erected next to the main building. Nicknamed 'The Cowsheds' they have proved remarkably resilient and are still a feature of the campus in 1995. The Trent Building (as the main College was later named), Florence Boot Hall, Hugh Stewart Hall, a few scattered hostels, and a string of 'temporary' offices: that was essentially the University of Nottingham in 1948. Yet all round it, there were acres of green fields, and in Hallward's mind's eye those fields were already populated with eager students and adorned with fine buildings. The dream became reality, but there were many nightmares to be endured along the way.

The first meeting of the University Court took place on 21st September 1948 and at a meeting of the Council held immediately afterwards two crucial appointments were made. One was that of J.W.F. Hill as President of Council, and the other was that of W.G. Briggs as Chairman of the Finance Committee.[8] Francis (Frank) Hill was a solicitor in Lincoln and an Alderman of that City, whose history he wrote in a number of scholarly volumes. A bachelor, he devoted his life to a heavy programme of public work and he had been a member of the University College Council for many years. He was mild-mannered, sensible, very shrewd, and always the perfect gentleman. He was President of the Council throughout Hallward's vice-chancellorship and the Hallward-Hill combination proved to be an ideal working relationship, Hill encouraging the Vice-Chancellor's enthusiasms, yet imposing a gentle but restraining brake when necessary. Gerald Briggs had been the Chief Education Officer for Derbyshire and proved firm and shrewd in his control of financial matters. As neither of these men came from the City of Nottingham the appointments caused some resentment there, though they emphasized the extent to which the new University was no longer in thrall to the City Council. Hill and Briggs were not, of course, appointed by the Vice-Chancellor, but behind the scenes Hallward had worked to encourage their election, after conferring with Professor Peers and others who knew the situation well. The same meeting of Council appointed Robert Peers Deputy Vice-Chancellor and Hallward took great care, by diplomatic handling, to ensure that this former rival for his own post should become a loyal ally.[9]

The number of students at Nottingham had risen dramatically in the previous few years. Just before the War there had been 545 full-time students, but by 1948 there was a massive escalation to 2,000, which itself presented many problems, both administrative and social. At the beginning of term in October Hallward made his first Vice-Chancellor's speech of welcome to new students in the Great Hall of the University, and because it made clear his general views and illustrates his speaking style, it is worth reproducing in full.

> This is a unique and historic occasion. You are about to matriculate as the first undergraduates reading for the degrees of a newly-founded university.
>
> I hope and believe that there will be few, if any, of you whose only reaction will be, in the phrase of modern decadence, 'I couldn't care less'. Because the start of a new university is a great enterprise fraught with immense possibilities for good or ill. For the next two or three or four years you are the living University. You will make its traditions and you will largely determine its light or darkness.
>
> Why do you come to a university? I hope you will ask yourselves this fundamental question more than once. What do you expect to get from it? And more important, what do you intend to give to it? I heard a modern university described as a degree factory to enable students to get better jobs. Is that what Nottingham University is going to be?
>
> Or, will it be the centre of culture and learning and research where men

and women will be inspired to live lives devoted to great causes such as the worship of God, the pursuit of truth, the pursuit of freedom, the pursuit of peace on earth, or the service and welfare of their fellow men?

In the end the quality of life in an institution depends not upon its site and buildings, not upon the standard of its physical provision and amenities, but upon something quite intangible and difficult to assess which can best be described as The Spirit of the Place. This spirit is an atmosphere which one senses at once when one joins a new community, whether it be a school or a regiment or a university. Is there a great wind of enterprise and endeavour blowing through this place? Or is it cynical, hard-boiled, frustrated and dead?

Let the spirit of Nottingham University be one of freedom and enterprise inspired by high ideals. There lie before us the most wonderful possibilities of growth and development if we build aright.

Our motto which is also the City's motto *'Sapientia urbs conditur'* tells us that good building depends upon wisdom. And note that the word *'Sapientia'* means wisdom and not 'knowledge' in this phrase.

And here I think we have struck the answer to the question I put at the beginning — why do you come to a university? You come to seek wisdom and to learn a philosophy of life. The philosophy of life which transcends and embraces all others is the religious one. The Fear of the Lord is the beginning of Wisdom.

On the University Coat of Arms there is a second Latin phrase — *'Quaerenti ostium'* which may be translated as 'an open door to the seeker'. What I want to stress is that the word *'quaerenti'* implies the active pursuit of something — which is very different from just sitting through lectures and 'mugging up' lecture notes to get through an examination.

The active pursuit of knowledge implies the buying of books to form the beginnings of your own library, the frequent use of libraries and a restless enquiring spirit which is not satisfied by partial and superficial knowledge, but is driven on by a deep urge to get to the bottom of things. That is the kind of wind which I hope will blow through Nottingham University.

The athletic and social sides of the University are equally essential parts of a full university life.

Give to each of these spheres of life their rightful share of your energies and time, but no more than this. An American Middle-West University was once described as 'One long Café'. That is not a university.

The good life at a good university is the many-sided balanced life in which every activity plays its part.

Finally one last word of advice. Do not allow yourself to be rushed or to be driven or to become anxious.

Plan your time wisely and show strength of mind in sticking to your plan. Do your work steadily through each year in the term and in the vacations.[10]

This Vice-Chancellor's address to 'freshers' at the beginning of each academic year was one of the occasions when Hallward came into close contact with the students. Otherwise, his job was now predominantly administrative and he was mainly concerned with chairing committees of the academic staff and safeguarding the multifarious interests of the University. He did not teach, or lecture, or do academic research. On the other hand, his horizons had been dramatically extended: he was expected to know what was going on within the complex structure of the University and its many departments, and he needed to keep abreast of all the latest ideas that swirled round the educational Establishment both in Britain and abroad.

On May 3rd 1949 the first State Occasion of the University took place when in Nottingham's Albert Hall, Lord Trent was installed as Chancellor, and the University's first honorary degrees were bestowed. Jesse Boot had regarded his son John as a playboy and that was perhaps why he had sold his business in 1920. But John Boot had been retained as a Director and it was largely as a result of

Hallward with the Chancellor, Lord Trent.

his initiative that a vast new Boots empire grew up, centred on Owen Williams' renowned 'Wets' factory, and sited within a mile of the University, beyond University Boulevard.[11] By 1948 Trent was firmly in control of the Boots Company and a natural choice as Chancellor. Hallward sat on his left at the ceremony, both men wearing the new official robes that Hallward had designed — black gowns liberally spangled with gold embroideries — and in his speech he referred to this occasion not so much as the University's birthday as its christening. 'My youngest daughter at breakfast last week asked this question: "Daddy, who came to *my* christening?" The answer "Your godparents came, of course," did not satisfy her. Further questions and answers explored the ramifications of grandparents, uncles and aunts, cousins and more distant relatives and connections, until a timely ring at the front door bell cut short the torrent of questions.'[12] He then went on to name the City of Nottingham and the Universities of Cambridge and London as the 'godparents' of Nottingham University. During this ceremony he also read the citation conferring the honorary degree of Doctor of Law on Lord Trent, the first degree ever conferred by the University. Further honorary degrees were then conferred on Mr W. Hives, the Managing Director of Rolls Royce; Professor G.M. Trevelyan, Master of Trinity College, Cambridge; Lord MacMillan, a Lord of Appeal, and Sir Walter Moberly, Chairman of the University Grants Committee.[13] The UGC was the body which supplied universities with government funding, so this was a tactful move. Also present on this occasion, at the invitation of the Vice-Chancellor, was the Provost of King's, Dr John Sheppard, still smiling as his Apollo stood firmly in the centre of an even grander stage.

Looking back more than forty years to his period of office as President of the Students' Union from 1948 to 1949 Ralph Townley wrote: 'The whirlwind arrival of Bertrand Hallward as our first Vice-Chancellor presaging the Royal Charter granting full University status, accompanied by the continuing influx of ex-servicemen and women, all coincided with my presidency. Almost overnight, a small provincial college was swept up to become a university of the first rank.'[14] Unfortunately, towards the end of the summer term of 1949 relations between the Vice-Chancellor and the Students' Union became strained over 'the Sutton Bonington Affair.' It seems that a number of students at the Agricultural College amused themselves by manhandling the female Warden of the women students and tying her up with cords. Together with the Registrar, Hedley Pickbourne, Hallward held a full enquiry and subsequently sent down eight students, a move considered rather too headmasterly by many under-graduates. There were distinctly unpleasant scenes when groups of students chanted threats outside Highfield House, and hostile messages were etched into the lawn with weedkiller.

'Mr Hallward was not popular in the first years of the University,' a student recalled. 'Partly this was because we felt that he was rather a headmaster. We thought (perhaps unjustly) that he was vain and always turned his elegant profile to the camera when being photographed by the press. In retrospect we did not understand the difficulties he had in putting a new university on the right path.'[15] Nottingham University's student newspaper, *The Gongster*, in June 1949 printed a parody of A.A. Milne: 'Christopher thought of sleek *Tigger*, with his energy, his great enthusiasm for new ideas and his disturbing eagerness to organize people and to bounce them into doing things.'[16] The nickname caught on, and Hallward was 'Tigger' to most students for years: academic staff tended to call him 'Bertie', though not to his face.

During the first months in Highfield House Hallward had been turning his 'elegant profile' not to the camera but towards the easel of the distinguished artist William Coldstream R.A., who had been commissioned by Clifton College to paint his portrait. With the Chairman of the National Gallery on the Clifton Council (Sir Robert Witt), it is not surprising that an artist of the front rank had been chosen, especially as all the official portraits of Clifton's headmasters before Hallward had been destroyed by a fire in the crypt of Clifton Chapel where they had been stored 'for safety' during the War. But Coldstream did not find it easy to transfer Hallward's larger-than-life personality to canvas; even after about forty sittings he produced an image which is not a striking likeness; the nose is not quite right. However, admirers of Coldstream consider it a fine example of his technique. Those who knew Hallward well doubtless marvelled that anyone at all had been able to keep him still and quiet for forty sittings.

The Sutton Bonington affair had not been forgotten by the time Hallward began his second academic year. In his address to the new students in October 1949 he asked them to bear in mind that they were 'the fortunate ones, the cream of the country'. 'If you waste your time here', he said, 'you are not being fair to those who failed. It has been said that a university is "all green fields and midnight oil" and I am convinced you cannot omit the midnight oil. The pursuit of the male by the female (and the female by the male) should be an unimportant by-product, not a main industry of university life.' The Vice-Chancellor's address, it seems, 'was received with varying degrees of enthusiasm'.[17] Putting his head right into the lion's mouth, Hallward spoke in November at the Annual General Meeting of the Students' Union in the Great Hall and explained that he could not reconsider his decision to send down the eight agricultural students at Sutton Bonington; he also expressed his willingness to co-operate with the Union as much as possible. Concerning the past and future years at the University, he announced that the first quarter million of the University's one million pound fund had been raised. Other sections of his speech dealt with the

Hallward as Headmaster of Clifton, painted by Sir William Coldstream, RA.

University's standing in the outside world and with its internal cultural activity; regarding the latter he lamented the fact that Saturdays and Sundays in halls of residence were 'rather barren'.[18]

According to a former student, Geoffrey Sayer, it was about this time, and on an occasion such as this, that an elaborate prank was played upon the Vice-Chancellor. 'As he was speaking in the Great Hall,' he recalled, 'a huge dial was gradually lowered from the ceiling. It was behind him so he could not see what we in the Hall could see. There was a needle on the dial (the "Oxometer") which swung from "Half Bull" to "Full Bull" to "Three-Quarter Bull" as he was speaking. As far as I remember, the Vice-Chancellor took it in good part.'[19] The Students' Union continued to put pressure on Hallward, chiefly for a formal Staff-Student Committee. However, in November Hallward informed Union representatives that he had discussed the matter with Deans of Faculties and that the matter of a Staff-Student Committee 'could not be discussed now, or ever in the future'.[20] The issue was not killed off as easily as that, however, and a Liaison Committee did meet the following year.

Before 1949 was over, Highfield House was given over to a most congenial occasion when, late in December, Hallward's eldest daughter, Ruth, married Owen Chadwick. Looking, as all the Hallward girls did, far more like her slim, dark-haired mother than her robust, blonde father, Ruth was now twenty-two and had studied at Westfield College, London, where she had been Student President. Owen Chadwick was thirty-three and had first set eyes on Ruth when she had been a bridesmaid at the wedding of a Clifton housemaster's daughter. Already ordained and a Fellow of Trinity Hall, Cambridge, he was to become, during Hallward's time at Nottingham, a very young Master of Selwyn College, Cambridge, in 1956, and Dixie Professor of Ecclesiastical History in 1958. As well as providing the Hallwards with four grandchildren in due course, the Chadwicks were a valuable link with Cambridge and the internal manoeuvres of academic life. After Hallward's retirement from Nottingham, Owen Chadwick reached new heights of eminence as Regius Professor of Modern History (1968), Vice-Chancellor of Cambridge (1969), President of the British Academy (1981) and Chancellor of the University of East Anglia (1985). He was knighted in 1982 and awarded the Order of Merit in 1983. The wedding ceremony took place at St Leonard's, Wollaton, and the reception was held at Highfield House. This was the first of what were to be four occasions when, as Hallward put it, 'Proud father escorted lovely daughter up the aisle'.[21]

Development Plans

Hallward's vision of a well-populated university on an extensive site and endowed with fine buildings presupposed three requirements. One was a healthy number of student applications, another was the availability of the surrounding land, and the last was plenty of money. Student applications were only a problem in that by 1950 there were five applicants for each place and (before the introduction of graded A levels) it was difficult to be sure that places were given to the best candidates.[1] Nor was the surrounding land a political problem thanks to a vital decision taken by the Nottingham Planning Committee in 1949 to give 'planning permission' for the University to develop a total area of 382 acres on the Highfield site.[2] Money to buy the extra land and to pay for new buildings was, however, always a difficulty.

The University Grants Committee funded universities on a five-year basis and had last made its grant in 1947. However, a number of factors had changed the situation at Nottingham since the 1947 estimates had been made. Student numbers had increased more than expected, the College had become a full University, and the years 1947 to 1950 proved to be a period of inflation and rising costs. Some money was available for building projects but not enough for any grandiose schemes. A new hall of residence for women students, the foundations of which had been laid before Hallward arrived at Nottingham, proceeded according to plan and was opened in 1951. Standing on Beeston Lane and named Florence Nightingale Hall because of a historical connection between Florence Nightingale's family and the old University College, it was designed by Cecil Howitt in an ultra-modern style. 'A visitor to the University', a student wrote, might gaze at this 'huge building of glass and pink brick', at 'the slopes of the roof, with its suggestion of a castle, note the rows of windows, count the five storeys and might well murmur "It tries so hard to look attractive that there is a kind of beauty in its ugliness".'[3]

So far the University had three halls of residence, all in different styles. Florence Boot was neo-Georgian, Hugh Stewart was genuinely Georgian with additions, and Nightingale was 'modern'. Hallward had exercised no control over their design, of course, but he was clear in his own mind that he did not want the University to develop from now on in a variegated, piecemeal fashion. There must be a master plan. For this reason he persuaded the Council to appoint Sir Percy Thomas to draw up a scheme for the development of the University site, and to be the University's Consultant Architect. Thomas had been the youngest ever President of the RIBA in 1937 and had designed many public buildings, such as the Civic Centre at Swansea and parts of the Universities of Aberystwyth and Bangor. Only the outbreak of war in 1939 prevented his design for a new Euston Station being built. He adjudicated the architectural competition for Coventry Cathedral and, according to his own account, 'completed all the design part of the towers, piers and anchorages' for the Severn Bridge.[4]

Hallward now turned to this distinguished and widely experienced professional to produce a long-term Development Plan. 'My constitutional position', he recalled, 'was Chairman of the Buildings Committee There was a staff headed by the Buildings Officer, O'Dell, a rough diamond, but a diamond. A separate officer dealt with maintenance, with engineers, etc. All my thinking about choice of architects and planning of buildings was subject to consultation with Percy Thomas. These matters were not regarded as the business of Senate. Council Minutes would show how they were brought to Council by me as Vice-Chancellor. There was no Planning Committee. In effect I was the Planning Committee acting closely with Sir Percy Thomas.'[5]

We have already seen how, while addressing architects in Bristol, Hallward had stated that 'his own interest in the subject of architecture sprang up first as a result of his visit to Greece.'[6] Percy Thomas's work was deeply influenced by classical models and he explained in his autobiography how three of his buildings in Cardiff 'show fairly well the development of my ideas from the neo-grec of the original College, through the simplified classicism of the Temple of Peace, to the more modern treatment of the College of Advanced Technology'.[7] With Hallward and Thomas in control of Nottingham's architectural future, neo-classicism would triumph over what Hallward termed 'brutal modernism'. Future designs would take their theme from the Trent Building and the simple Georgian style of Florence Boot Hall. In making this decision, and keeping to it, Hallward in due course encountered storms of protest from those who supported the modernist movement and ridiculed 'traditionalist' structures. The architectural style of the developing University was, as we shall see, a constant source of controversy and acrimony, and those who did not share the Vice-Chancellor's tastes became tenacious critics of his influence over new designs.

At first the attempts to build anew were frustrated by lack of finance. Percy Thomas was appointed assessor of an architectural competition to design a new hall of residence, but it soon became clear that there was no money for it. After the War the College had acquired a rambling house called Lenton Firs where sixty women students had been accommodated. In 1951 they were moved out and, with additions, the house became a new hall for men students named Wortley Hall in memory of the College's last Principal. This jumble of buildings that had not been purpose-built was a disappointment to visionary planners like Hallward and Thomas, but it was the best they could do at the time. An even bigger disappointment was the necessity of abandoning an ambitious but very expensive scheme for new Botany and Zoology buildings, designed by David Aberdeen. This did not conform to the neo-classical style but its modernism was restrained, and its scale magnificent. In any case, Hallward had accepted that science complexes would be built in practical modern style. It was the University's formal public buildings and halls of residence that would constitute the new Athens at Highfields.

In a unique report which Hallward wrote for the Council in 1950, after two full years as Vice-Chancellor, he set out clearly what he considered to be the needs of the University for the future. He pointed to the lack of a Music School and considered the facilities for sport totally inadequate. 'Provision for Physical Education', he wrote, 'is urgently wanted in the form of a comprehensive building with rooms for staff and gymnasia, indoor swimming-bath, squash courts, badminton courts, etc. All the larger boarding-schools and many of the day schools of this country have far better provision for these needs than the University.' 'It is certain too', he went on, 'that the building of further large laboratories will, in due course, have to be faced, if the needs of teaching and research are to be properly met.'[8] He also made some suggestions that ultimately never found favour, such as the building of a chapel, and extension of the Library by constructing another floor in the main reading room. The problem of what to do about the lack of sufficient library space was going to be a recurrent source of controversy in the next decade.

In his conclusion to this nine-page report, Hallward made clear his own view that a university must enjoy an attractive environment and that, like a Cambridge college and an English public school, it must strive to be a family of teachers and students. 'We must not forget that a university is not simply a matter of lectures and classes, but a society with its own way of life, and that graciousness in that way of life does have its physical prerequisites in the necessary buildings. In our present world we have got to try and find new ways of combining graciousness with simplicity of living. But the need for due economy must not obscure the fact that the ideal of English university education has been the life in a college, a social life shared between teachers and taught. At its best a college has been one great family of teachers and students living together under one roof. No more valuable source of true education has ever been invented.'[9] Behind these words lay Hallward's own experience of collegiate grandeur — of Wilkins' classical façade at Haileybury, of the Gibbs building at King's and the magnificent mediaeval Chapel, of Charles Hansom's gothic Clifton. Just as Oxford and Cambridge had their colleges, and public schools had their houses, so Nottingham would eventually have halls of residence that were not merely hostels but, with their wardens and resident tutors, something midway between an Oxford or Cambridge college and a public-school boarding-house.

American Journey

Knowing that in the next period of five years (1952-57) the University Grants Committee would fund some of Nottingham's Development Plans, particularly a central building incorporating a Students' Union, Council gave their Vice-Chancellor permission to be absent early in 1952 so that he could visit universities in North America and see what could be learnt from them. Margaret Hallward accompanied her husband on this long adventure, which involved 113 days away from Britain. Hallward announced proudly in 1994 that he 'had never kept a diary in his life' but fortunately his wife sometimes did, and she made jottings about this journey in a flimsy memo pad and a disused laundry book dating from Clifton days, both of which have, fortunately, survived. It was their first visit to either Canada or the United States, and Hallward's experiences there undoubtedly had a big influence on his plans for Nottingham.

They left Southampton on 23rd February in the Norwegian ship *Reyndam* and docked at Halifax on March 1st. Three days later they were in Washington, where they dined at the British Embassy with Sir Oliver and Lady Franks. After a tour of the sights of Washington and Mount Vernon there was a drive across the Blue Ridge Mountains to the University of Virginia, where the Hallwards were amazed at the excellent, cheap food available in the cafeteria and impressed by the 'very good-looking lot of students'. The President of the University received them and they took note of the 'magnificent layout by Jefferson ... in classical style, having copied from French and Italian buildings. It is in red brick with white columns with lots of spacious lawns and trees.' Jefferson's home, Montecello, stood on the heights overlooking the town and the Hallwards took note that 'he is said to have watched University building from his telescope and noticed if the workmen were idling.'

After stopping at a 'negro Technical and Agricultural College' the Hallwards moved to the University of North Carolina at Chapel Hill where they were impressed by the Drama department and astounded by the gym and swimming-pool. They stayed with the Chancellor of the University and met several members of staff at dinner. The next day they were admiring the 'fine gothic' buildings of Duke University and its magnificent chapel, where Margaret had a good look round a sorority house. By March 15th they were at William and Mary College, Williamsburg, lunching with the President and again meeting many members of the academic staff. Margaret looked round the colonial houses of the town while Hallward was initiated into the mysteries of baseball. Four days later they had driven to Pennsylvania State College where they had a good look at the spectacular Home Economics department, and moved on to stay at St Andrew's School in Delaware, a private school for boys. Here Margaret, who took a keen interest in birds, found a kindred spirit in her host: 'he could tell us about every bird we saw. A magnificent flock of Canadian geese ... black duck, pintail, shell duck, shoveler and various others: also the redwing with their lovely trill'. The next stop was Bryn Mawr, 'a girls' college with very high standards,' before reaching Princeton, lunching with the President, and touring the campus where they admired particularly the magnificent new library, with its capacity for two million books (the Nottingham Library had 170,000 at this time). By March 26th they had reached Rutgers University in New Brunswick, which Margaret found 'a rather grim group of buildings', though its School of Adult Education and School of Agriculture were impressive. From there, after a stop at Kent School, the Hallwards reached Yale where they were entertained a good deal in the impressive Faculty Club, 'an extremely nice seventeenth-century house', and met many members of the staff, including the President 'a dynamic and charming personality' who welcomed them to his magnificent house. After several enjoyable days at Yale the Hallwards moved on to see Brown University at Providence, Rhode Island, where they lunched in the Refectory with six Faculty members, and stayed in the University Guest House. Again, there was a Faculty Club where they met many members of staff.

Naturally enough, the next port of call after Yale was Harvard, near Boston, where the Hallwards admired Walter Gropius' new Graduate School, as well as the Massachusetts Institute of Technology, 'a vast factory of a place'. The restless tour continued on to Groton School, Bowdoin College, and Colby where the President put them up for the night and made sure they saw the University sights. By April 10th, driving northwards, they had crossed the frontier into Canada and reached Montreal where they stayed with their cousin, Bernard Hallward, and were taken round McGill University as well as the new premises of Montreal University, a 'very ugly, factory type of building'. At St Anne's the Agricultural College was inspected and also the Victoria College for Women. On April 14th they took a bad road to Ottawa, had a look round the capital, and moved on to Kingston with its 'fine University built in grey stone'. The next day they were at Toronto where, for once, Hallward went off alone to look at the University while Margaret had her hair washed.

The relentless hunt of universities continued on April 16th when the Hallwards were at Hamilton, 'the Birmingham of Canada,' looking round McMaster University with its new buildings, one-year-old library, and new Students' Union. There was dinner with the President, his daughters, assorted academics and an Indian bishop. Pausing to admire Niagara Falls, they drove on to the University at Rochester, New York, and its University Hospital, before reaching Cornell where again they were entertained in the Faculty Club and looked round the Horticulture department. The next two days were taken up with Oberlin College and Wooster College before driving on to Michigan University with its campus hospital, stadium and law school. Next followed the Kellogg Centre for Further Education and Michigan State College where they had a long talk with the head of Landscape Architecture and looked at many plans. They also saw some of the accommodation built for students by Frank Lloyd Wright. At this point the Memo notebook runs out, but, the tour far from finished, we move on to the Clifton laundry book.

This begins in Chicago where they saw the University of Chicago campus and then the 'most beautiful campus' of Madison University on its lakeside site. On May 1st they were in Iowa City looking round another 'very lovely campus with a small lake in the middle'. On May 3rd they were driving through the prairies of Nebraska, admiring vast herds of Herefordshire and Aberdeen Angus cattle. The Missouri River was flooded but they found their way to Denver, Colorado, and Boulder University with its Spanish-style buildings with roofs at different levels. Then a drive into the Rockies, where the views of snow-peaked mountains excited Hallward, and on to the adobe huts of New Mexico, and Arizona's Grand Canyon before driving to the Pacific Coast and the city of Los Angeles. Visits to the Huntingdon Library, the art galleries and Paramount Studios were fitted in, as well as many campuses in the city. Then a drive northwards to San Francisco to meet the President of Berkeley and look round the 'lovely buildings in Spanish style, and very well laid-out'. A long drive after this took them to Seattle and the university there and soon they were on Vancouver Island and then in Vancouver itself where the President of the University 'put us up for the night in their very attractive new house right on the headland and drove us round the campus after supper'. Then there was a drive back to Seattle where they sold the car they had been using for the last few months and took a plane to Minneapolis for a quick look round the University there before flying on to New York, where former Nottingham student president Ralph Towneley acted as a guide round the cultural sights of the city.

On June 6th the Hallwards flew from New York to Montreal to catch another aeroplane for Halifax, but shortly after taking off it ran into a 'terrific thunderstorm' and had to land at Morristown, where they were bundled into a train and continued the journey overnight. Their boat sailed from Halifax the next evening but not before a last university campus — Dalhousie — had been thoroughly inspected. Margaret's journal ends here, with a list of twenty-four rare birds, and where she had spotted them.[1] If the Hallwards' stamina was ever in doubt, this American journey should settle the matter. It was planned with the meticulous detail of a military campaign, for in each of the dozens of institutions visited the couple were expected and generously entertained. Very little time was spent merely sightseeing and almost none resting. Moreover, the need to exude charm, good manners and vitality with a series of different hosts almost every day can be utterly exhausting. Yet they thrived on it: Hallward had been full of ideas even before he went to America, but he had seen enough there to keep him fizzing away for another decade.

Perhaps the most important effect of the American journey was to re-assure Hallward that the Percy Thomas Development Plan, which envisaged the growth of the University over a 382 acre park, was the right way forward. This, after all, was what the Americans called a *campus*. 'My experience in America', he wrote, 'showed me the value of a fine campus. I brought the word to Nottingham. At first it was greeted with anti-American shudders.'[2] He had also been entertained in many a university staff club and he was keen to get one established at Nottingham. 'Through my experience in America I was quick to see the social value of a very good University Club. I had also noticed in America that a fine private home, added to and modified, made a much more delightful Club House than a purpose-built erection of concrete and glass, however efficient. And it must be central and have a good garden round it. It was also deliberate that I took no part personally in launching the Club but found the ideal professor and wife to do it.'[3] Council sanctioned the purchase of Lenton Mount, a large private house already existing in the centre of the University area, and it was opened as a Staff Club in February 1954.[4]

Portland and Cripps

In 1953 Council gave permission for the most important project so far of Hallward's period in office. This was the construction of a large new social amenities building alongside the main College. It was also agreed at this time that the original College should henceforth be known as the Trent Building while the new structure would be known as the Portland Building in honour of a former Duke of Portland who had been President of the University College.[1] Different groups in the University had different ideas about the function of the new building. The Students' Union, for instance, campaigned from the outset for it to be a union building under their exclusive control and for their exclusive use. Socialist philosophy taught that unless students had such a facility they would be overwhelmed by the University authorities and Establishment. Hallward was in no doubt, however, about his own position on this. 'All universities must have considerable offices and other technical rooms for the students. There must also be an area of social accommodation for the dons and senior administrative staff. There must be a variety of restaurants, coffee bar, tavern, lounge rooms, etc. With my wife I investigated what a union building meant in Lund, Aarhus, Uppsala and in the USA on a lightning tour of American universities and colleges. I also arranged for the Nottingham City Architect Howitt to go over and see union buildings in America. In discussion with Howitt I suggested it should be ONE building … and no Student Union separate building.'[2]

The decision to name the new building 'Portland' (in addition to the fact that it was built in Portland stone) seemed all the more suitable when in 1954 Lord Trent was forced to resign as Chancellor because of ill-health, and William Cavendish-Bentinck, seventh Duke of Portland, was appointed to succeed him. Apart from the fact that he was himself an influential local grandee, the Duke's family had been supporters of the University College in its early days and he certainly provided a dignified figurehead, though his interests, by all accounts, were not primarily academic. 'Do you shoot, Hallward?' he asked at their first

Courtesy of John Laing plc

The Portland Building.

meeting. 'I'm afraid not, sir.' 'Do you hunt?' 'No sir.' 'Do you fish?' 'No sir.' 'Well, I'll send you one of my Boy Pigs to breed from at Sutton Bonington.' 'Thank you sir.'[3] At degree ceremonies Hallward would sit next to him and the Chancellor would say, 'You turn over the pages for me.' On one occasion he gave a slightly notorious past student a degree *in abstinentia*, and on others he would say audibly into the microphone 'damned pretty girl, that' as a particular female student came up to receive her degree.[4]

In January 1953 the students' newspaper *The Gongster* printed a handsome drawing of the projected Portland Building and provided details about the architect, Cecil Howitt, listing his many commissions, chief of which was the new Council House in Nottingham itself. 'Mr Howitt has recently returned from America', the article observed, 'where he visited many universities. He comments that he found only one that could compare with Nottingham as regards its fine parkland setting.'[5] On February 12th a meeting took place between the President of Council (now *Dr* Francis Hill thanks to a *D.Litt* from Cambridge gained by his local history books) and the Student Executive. Hill told them that their demands for total control over the new building could not be conceded. 'Dr Hill said that to call it a union building was a misnomer. The building, he said, was a multi-purpose building and had formed part of a consistent plan of the University to encourage social intercourse between staff and students.' Hill also explained that Council could not accept the students' scheme for a sharing of power within the University. 'Council is responsible to many bodies, including the Queen in Council, University Grants Committee, the local authorities, industry and public opinion,' he said. 'With all these controls and semi-controls we sometimes feel, at least I do, that I am walking on a tight-rope.' The only way, he felt, that Council could discharge all its functions with regard to these bodies was by adhering to the Statutes.[6]

This prompted an outraged editorial in *The Gongster's* next issue which declared, 'the multi-purpose building has shocked the Union in a way that has not been known for some years. Many members have a feeling of angry resentment'.[7] However, the Council and Vice-Chancellor were not easily blown off course, and the Portland Building went ahead, though comparatively slowly. It was opened on November 9th 1956 by Viscount Kilmuir, the Lord Chancellor, who spoke of it as being 'brilliantly built' and 'truly unique among university buildings'. Hallward in his speech described how he had visited many American union buildings and had suggested modifications based on his experiences. He paid tribute to everyone concerned, especially Sir Hugh and Lady Casson who had been responsible for the internal decorations.[8] In 1958 Senate reported to the Council that 'the Portland Building continues to make an enormous contribution to the life of the University and also to that of the City, the region, and indeed the country. Professional and other bodies make extensive use of its amenities for conferences, dinners and other gatherings, and parties of visitors are continually coming to inspect its planning and decoration'.[9]

In addition to his responsibility for the overall concept and design of the Portland Building, Hallward made a remarkable personal contribution to the small chapel that was constructed in the nether regions of the building in a space originally intended as a boilerhouse. Acting on a suggestion of his wife's, he decided to pay (anonymously) for the installation of a fine Willis organ in the chapel by donating £1,000 of his salary for six years; and given that his salary was in the region of £5,000 p.a. during these years, the gesture amounted to no small sacrifice. In the 1980's the University deemed it appropriate to dispense with anonymity and affix a discreet plaque to the organ commemorating the generosity of its donors.

Although the Portland Building was the showpiece, it was not the only addition to the University in these early years. A new boathouse was built on the Trent near Lady Bay Bridge and opened in 1952 by the famous oarsman Roy Meldrum, and during 1953 four staff houses were built at Nightingale Hall and another five were begun near Wortley Hall. Lenton Grove and Lenton Mount, two large private houses within the campus area, were bought in 1952 and converted for use, one as a School of Music and the other, as we have seen, as the Staff Club. By 1953 the departments of Botany and Zoology were housed in a new building at the north-eastern end of the campus where, by now, it had been agreed that future provision for science would be made.[10] In 1954 Council appointed the landscape architect G.A. Jellicoe to 'work in close consultation with Sir Percy Thomas, the University Consultant Architect, whose advice is sought by Council on all major building projects'.[11] In 1955 Jellicoe produced a magnificent new plan, complete with model, the main feature of which was a spectacular Great Hall in the shape of a rotunda.

Very little came of the Jellicoe Plan, and Hallward was later able to explain why. 'Jellicoe had established a reputation as the leading landscape architect of the country. I admit the decision to invite him to do a report on Nottingham's campus was rather late in the day since most of the decisions had been made ... and the remit which he was given was confined to the central area behind the Trent Building. The question put to him, if I remember right, was the siting of a University Library and a Great Hall and the layout of land between and around them. The inclusion of the Great Hall was with the idea that some benefactor reading the Jellicoe Report might come forward with the offer to pay for it if he got his name upon it. This of course did not occur. In my opinion a lot of [the Jellicoe Report] is "airy-fairy" and a way of spending money on architects' fancies.'[12]

Certainly there was no point in dreaming up fanciful and expensive schemes when money was still extremely short. As early as 1953 Hallward had realized that he would have to make a direct appeal to benefactors and entrepreneurs. 'I took charge of this important occasion myself. Who should I ask to address this gathering of largely manufacturers and industrialists and financiers in the Great Hall? I had a brainwave. The name is almost forgotten now, but Sir Ernest Barker (Fellow of Peterhouse) was a retired Professor of Economics at Cambridge and had been for some years Principal of University College London. With Professor Joad he was known to every household in Britain because of his regular performance in *The Brains Trust*, the first and greatest of the regular general knowledge quiz sessions. With me presiding to introduce him he addressed the gathering of about 300 in the Great Hall for three quarters of an hour on the subject: What is a university? What is it for? What makes a good or great university? etc. etc. *It needs money.* He spoke in a deliberately broad Lancashire accent and was exceptionally amusing yet intellectually compelling. It was a great performance for the occasion. The accent and the man-to-man language was exactly right for these men of the machines and men of money. In the Hall that day were Cyril (father) and Humphrey (son) Cripps. After an interval of about a month, possibly longer, a letter arrived for me signed by Cyril and Humphrey Cripps with the heading at the top of the paper *Pianoforte Supplies Limited*: the substance of the letter was a wish to come and see me in reference to the Appeal. They came to see me. I introduced the talk by saying that we very much wanted to fund a Chair in Music, at which they laughed, saying "Oh, you saw Pianoforte Supplies Limited on the notepaper". Gradually it became clear that they had undertaken quite a lot of private investigation about Nottingham University and about me in particular, and that something really munificent was in their minds.'[13]

The story of Sir Cyril and Sir Humphrey Cripps is almost as remarkable as that of Jesse Boot himself. Cyril Cripps started as a cockney lad working as a clerk in the music business and in 1919 he borrowed some money to set himself up making piano hinges and other parts in a small shop off the Lambeth Walk. In 1923 he bought an old shoe-polish factory in Roade, Northants, where he set up Pianoforte Supplies Ltd and diversified into producing parts for motor cars and, later, Hurricanes, Spitfires and Lancaster bombers.

Meanwhile his son Humphrey had attended Northampton Grammar School and gone up to St John's, Cambridge, in 1934, when Hallward was Proctor. 'I went prog-baiting, but never got caught,' Cripps recalled. He went to work in his father's firm after graduating in Chemistry and during the 1939-1945 War

Cyril Cripps and his son Humphrey with the architect of Cripps Hall, Donald McMorran (centre).

the family business worked flat out to provide important supplies for the forces. After the War the business expanded and prospered to such an extent that Cyril Cripps and his son were able to embark on their first major acts of philanthropy. They chose Nottingham University because they were impressed with the site, and they saw a kindred spirit in the dynamic Vice-Chancellor. 'That man!,' said Sir Humphrey, leaning back in his office chair in 1994, 'it's unbelievable what he did for Nottingham.'[14]

Cyril Cripps' generosity began in October 1953 with a gift of £50,000 to endow a Chair in Metallurgy. This was followed in December by another £50,000 for a Chair in Production Engineering.[15] Then in 1956 came the magnificent offer to fund a new hall of residence for men with an advance payment of £250,000 for the University to invest.[16] Donald McMorran was chosen as architect and he produced a hall of 'classical' design with many of the features of a Cambridge college, and built to last. In *The Gongster* early in 1959 he answered the many modernist critics of his allegedly unimaginative design by arguing that 'function' was more important that 'fashion'. 'To-day', he wrote, 'the very familiarity of my buildings may seem strange.' Harold Cohen, University Fellow in Fine Art, replied in the next issue that this was 'the familiarity which breeds contempt'.[17] Cripps Hall was formally opened on 15th

Courtesy of John Laing plc

Cripps Hall.

October 1959 when, according to *The Gongster*, 'Mr Cyril Cripps fulfilled the dream which ... inspired the building of the University's third men's hall. More than £400,000 of the total cost of £500,000 was provided by the Cripps family, and the new building will house 220 students.'[18]

'It would cost about £22 million now', mused Sir Humphrey Cripps in 1994, speaking from considerable experience.[19] After his father's death, and thanks largely to his major share in Velcro with factories world-wide, Sir Humphrey came to be thought of as a British Howard Hughes, with the Cripps Foundation pouring millions into new buildings at St John's and Queens', Cambridge, Northamptonshire General Hospital, and Northampton Girls' High School, among many others. In 1994 he was still sitting amiably in his office at Roade, and the company was still called Pianoforte Supplies Ltd. Moreover, Cripps Hall not only survived its architectural critics but in 1988 it was one of only eighteen post-war buildings listed by the Department of the Environment as 'having special architectural or historic interest'.[20]

Student Opinion

The first issue of the University College's literary magazine *The Gong* appeared in February 1895 and took its name from 'the extremely dissonant instrument in the front hall of the Old Shakespeare Street buildings'. *The Gongster* first appeared in 1939 as the official student newspaper, choosing a name that suggested its literary merit was less than *The Gong*, though in its daring journalism it was something of a villain. As a university student newspaper it reached a very high standard during the Hallward years, with informative, well-written articles and some excellent pictures. It ranked high in the *Daily Mirror's* table of student newspapers, reaching second place in 1962 after Birmingham's *Redbrick*, with the Bristol and Oxford newspapers third and fourth.[1] Alan Sillitoe, John Izbicki and Ray Gosling wrote for the paper as students, as did Christopher Dodd, an Old Cliftonian who became editor in the early 1960's. 'The Hallwards invited all the new O.Cs to Sunday lunch in about my second week in Nottingham in 1960,' he remembered. 'He was tremendously supportive of the student newspaper and this early contact stood me in good stead in my second year when I became editor, and he was very accessible on University matters.' Dodd, who became a well-known writer on rowing later in life, also recalled that Hallward was 'proud of what the Boat Club was doing at that time — high in the Tideway Head and going through a few rounds of the Thames Cup at Henley.'[2] Despite his many sporting attainments, Hallward had never been a rowing man, though he had the ideal physique for it. Yet rowing was a sport he did a great deal to encourage in his career, with a new boathouse at Peterhouse and at Nottingham.

   The Gong had recognized as early as 1949 that 'we have a Vice-Chancellor of great enthusiasm and quite extraordinary energy, a man who, we can confidently expect, will do a great deal for this University.'[3] Then the Sutton Bonington Affair gave Hallward a bad press in *The Gongster* for several issues, though in April 1950 he was anxious to patch up relations with the Students' Union. After the visit of the Duchess of Gloucester at an Open Day, the paper printed his letter to the President of the Union, thanking him 'for the invaluable assistance which the student helpers gave so willingly in the Open Days. I am anxious that the thanks of the University and my own personal good wishes be conveyed to these students so that they may learn how much their courtesy, efficiency and friendly help was appreciated, both by the staff and the University and by the thousands of visitors.'[4] His 'freshers address' of 1950 emphasized 'the old Greek ideal of friendship as the basis of education'. He felt that 'the contact between student and student and between student and teacher in friendly discourse was an important element in a rich university life'. 'In substance,' *The Gongster* thought, 'the Vice-Chancellor's address did not contain anything particularly striking or profound, but the conciseness and coherence with which he made his points, together with the easy urbanity which older students know so well, combined to make his talk almost ideal for the purpose for which it was intended.'[5] However, in February 1951 there were complaints in the paper that the Staff-Student Committee, which Hallward had reluctantly set up, had not worked. 'All the big issues that were outstanding between the staff and ourselves last year', wrote a student, 'are in fact still outstanding.'[6]

In the summer of 1951 a custom was revived of holding a Student Carnival procession in the City (the last 'rag' had been banned in 1938). 'Just before the column left University Park we spotted the VC among the crowd at the gate,' reported *The Gongster*. 'Asked if he would care to make a statement, Mr Hallward replied "No, I think it's simply grand".'[7] The citizens of Nottingham stood in crowds ten-deep to watch as the floats trundled by and did not seem too upset by the disruption to traffic, so the affair was considered a public relations success. In October Hallward was encouraging his fourth intake of students not to become 'sponges', a method of soaking up facts and data which could lead to mental stagnation and loss of that natural enthusiasm and passion for the subject which distinguished every great lecturer and scholar. 'In conclusion,' *The Gongster* reported, 'Mr Hallward urged his audience not to neglect physical pursuits — walking and friendly games; to develop or acquire some of the accessible arts — Music, Drama and the Film; to take an active part in the Union and its Societies and, above all, to organize and direct their time. Hell was to drift; heaven was to steer and control.'[8] The next year he continued to mingle Sparta with Athens. 'Once again it was pleasant to listen to the VC when he gave his address of welcome to the freshers. He urged his audience not to neglect physical pursuits (a walk at night round Wollaton Park interspersed with cold showers). Those who kept fit were the ones best able to work with their minds.'[9] The sports section of the paper naturally seized on this advice with enthusiasm.

The Hallward message was certainly consistent, and as the years rolled by, it seeped into the student consciousness. In 1953 he insisted that a university was for 'all round education. A man gets a first on what he reads *round* his subject,' he urged. 'As has become customary', *The Gongster* noted, 'the VC emphasized the importance of the accompaniment of hard mental effort with sufficient bodily exercise.'[10] Not that his reputation for intellectualism was at all dimmed. His talk at Sutton Bonington in 1954 on Foxes, Hedgehogs and Tolstoy was considered way above the heads of most students. 'Mr Hallward said that specialization in education, although necessary, was only part of the learned person's armour and to command a knowledge of one subject only was barbaric. The fox's many wiles and the sole defence of the hedgehog can be compared with this. Tolstoy in his writings exemplified both the fox and the hedgehog.' 'Everyone who heard this enlightening lecture will, I am sure, wish to delve deeper into Tolstoy's works,' the report concluded, perhaps with a touch of irony.[11] Friendship and health were again the themes of Hallward's 1954 freshers talk, when he confided to his audience that he regularly ran round the University lake during the winter evenings.[12]

The view that the Vice-Chancellor was a notable character, whose obvious dynamism was no bad thing for the University, in general prevailed among student opinion; though he continued to have tussles with the Union. The Staff-Student Committee witnessed some stormy sessions while the Portland Building was being planned and, according to Frank Copplestone, President from 1952 to 1953, 'The Vice-Chancellor on one occasion led a walk-out of the staff side of the Staff-Student Liaison Committee; and I, contrary to protocol and good manners, attacked the University administration in my after-dinner speech at the Union Ball.'[13] When the Portland Building was opened and the students saw that only part of it was devoted to the Students' Union, there was further outcry. 'Not for a long time has there been such a wealth of controversy at Nottingham' reported *The Gongster* in October 1956. 'A speaker at the last Executive Meeting went so far as to say that the Vice-Chancellor was in grave danger of alienating student opinion — others have talked of "open revolt". Everything centres on the philosophy of the Portland Building.'[14]

At a 'very poorly attended' Union A.G.M., Hallward appealed for calm. It was reported that the Vice-Chancellor said 'he had heard of some anxiety and unrest. Much of this he thought was the "natural psychological result of change". There was laughter when Mr Hallward remarked that "the letters VC seem no longer to be a decoration". Nottingham, he suggested, was suffering from growing pains. Furthermore, we were not yet used to this rather magnificent form of life in a "new and very splendid building". Indeed, he thought the Portland Building "one of the finest university buildings in the country, and possibly the world". The VC said that if the bar were properly used he would give his assurances of reasonable freedom.'[15] Here, however, Hallward touched a raw nerve because at first he not only claimed to have control over opening times of bars in the Portland Building, but also refused permission for bars to be opened at all on certain occasions. In January 1957 *The Gongster* was claiming that 'only concessions by Council or very strong measures by Executive can save this Students' Union from complete emasculation. For, make no mistake about it, the question of a private bar at Union Ball brings to the surface the issues of Union responsibility in the face of an increasingly repressive and unco-operative attitude from Authority'. The Vice-Chancellor had not only banned spirits at the Union Ball, they complained, but had banned a private bar as well. This, the headline ran, was THE LAST STRAW.[16] In the end Hallward let them have the private bar and in March 1957 the situation was stabilized when the Portland Building was granted a full, seven day licence, and a notice went up over the door 'Bertrand Leslie Hallward, Licensed to sell Beer, Wines, Spirits and Tobacco'.[17]

Hallward was no doubt upset by these wrangles, and in a speech at a Sutton Bonington dining-in night, he allowed himself a nostalgic comparison with the Cambridge he used to know. 'The fault of the students at Nottingham', he suggested, 'seemed to lie in their attitude towards the don, tending to cling to the old idea of "the bloody old don". In contrast, at Cambridge the well-mannered undergraduate greeted his professor in the cloisters'. He went on to hope 'that the erection of university huts in the mountains, for week-end visits by walking or climbing parties, might help to encourage a more friendly attitude — the dons were "sensitive human beings" after all.'[18] Here, indeed, was a return to the philosophies of Pigou.

However, these complaining students of the 1950's in their sports jackets and ties, grey flannels and tortoiseshell spectacles, were not the same breed as the determined agitators who descended upon universities a decade later. They might skirmish with authority but they knew there were limits, and a determined stand by the Vice-Chancellor, together with a few judicious concessions, was enough to win the day. Clive Priestley, the Student President during the controversies of 1956 and 1957, wrote later: 'The Lord Chancellor opened the Portland Building … [and] … thus was put in place a cornerstone of the Hallward masterplan for a university splendid academically and in all other respects. Indeed the radiant beams of the Vice-Chancellor's intellect and personality lit up the University'.[19] It was Priestley's successor, Tony Burkett, who in October 1957 presented the Vice-Chancellor with the 'Ordo Caligulae', a special mark of esteem which the Union reserved, by tradition, only for those whom it considered had done the University, and the students, great services. A mixture of references to Jesse Boot and the Latin for 'Little Boot' (the nickname of the Roman Emperor Gaius 'Caligula'), the 'Ordo Caligulae' took the form of a miniature bronze boot on a wooden plinth inscribed with the name of the recipient. 'The Vice-Chancellor in his address', reported *The Gongster,* 'thanked the Union for what he called "the Order of the Little Boot" and was thankful it was not "the Order of the Big Boot".'[20] The trophy still stands, in 1995, a prized possession on the Hallward bookshelves at Gretton Court, and it symbolizes not only the half-way mark in his period of office at Nottingham, but the acceptance — even among his critics — that he was doing a remarkable job.

Part Five

Nottingham 1957-1965

Science City and the Halls of Residence

The year 1957 was a landmark in the development of The University of Nottingham. As well as marking the half-way point in Hallward's reign as Vice-Chancellor and being the year in which he received the official approval of the students, it was the year when, as a result of government policy, Council took the decision to plan for a big increase in the size of the University. The Scientific Manpower Committee's report to the government had called for a doubling of the output of scientists and technologists by 1970 and the University Grants Committee's response to this was to encourage expansion in the universities. At Nottingham, Council received a request from the UGC early in 1957 'to consider the possibility of an increase (of the University) from its present number of some 2,300 students to 4,000 by the late sixties'.[1] This explains why in the second half of Hallward's period of office a 'building boom' got under way with the construction of six new halls of residence and a veritable 'Science City'. The Percy Thomas Plan and the Jellicoe Plan had set aside areas on campus where the new construction could take place: halls of residence to the south-west, Arts Faculty buildings in the centre, and 'Science City' beyond the existing Biology Building on the north-east. There was plenty of space and money was promised: all that was needed was the dynamism to go ahead. It was this dynamism that Bertrand Hallward provided. 'As the years go by, the results of the high ideals and the vigour of the Vice-Chancellor become apparent to all', Council reported in 1956, and in 1959 it recorded that 'To the Vice-Chancellor, in whose fertile and unresting mind so many developments are born, the University will never cease to be grateful.'[2]

The Chairman of the University Grants Committee, whose role during these years was crucial, was from 1953 to 1963 Sir Keith Murray. Sir Walter Moberly, who had been given an honorary Nottingham degree in 1949, had retired in 1950 to be replaced by Sir Arthur Trueman, a former student of University College, Nottingham. The extent to which he might have favoured his *alma mater* was never known because over-work and ill-health forced his resignation in 1953.

This brought to the post Keith Murray, Rector of Lincoln College, Oxford, and previously Bursar there, an expert on agricultural economics and a former chairman of an inquiry into university halls of residence. 'Keith Murray was a bachelor and fond of dancing, and a good dancer,' Hallward recalled. 'Margaret and I attended great occasions when Keith Murray was present. Margaret was a superb dancer (I was *not*). At a dance her exquisite figure and gay laughing face were adorable. Keith Murray traced some cousinly connection between our families.'[3]

In May 1955 Keith Murray headed an official visit of the University Grants Committee to Nottingham and 'indicated that the Committee had been greatly impressed by developments which had taken place since their last visit. The physical assets had increased to an extent which they had then not thought possible, and he expressed their appreciation of the careful planning of the various projects.'[4] 'I had an extraordinary affection for Hallward,' Murray recalled. 'He was difficult from time to time ... but he was so whole-hearted about the University. He was an imposing figure, rather enthusiastic, exuberant from time to time. That's all impressive. And he was so whole-hearted about the thing. Immediately one was affected by that regardless of the subject matter. There is no question that Nottingham became an outstanding and prestigious University, entirely, I think, due to Hallward's energy, drive and imagination.'[5]

In 1955 Council had sanctioned the building of a new Agricultural Sciences block at Sutton Bonington and the architect chosen was Basil Spence, who had won national fame with his designs for the new Coventry cathedral. At this time he was also commissioned to prepare a layout for science and applied science buildings at the north-east end of the campus, as designated by the Thomas-Jellicoe plans. When, in 1957, it became clear that the UGC was prepared to provide the financial backing for expansion at Nottingham, Spence produced a detailed model of his projected 'Science City' which was revealed towards the end of the year. Although Hallward played a major part in the planning and design of most of the University's new buildings, he recognized that his expertise did not extend to the technicalities of science. As he put it, 'Engineering and Science Labs were built to the detailed wishes of their heads of department, guided by UGC limitations, and with quality surveyors guided by the Buildings Officer O'Dell, under my overall knowledge and chairmanship of detailed building committees.'[6]

The first of Spence's buildings to be completed was the agricultural science block at Sutton Bonington which was gradually occupied during 1959 and formally opened in January 1960. To the great joy of the modernist camp, it was a creation in concrete and plate glass. 'Press and TV coverage was given to the opening of the £235,000 Agricultural Sciences Building at Sutton Bonington last week', *The Gongster* reported on January 29th. 'This building's large expanse of glass contrasts greatly with the drab solidarity of Cripps and offers a tremendous range of facilities for scientific teaching and research. In fact it is claimed that it is without par in the universities of the Commonwealth and it is surely something of which all members of this University can be proud. It will also do much to disprove the idea that agriculturalists are merely muck-shifting, straw-chewing yokels that some misinformed people believe.'[7]   Hallward made a point of hosting the ceremonial luncheon to mark the opening at the newly completed Cripps Hall, to underline the fact that Sutton Bonington was, despite its distance from the main campus, nevertheless an integral part of the University.[8]

Having chosen Basil Spence to develop 'Technopolis', Council in 1957 gave responsibility for the design of a new social sciences block to Donald McMorran, the architect of Cripps Hall, and announced that it was intended to build up to six new halls of residence in the next few years. Work began on the Social Sciences building and thought was being given to the choice of architects for the halls when the National Coal Board suddenly lurched onto the stage and threatened to destroy, like a pantomime ogre, all that the good fairies had accomplished. In September 1957 the Coal Board announced proposals to mine underneath the University site.[9]

The Nottingham area is, of course, famously one of the great coal-mining regions of Britain, and underground seams had been worked right up to the edge of the University campus where Wortley Hall stood. The Coal Board's argument was that they simply wished to continue these workings. For the University, however, the implications were appalling. Mining resulted in subsidence which, even if slight, caused damage to buildings. If mining on a large scale were to take place under the University, all confidence in the site's suitability for expansion would evaporate. Hallward lost no time in enlisting the support of Sir Keith Murray: surely the Coal Board could not mine under buildings erected by Treasury funds?[10] For the next three years battle was joined and, in a very real sense, the fate of Nottingham University hung in the balance.

Hallward was at the forefront of the conflict, and the Minutes of Council and Senate reveal how active he was, together with Francis Hill, in lobbying for support and presenting the University's case in legal and political circles. An approach to the Chairman of the Coal Board produced no result, so in the autumn of 1958 Council appealed directly to the Prime Minister, Harold Macmillan. In his reply, Macmillan 'stated that it would be wrong for the government to intervene at this stage. He suggested that the University should make one further effort to reach agreement with the NCB and outlined the procedures which should be followed if these further discussions were not successful.'[11] The Coal Board, undeterred, applied in 1959 to the Minister of Housing for permission to mine under three acres of land which included the site of Wortley Hall. After a Public Enquiry in October the Minister granted permission to mine these three acres 'for experimental purposes', and, encouraged by this victory, the Coal Board indicated that it would apply for permission to mine under the entire University site in 1960. Council then employed a firm of consultant mining engineers to monitor the extent of damage to Wortley Hall. Frank Barnes recalled that 'of course many people were worried at the time and indeed indignant at the prospect. We were living on Wortley Close then, having sold our house on Parkside under the threat of subsidence, and I remember the metal studs driven into the ground in the Wortley area, indicating that mining was to proceed on an experimental basis, with subsidence expected and to be measured ... I well remember also the sudden dip in the main Derby Road and the breach of Wollaton Park wall alongside it that occurred overnight, caused by the very shallow workings from Wollaton Colliery which interfered with the levelling and drainage work on Beeston Lane playing fields.'[12]

In fact the consultants reported eventually that the damage to Wortley Hall had been minimal and this encouraged a compromise between the University and the Coal Board in the summer of 1960, by which the University agreed to partial extraction of the deep hard seam by two panels, one on either side of Lenton Hall Drive. The calculated subsidence was negligible and Cripps and Hugh Stewart Halls would not be affected. It was also agreed that there would be full extraction of a seam to the west of Beeston Lane under the new playing fields, for which the calculated subsidence was about two feet six inches.[13] These operations duly took place, there was very little damage, and the threat passed. Nevertheless for the period of three years during which this controversy was alive, the Vice-Chancellor and Council had been given good cause to worry.

Meanwhile, Science City was taking shape and one of the first new buildings to open there in 1960 was, appropriately enough, a laboratory block for the department of Mining. It carried the stamp of Professor Joseph (Joe) Pope, who left the University shortly after its completion to pursue a career which ended at the University of Aston, where he was Vice-Chancellor. 'It is utilitarian,' he explained to a student reporter. 'We can do anything in it at any time. It is not a series of boxes with little benches in, but an extremely adaptable workshop. We have spent money on the things that count. You will find here no marble halls, but that does not stop the place from being attractive, pleasant, light and airy.' *The Gongster* approved, calling the building 'a masterpiece of engineering', and '60,000 square feet of progress'.[14] The other main features of this initial phase of Science City were a first year engineering building, laboratories for civil and mechanical engineering, and a massive new Chemistry block, all

An aerial view of 'Science City'.

complete by 1961. The contractors were Costain's and their foreman, Mr Housego, announced proudly that 'we are up to schedule and we have had no labour troubles on this job at all'.[15]

Phase Two of the Science City development was made easier in 1961 when the Ministry of Works released its hold on a series of prefabricated office buildings that had occupied part of the site since before the War. However, Nottingham City Council refused to sell the open-air lido built by Jesse Boot for the enjoyment of Nottingham's citizens, and also retained control of the pavilion on the boating lake. Moreover, the residents of the Dunkirk district were becoming alarmed at the expansion of the University in their direction. Basil Spence's schemes for Phase Two featured a physics and mathematics block, a laboratory for cancer research, new buildings for chemical and production engineering, and, surmounting all, a sixteen storey tower block. This was, and remains, a controversial feature of the campus. It was begun in 1962 and finished in 1965, just before Hallward left. He never liked it but Basil Spence was adamant that there should be a 'vertical feature ... to set off the profile of the whole complex'. Tower blocks were certainly the fashion in the 1960s; but fashions change.[16]

In the summer of 1960 Council's plans for six new halls of residence, five for men and one for women, were made public. Lincoln Hall was to be designed by

F.E. Woolley, Derby Hall by Brian O'Rorke, Lenton Hall by Donald McMorran, and Sherwood and Rutland Halls by J. Fletcher Watson. The women's hall (Willoughby) was designed by W.H. Williamson. *The Gongster* announced that 'work will begin in 1961 and it is hoped that all six will be more than keeping pace with the growth of the University. Our photo shows that their architecture is very similar to that of Cripps which came under heavy fire last year!'[17] Poor Cripps Hall had certainly attracted the wrath of the modernists. In 1959 the *Architects' Journal*, so *The Gongster* reported, 'included a picture of Cripps with five other buildings. And, in the opinion of the *Architects' Journal*, these are the six poorest buildings to be erected recently in both Britain and America.'[18]

This was not a view shared by Bertrand Hallward. 'We were in the middle of the violent controversy over new styles in architecture,' he explained. 'The Secretary of the Cabinet got me onto a sofa in the Athenaeum to complain to me that a new University was not choosing new style architects. I said we have Basil Spence for the Engineering, Chemistry, Physics layout and buildings. But clearly the Cabinet Secretary had been "got at" by the new style crusading and brutal architects. Fortunately with Sir Percy Thomas' help and advice we found Mc Morran for Cripps Hall and the Education Building, and a series of other competent architects, whose previous buildings we either saw or had photographed, for the building of the other halls.'[19] As far as the Vice-Chancellor was concerned, architecture critics could go and boil their heads.

In 1961, while the foundations were being laid for some of the new halls, McMorran's Social Science building was formally opened by R.A. Butler. It housed the department of Education, the Institute of Education, and the departments of Geography, Economics, Industrial Economics, Social Science and Psychology; and whereas Hallward had left the detailed planning of the pure science buildings to the relevant heads of department, this building had gone ahead 'under my closer chairmanship and supervision'.[20] The Boots Company had made the site available, and the UGC paid the construction bill, which was nearly £450,000. 'There has evidently been the closest understanding between the University authorities and Mr McMorran, the architect, who deserves to be congratulated,' observed Butler in his speech at the opening. 'Mr McMorran is no doubt acquainted with Le Corbusier's dictum that "A house is a machine for living in" — but while giving you a building with all the efficiency of a machine he has succeeded in clothing it in those elements of art and imagination, proportion and beauty, which are necessary to the sustenance and nourishment of humane minds.'[21] A modern design based on traditional lines, the new complex blended well with the nearby Trent and Portland Buildings, and set the tone for the new halls of residence.

The Duke of Portland with R.A. Butler at the opening of the Social Science Building in 1961.

Courtesy of John Laing plc

Unfortunately the Conservative government went through a bad patch economically in 1961 and 1962, and financial cutbacks were made in many aspects of national life. The UGC found that it was unable to meet its financial commitments to Nottingham, as to other universities, and this caused grave anxiety. 'It cannot be said too bluntly to HM Government that it is not honest to will the end without also willing the means. Council cannot reiterate too often its utter dissatisfaction with the position in relation to external pressures on universities of the whole country,' Council complained in its 1962 report, clearly incensed at the 'wind of small change blowing from the Treasury'.[22] Despite this, all six halls were complete and in operation by the end of 1965. On the whole they were well received, by *The Gongster* at least. A photograph of Lincoln Hall, featuring one of its classical portals and a site almost ready for occupation by students, appeared in May 1962. A photograph of the 'picturesque' quad of Derby Hall, which 'opened as planned at the beginning of term', appeared in January 1963 under the headline 'Derby Hall is right on schedule'.[23] Willoughby Hall, which was different from the others in that it was not designed on a 'college' quadrangle plan, and that it was for women students, was ready in 1963. *The Gongster* devoted a double page spread to it in January 1964 and the reporters congratulated the architect (W.H. Williamson) 'on what is probably

Courtesy of John Laing plc

Willoughby Hall.

Sherwood Hall.

Courtesy of John Laing plc

the best designed exterior on the campus. One welcomes the departure from the quadrangle style employed in the latest three halls, and evident in two of those under construction. This style would appear to achieve nothing other than a wastage of space and discomfort for the residents during the bad weather. However, this is as far as one can pursue unqualified praise. The interior of the Hall repeats the all-too-familiar story of inadequate finance necessitating the cramming of 151 students into a space large enough to take about 100 in comfort.'[24]

Sherwood and Rutland Halls were both designed by J. Fletcher Watson on complementary sites and with the intriguing use of exterior wooden panels. An atmosphere of 'dreaming spires' was evoked by several cupolas and towers, and, in the case of Rutland, a remarkable polygonal library. 'Few serious criticisms were forthcoming from the inhabitants,' *The Gongster* reported of Sherwood, which opened in October 1964. 'Comments ranged from "It's marvellous really" to "I can't see anything wrong with it". Even the American colonial or possibly Scandinavian exterior, with its white wood, its pillars and useless towers, seems to be generally accepted, but one can't help wondering why the architects ... have apparently been encouraged not to use more modern building materials.'[25]

Most of the new halls were fully in use by the time Hallward left in March 1965 and Lenton Hall was ready for the following October. Cavendish and

An aerial view of the new halls of residence.

Ancaster Halls, begun in 1964 and designed by the same architects who had planed Willoughby Hall, both opened in 1966.

Hallward had inherited three halls of residence in 1948 and he left thirteen completed or planned in 1965. With the advice of Thomas, Jellicoe, McMorran and others, it had essentially been he who had acquired the necessary land, he who had determined where the halls should be built, and he who had influenced their architectural styles. More than that, in determining how the halls should be run, the Vice-Chancellor's influence was crucial. 'In general', he wrote, 'my halls had Wardens who were *not* professors but qualified academic dons who were accepted by heads of departments as members of their departments for lecturing and teaching. I tried to introduce the view that the warden's job needed a scholar with special pastoral gifts. I wanted them to develop a High Table of tutors belonging to the hall, and I built tutors' houses close by.'[26] The concept of mixed halls, accommodating both sexes, was not something Hallward took very seriously, though the issue was raised by students during his time, and Rutland Hall pioneered co-education in 1970.

Don Varley, the second Warden of Rutland Hall, wrote to Hallward in 1989: 'I clearly recall the day you literally swept me from Trent quadrangle to see the architects' models of the planned new halls. It did not enter my head that I would ever become Warden.' When he did, however, his mission 'had been set years before by you — the collegiate concept in a twentieth-century context. In a small way, I have worked with a succession of talented deputy Wardens, Senior Common Room tutors and Junior Common Room leaders to try to shape the kind of community you made clear to me was your vision for the residential side of Nottingham University's strategic plan. And the University — it is now the truly international community of scholars you envisaged, a far remove from the Borough Council "Tech" you took over so firmly in 1948.'[27]

Renaissance Prince?

'Something which has gone down in the history of statements about Bertie is that when you went in for an interview for a job, he would always say "Come, form a circle,"' one head of department remembered.[1] Hallward was well aware that it was no use having magnificent buildings without first-class academics to teach in them, and, as we have seen, the recruitment of excellent staff was one of his priorities. He presided over virtually all appointment committees, especially the joint committees of Council and Senate which appointed professors. During his period as Vice-Chancellor there is no doubt that the University gained a reputation for excellence in research and teaching as a result of many good appointments made between 1948 and 1965. In addition to the existing professorships, nearly forty new ones were created, as well as scores of posts of reader, senior lecturer and lecturer. To judge by the number of staff who were appointed Fellows of the Royal Society, the Chemistry department had the best record of achievement. Even in the days of the University College F.S. Kipping and J.M. Gulland had been Fellows, but when Gulland's successor as the Sir Jesse Boot Professor of Chemistry became a Fellow in 1954 he was only the second at the University, following the Deputy Vice-Chancellor, Professor L.F. Bates.[2] A further three members of the Chemistry department, all appointed in Hallward's time, became Fellows in due course — Professors D.D. Eley, A.W. Johnson and C.C. Addison.

Sir Harry Pitt had been a Fellow of Peterhouse with Hallward and he was appointed to Nottingham as Professor of Mathematics in 1950, becoming Deputy Vice-Chancellor in 1959. Also a Fellow of the Royal Society, he left Nottingham in 1964 on his appointment as Vice-Chancellor of Reading University. An admirer of Hallward, he had been attracted to Nottingham because of him, and found him 'extremely easy to work with', a man of 'tremendous energy and enthusiasm and great kindliness who could be depended upon to help people'.[3] 'A marvellous Vice-Chancellor in my view; a man of great vision: I give him full marks.'[4] This was the opinion of Sir Joseph Pope, FRS, Professor of Engineering at Nottingham in Hallward's time, who became Vice-Chancellor of Aston University in 1969. Both these scholars were innovative researchers of high distinction as well as men with great administrative gifts.

A considerable list of Fellows of the British Academy (for scholars in the Arts) dates from the Hallward period. Sir James Holt came to Nottingham as a young mediaeval historian in 1949 before moving to professorial posts at Reading and Cambridge where he was Master of Fitzwilliam College. E.A. Thompson, who came to Nottingham as Professor of Classics in 1948 won a national reputation as an historian of the late Roman Empire and remained at the University until 1979. His colleague John Rich remembered that 'in the early days, there was the vigour and enthusiasm of Vice-Chancellor Hallward to contend with. Hallward himself was a classicist, which put the department a good deal in the firing line, as when he decreed that the University should have a Greek play, or even that the Classics staff should come to Highfield House for instruction in Modern Greek'.[5] There were some, however, who found the Hallward style too irritating: one of these was Dr Harry Street, Head of the Law department, who moved to Manchester University in 1956.

Professor Brian Tate, FBA, who was appointed to the Chair of Hispanic Studies in 1958, recalled that Hallward 'wanted to appoint men with "fire in their belly"', and considered him 'a big man in every sense who was never devious and never bore grudges'. Indeed, he 'was the least resentful person you could ever meet, always laughing and smiling'.[6] Seldom singing, though, for Hallward was not gifted in that direction, nor did he play a musical instrument. However, he enjoyed listening to music and both at Clifton and Nottingham frequently had students and friends in to hear records from his extensive collection. He was particularly pleased to attract to Nottingham Ivor Keys, who had been Professor of Music at Queen's, Belfast. Keys had clear aims: 'We want to establish this University musically so that anyone seeking higher education in music will automatically think of Nottingham as the place to come. We must, too, make an impact on the City. They have a fine musical tradition, but we must make them turn to us more for their music.'[7] Hallward was delighted also with the art galleries that he had incorporated into the Portland Building, and with the work of Professor Alistair Smart, an enthusiastic proponent of eighteenth-century style and taste in architecture and painting.

Hallward enjoyed the music of Purcell and was the driving force behind the staging of his operettas *Dioclesian* and *King Arthur*, the latter in the summer of 1956. 'The productions of Purcell', he wrote, 'were I think our greatest musical achievements. The wooden staging for transformation scenes was manufac-tured and set up by the maintenance department in the authentic style of

Purcell's day. These performances drew audiences from schools across Britain.'[8] Dr Barbara Reynolds, writing to the novelist Dorothy Sayers, described *King Arthur* as 'a triumphant achievement, involving the co-operation of most of Nottingham, let alone the whole University'. Clearly, she had fallen under the spell of the Vice-Chancellor. 'I don't know if you have ever met Hallward?' she enquired. 'He is something of a super-man, I think, in an amusing and rather endearing kind of way. He gets very lit up by ideas and schemes and carries them through with tremendous *élan*. As he strides about the beautiful grounds of Nottingham University with its rolling parklands, country houses, and wide vistas over the Trent, he always seems to me to be the last remaining Renaissance Duke.' Like the rulers of Ferrara, she went on, Hallward set the ladies of the Court (led by Duchess Margaret) busily stitching, and summoned Hugh Willatt to produce, Ivor Keys to conduct, and scores of students to act and sing. 'It was a most joyous occasion, and I was so glad I went up for it.'[9]

'He was like a Greek god, with golden burnished hair,'[10] enthused another female academic, echoing a theme which ran from Hallward's years as a public school Apollo at Haileybury to his being, in T.E.B. Howarth's view, 'a perfectly type-cast Apollo' at Cambridge.[11] Even at Bude, Clifton boys had used the phrase 'Greek god'. Yet at Nottingham he was not so much the Renaissance duke or Greek god as the English country gentleman, issuing forth from Highfield House to inspect his estate, striding about at energetic pace, compass in hand. Little escaped his notice, particularly details of the gardens. 'They have planted the wrong shrubs!' he exclaimed to one of his sons-in-law while walking round the campus. 'Why wrong?' he was asked. 'These flower in vacation, not in term time. I ordered a species that flowers in term time.' 'How do you know the difference?' 'Years ago I was ill. I learnt about shrubs in convalescence.'[12] 'They were the twenty-three happiest years of my life,' recalled Arthur Smith, head gardener from 1947 to 1970 — 'Well, they were when you got used to Hallward, and he took some getting used to!'[13]

'He gave marvellous parties,' one colleague recalled. 'Hallward would greet people in a loud voice: "Yes, come in — talk", or "Come in — cheese", and there would be poor Margaret sawing up bread and cheese endlessly.[14] Margaret Hallward did not have a great deal of help in Highfield House and the burden of frequent dinner parties and drinks parties as well as the need to provide accommodation for a constant procession of distinguished visitors to the University was a considerable burden. Her wide knowledge of members of staff and concern for their welfare made her one of the most popular and respected people on the campus. Ralph Townley, a student president, was invited to dinner at Highfield House in the early days and mistook Margaret for one of her daughters. 'For Margaret then and always was young, slender, upright, alert,

A family meal at Highfield House.

charming and ever with a spring in her step', he wrote. 'Her eyes brightened to greet the visitor who soon found himself enfolded in warmth and comfort.'[15] 'I never knew anyone who was not immediately drawn to her,' wrote Professor Alistair Smart, 'for she inspired both affection and admiration, and by her sweetness added to the sweetness of life at Nottingham in those unparalleled years.'[16]

Hallward owned a rather splendid car, a silver Humber Super Snipe, which he drove, so his family thought, looking rather like Toad of Toad Hall, and generally driving far too fast, even with a caravan in tow. Between 1947 and 1956 there were five family camping holidays for the Hallwards and Macklins together, visiting French cathedrals and bathing in French rivers, and driving on two occasions down to Italy. In the winter, Highfield House was the ideal location for a family Christmas, with the King's Carol Service compulsory listening in the drawing room and the host in jovial form on Christmas Day in the dining-room, carving a vast turkey; and there would be china tea before bed.

As the years went by Highfield House ceased to be home for three of the Hallward girls. Ruth had married in 1949, and in 1956 Catherine, herself a graduate of Nottingham University, married David Corder, one of a numerous and well-known Nottingham family, who worked as a solicitor in the town.

Bertrand and Margaret Hallward relaxing at Highfield House.

Three years later Iola, an accomplished painter, and graduate of the Slade, married George Spafford, a barrister in Manchester. As with Ruth and Owen Chadwick, both weddings took place at St Leonard's, Wollaton, with 'proud father' escorting 'lovely daughter' up the aisle. The Corders and Spaffords between them produced another six grandchildren to add to the Chadwicks' four, and there was much sending of presents and cheques from generous grandparents at Christmas and birthday time. Meanwhile Christabel, the youngest daughter, was up at Girton where she became President of the JCR and soon embarked on a career as a history teacher.

Apart from the holidays during University vacations, Hallward was seldom away from the campus for long, with the one exception of his American journey in 1952. As the representative of the University, he attended the coronation of Elizabeth II in 1953, but, of course, it poured with rain; and even in Westminster Abbey, from where he was sitting he 'couldn't see a thing'. He attended the Jubilee celebrations of Leeds University in April 1954 and a few months later he was in Dublin at the centenary celebrations of the Catholic University of Ireland. In the summer of 1958 he was the guest speaker at a degree ceremony at the University of Chattanooga, Tennessee, and was himself awarded the honorary degree of Doctor of Laws, being presented to the assembled audience as 'an advocate of sound scholarship who recognizes the value of campus comrade-ship in the university experience'.[17]

In October 1960 Hallward missed the start of the new academic year to be in Nigeria at the invitation of the government, and in the winter of 1961 he attended a conference of heads of universities, in the United States. The next year he was in Cyprus, inspecting RAF educational establishments for the Air Ministry. In general he did not like to be rushing from one place to the next on business that was not essential to the University and its development. Nor did he relish being a member of public committees or seek to be appointed to them. If he were on a committee he preferred to be the chairman and to get through business quickly. His activities in the Nottingham area were strictly limited. He was a member of the governing body of Trent College, a local independent school, and he would be the guest speaker at other school prize days from time to time. He did not become involved in national or local politics and tended to keep his political views (which were generally left of centre) to himself. A lifelong admirer of Samuel Johnson, he accepted the Presidency of the Johnsonian Society in 1962, though this involved little more than giving a Presidential lecture (on 'Johnson Today') to a gathering of enthusiasts in Lichfield. In 1963 he was guest lecturer on a Swann's Hellenic Cruise, providing Margaret and himself with a fairly free holiday. Towards the end of his time at Nottingham he became a member of the National Standing Commission on Museums and Galleries which, as an observer at another university remarked, 'sounds a somewhat static body for so dynamic a person'.[18]

A number of honours had come his way, apart from the doctorate at Chattanooga (which he kept quiet about at first). The Duke of Portland made him a Deputy Lieutenant of the County, though in this capacity he did 'absolutely nothing', and in 1956 he was delighted to be made an Honorary Fellow of Peterhouse. Clive Priestley, who joined the Administrative Class of the Civil Service shortly after his term as student president ended in 1957 was asked whether, in the patronising jargon of Whitehall, the VC was 'K-worthy'. 'The then Establishment', Priestley wrote, 'evidently did not think so'.[19] Being a Vice-Chancellor would not, in itself, necessarily be enough to secure a knighthood: in a list of twenty-one Vice-Chancellors in 1964, for instance, only five were knights and some had been knighted before taking office. Public service beyond the call of normal duty — such as chairing important government commissions — were often rewarded with knighthoods but, as we have seen, Hallward preferred to concentrate on developments at Nottingham. By the late 'fifties he had done little for the government except to chair a War Office Enquiry into conditions of service for boy soldiers, and this in itself was not, it seems, thought worthy of reward. The late 1950's were precisely the years when Hallward was hounding the Ministry of Housing and the National Coal Board, and indeed the Prime Minister, over the Nottingham campus mining issue, so it is not perhaps surprising that he had offended somebody in Whitehall. To be fair, in the late 1950's Bertrand Hallward was not thinking of knighthoods. Sitting in his vast office in the Trent Building and flanked by his loyal secretary Rosemary David and the Registrar, Alfred Plumb, he was thinking nearly all the time about the University of Nottingham.

The Nottingham Playhouse

The one major commitment of Hallward's which had nothing to do with the University was his chairmanship of the board of directors of the Nottingham Playhouse, a repertory theatre which had been founded in 1948 in a converted cinema in Goldsmith Street. Its facilities were comparatively primitive but it could seat about 460 people and had 'a true theatre atmosphere' according to John Bailey, its historian and lifelong supporter.[1] The Board of Directors consisted of about fourteen local professional people and under its first chairman, Councillor John Mitchell (Lord Mayor of Nottingham at the time), money had been raised, with the help of the Arts Council, to give the new theatre modest security. When Councillor Mitchell resigned in 1949 the directors (who included the University's Professor of English) decided to ask the new Vice-Chancellor of the University to be their chairman. He would bring prestige to the post and, from what they had heard, considerable dynamism. Hallward accepted, and remained chairman for fifteen years, during which time a new theatre, hailed as one of the best in Europe, was built against a remarkable background of party political strife in Nottingham's Council House. 'It was a tremendous tax on my time', Hallward recalled, 'fortnightly meetings in the old theatre, of two to three hours. But it was worth it.'[2]

The Board was responsible for the financial and administrative aspects of the theatre, and its most important task was to choose an Artistic Director who took charge of staging the productions. The first Director was André van Gyseghem who opened in November 1948 with Bernard Shaw's *Man and Superman*. The curtains came down on the last production in the old theatre on July 13 1963 (for nostalgic reasons the same play was chosen and the same producer), and it has been calculated that between these two dates there were 322 productions and 4,000 performances, as well as four Directors — van Gyseghem in 1948, John Harrison in 1952, Val May in 1957 and Frank Dunlop in 1961.[3] The theatre staged fortnightly repertory and every other weekend saw frantic activity as the old set was taken down and the new one erected all through Saturday night and Sunday morning.

The Playhouse Theatre prospered modestly in its early years and it was possible to acquire the freehold in 1956, and the freehold of adjoining buildings in 1958 with a view to the construction of a new theatre in due course. However, the controlling Labour Party on the City Council was keen to back a new social amenity for Nottingham out of profits from the municipally-run gas industry and, according to a local paper, decided to spend more than £250,000 'on rehousing the Playhouse Company because of the national reputation this theatre had won for itself and the City during its ten years' cramped existence in Goldsmith Street'.[4] Accordingly, it authorized the distinguished theatre architect Peter Moro to produce plans for a spectacular new design in Wellington Circus. The Conservatives immediately attacked this 'reckless and feckless' expenditure and gave notice that when they came to power they would scrap the plan. By February 1961 the estimated cost of the new theatre had risen to £370,000, and the Board of Directors' Theatre Trust guaranteed to raise £60,000. In view of this promise, the City Council gave the final approval to the scheme by a majority of one — the casting vote of the Lord Mayor, Alderman Green. Three months later the Conservatives swept to victory in the local elections, and although work had begun on the new site, they threatened to sell it to

The new Nottingham Playhouse.

Moss Empires. Fortunately the latter decided to rebuild the existing Theatre Royal, so the new Playhouse went ahead after all.[5]

As Chairman of the Board of Directors Hallward's rôle in all these events was central, though much of the detailed negotiation, planning and sub-committee work concerning the new theatre was undertaken by Hugh Willatt, a member of the Board with special expertise in the world of the theatre, who later moved to London and rose to be Chairman of the Arts Council. Hallward's main contribution as Chairman, in Willatt's view, 'came from his strong and vivid personality. He controlled a not always easy Board and was a good front figure on the occasions when he rather than the theatre director had to take the stage'.[6] On the other hand, Hallward had no particular experience of the theatre apart from a normal academic knowledge of drama, and contact with theatre people was generally left to Willatt, the Vice-Chairman. For drive and experience in fund-raising, however, Hallward could not have been bettered.

On December 11,1963, Nottingham's *Guardian Journal* produced a souvenir supplement of the opening of the new Playhouse. 'The long haul is over,' it announced. 'To-night, the new Nottingham Playhouse, Europe's most modern theatre — costing £370,000 and seating 760 — brings up its curtain for the first time. It has taken fifteen years, five of them clouded by political wrangling, to bring about this moment — a moment designed to put Nottingham squarely on the theatrical map of the world.'[7] Princess Margaret had accepted the invitation to open the theatre but, as she was imminently expecting a baby, her husband Lord Snowdon came alone and handed over the lease of the building to Bertrand Hallward, Chairman of the Theatre Trust. Standing before the classical pillars of the set for *Coriolanus*, Hallward spoke of the 'materialization of a dream', and thanked especially Alderman Roland Green, the ex-Lord Mayor whose casting vote had been so crucial. 'To-night', he ended happily, 'is a night of delight and congratulation.'[8] Then followed excerpts from Tyrone Guthrie's production of *Coriolanus*, starring John Neville, Leo McKern and Ian McKellen, after which there was an official reception at the Council House. Unfortunately the night of 'delight and congratulation' ended abruptly at this point because by the time Guthrie and his hungry company arrived at the Council House after changing, they found that the other guests had cleared the buffet table: according to John Bailey 'Sir Tyrone was for leaving the Council House to seek sandwiches elsewhere, and instead of everyone enjoying a celebration, a dreadful situation of confrontation (even physical!) developed and the reception ended very unhappily'.[9]

Huge headlines in the morning's local papers pilloried the Council and accused the Conservatives of a plot to discredit the Playhouse from its opening day. The situation was not improved when *Coriolanus* received very mixed reviews, some critics regarding it as 'an anthology of Guthrionics', while Bamber Gascoigne in *The Observer* considered that 'Guthrie's first act is a very severe embarrassment.'[10]

However, the critics were agreed that the new Playhouse was a superb theatre, and with a triumvirate of artistic directors of the stature of John Neville, Peter Ustinov and Frank Dunlop, it staged some fine and innovative productions that kept much-needed cash flowing into the box office. The Theatre Trust had committed itself to raising £60,000 to add to the £310,000 provided by the City, and though an appeal had produced more than £20,000 there was now a problem over the shortfall. The Conservative Council was not disposed to come to the rescue and eventually demanded a cash payment of £42,000 and raised the rent of the Playhouse to cover the rest of the deficit.[11] Hallward at this point resigned (on August 16th 1964), ostensibly in protest that the theatre's financial security had thus been compromised. In fact he knew that he would be leaving Nottingham the next spring and would have to resign anyway.

For fifteen years Hallward had presided over the affairs of the Playhouse, finding a dilapidated provincial theatre in 1949 and leaving a new building of international renown in 1964. Many others had also slaved away in the interests of the common cause and the credit is not Hallward's alone. On the other hand he had provided firm leadership and had not lost heart in the face of endless difficulties. Sitting in the Chairman's seat on the opening night he could reasonably have felt emotions of satisfaction. Sitting in an anonymous seat while this book was being researched in the autumn of 1994 the author could not but marvel both at the theatre itself, and the coincidence that had brought to the stage that night a drama based on *The Picture of Dorian Gray.*

A Medical School

In his last year at Nottingham, a great scheme that Hallward had sought to bring about ever since his arrival as Vice-Chancellor received official permission to proceed. On 27th July 1964, the Minister of Health announced that a new medical school would be built on the Nottingham University campus. The twists and turns of fortune which eventually led to this crucial decision have been mapped in careful detail by Dr Susan Ablett in her 1992 doctoral thesis on Nottingham's Medical School, in which she describes Hallward as a 'noble champion' of the cause.[1]

Nottingham's Medical School was the first to be built in the United Kingdom in the twentieth century; the dozen or so existing ones had been founded in the 1820's and 1830's, or even earlier. In 1944 the aptly named Goodenough Committee reported that there seemed to be no need for more medical schools and in 1953 *The Lancet* argued that 'the evidence suggests that England and Wales has an annual surplus approaching 200 doctors.'[2] However, this was contested by those who felt that the newly-established National Health Service needed more doctors. Another report in 1956 (the Willink report) argued that the supply of doctors was 'reasonably close to requirements', but by 1961 it seemed that many doctors were emigrating to Canada and elsewhere because they found the NHS unattractive, so there really was a crisis after all. In November 1961 a medical expert in the House of Lords called for 'at least three and preferably six new medical schools', and the Robbins Report of 1963 advocated a massive expansion of the whole of higher education, including medicine. In December 1963 the UGC recommended one new medical school: the question was, should it be at Southampton, Leicester or Nottingham? On 27th July 1964 Antony Barber, the Minister of Health, announced that Nottingham had been chosen. Tracing how this decision was made is a complex matter.

Principal Hugh Stewart had regarded the establishment of a medical school at Nottingham as a 'cherished aim', and in 1943 his successor Wortley was negotiating with regional health authorities on the subject of a 'suggested

Medical Faculty at Nottingham'. So the topic had been well aired by the time Hallward arrived in 1948 and it became part of his plan for the overall development of the University, despite advice he was given on the top of a Birmingham double-decker bus by a fellow Vice-Chancellor attending a conference at the University. 'Hallward,' said Sir Raymond Priestley (Vice-Chancellor of Birmingham University) 'don't have a medical school, it will eat up all the money.' 'I noted this', Hallward recalled, 'and found out some of the figures, and of course he was right. Yet ... if you have got to a certain development in a rising university, and you are pretty strong, then you needn't fear the Medical School.' During his American tour of 1952 Hallward looked at several medical schools and saw how essential it was for the school, the university and the teaching hospital to be close together on the same site, not least because 'it was important that the brilliant young researchers in biophysics and biochemistry, in the main part of the University, meet at lunch with the equally brilliant clinical people, and swap ideas. This is the importance of physical proximity and communication ... because the idea can go dead in a few hours.'[3]

As far as the location was concerned, it seems that Hallward made his mind up quickly because witnesses recall him pointing to the present site very early on and 'declaring adamantly that this would be the site of the new Medical School', despite the fact that in those days the land was occupied by the premises of several industrial firms. So to build the Medical School he envisaged, permission would have to be gained at the highest levels of national and local government, and a lot of money would be required to buy out the present occupants of the land.[4]

In the early years Hallward had the practical sense to realize that a medical school had to give way to other priorities. Some months after the American trip he wrote to an official at St Thomas's Hospital Medical School: 'My mind has been turned rather definitely against the creation of a medical school here, at least for the next ten to fifteen years. We have decided to develop Engineering and Agriculture. I am coming to the view that, with the limited financial resources of this country, the growing University will do better to limit its demands and to do what it can as well as possible. My wife and I spent three months in America last spring, and I was profoundly impressed by the financial difficulties which teaching hospitals and medical schools are running into in their private universities'.[5]

Early in 1953 Hallward wrote to Francis Hill: 'I am beginning to think that Engineering and Agriculture, together with the general development of the University, and our residential policy, provide more than enough for the next ten years of development.'[6] So the idea of a medical school was postponed — but not abandoned. Only the next year, when members of the UGC visited

Nottingham, Hallward took to one side Sir Melville Arnott and said: 'What about a medical school?'. 'I advised him against it', Sir Melville recalled, 'and said they are more trouble than they are worth and that he would never have any peace if he had a medical school.'[7] And there, given the prevailing official view that there were enough doctors in Britain anyway, the matter rested. The Jellicoe plan of 1955 contained no provision for a medical school and the statement by the University for the quinquennium 1957-1962 describes the medical school proposals as having been 'indefinitely postponed'.[8]

By January 1962, however, they were firmly back on the agenda with the publication that month of the *Hospital Plan for England and Wales*, which referred to the fact that the Sheffield Region had fewer beds in relation to population size than any other, and advocated the building of 'a new district general hospital on the south side of Nottingham'. Hallward seized on this opportunity to press for the new hospital to be built close to the University campus, with an adjacent medical school. The University Grants Committee had first to be persuaded to pay for it, then a site had to be made available, and finally the claims of Leicester and Southampton had to be argued down. The innumerable discussions and negotiations entailed in all this consumed a good deal of Hallward's time and energy in his last three years, but he saw a Nottingham Medical School as the logical next step forward for the University now that the new halls of residence and Science City were well on the way to completion.

The City Corporation proved a strong ally, well aware of the benefits a new hospital would bring; and for over two years it managed to stall requests from industrialists to develop further the forty-acre site on the other side of Clifton Boulevard that Hallward had long seen as the obvious place to build the new hospital complex. Hallward was faced with a major battle here because, as Sir Keith Murray wrote to him in June 1963, 'it is no secret that the Ministry feel that the site immediately opposite the University would be both expensive and difficult to acquire ... but the final decision will be taken by the Ministry and University Grants Committee, in the light not only of the financial consideration but of the other factors which are relevant to the choice of a teaching hospital site'.[9] Two other plots were being seriously considered at this time, one near Wilford Power Station and the other near the Teachers' Training College on the outskirts of the city. Hallward urged that a decision should be made soon because of the 'grave dissatisfaction' amongst the owners of the Clifton Boulevard properties, 'who state quite rightly that they have been forced to wait for months of indecision and that their business interests are being impaired'.[10]

On August 1st 1963 Hallward and Hill attended a meeting in London with representatives of the UGC and the Ministry of Health, at which Hallward's enthusiastic advocacy of the Clifton Boulevard site was by some considered 'over the top'. Dr Ablett states that 'there was a degree of concern among some of the University's representatives that the Vice-Chancellor's rigid determination to discuss only the Clifton Boulevard site might go against him, and lose Nottingham its advantage.'[11] Another important meeting followed, this time at the University on 22nd August, involving Hallward, Hill, the UGC, the Ministry of Health, the Sheffield Regional Board, and Nottingham's Town Clerk, City Engineer and Planning Officer. All possible sites were reviewed and the Ministry representatives seemed to have been convinced that the one on Clifton Boulevard was the best.

In October 1963 Enoch Powell, who doubtless recalled Hallward's Cambridge lectures, resigned as Minister of Health, to be replaced by Antony Barber. Months of delay followed and by May 1964 no decision had been made and the industrial firms in the Clifton Boulevard area were incensed at the inaction. The clinching move seems to have been made by the City Council, which offered the Ministry a grant of £100,000 towards the cost of a medical school at the University. The Town Clerk relayed this information to Sir Francis Hill on 15th July and on the 27th July came the official announcement from the Ministry that the decision had been made.[12]

It would be absurd to suggest that the Nottingham University Medical School was built simply because Bertrand Hallward wanted it to be built. Clearly, many other issues and individuals were involved. However, it would certainly not have been built had he been *opposed* to the idea, and it is quite possible that other sites would have been chosen had he not fought with relentless determination to see it established on Clifton Boulevard. Hallward's last major contribution to the Medical School was to seek out Sir George Pickering, Oxford's Professor of Medicine, to be Chairman of the Planning Committee for the whole project. Meanwhile Sir Francis Hill, as President of Council, was hoping to entice Professor Fred Dainton of the Leeds University department of Chemistry to succeed Hallward as Vice-Chancellor on his retirement in 1965. Dainton was a Fellow of the Royal Society and a former Cambridge don who had a particular interest in the teaching of Medical Science, and although he had refused other invitations to become a Vice-Chancellor he cold not resist what he described as 'the golden carrot' of a new Medical School when it was dangled before him by Sir Francis over a very pleasant lunch at the White Hart in Lincoln. In this manner, as Dr Ablett has shown, 'the University acquired a second Vice-Chancellor, as committed to the idea of a medical school and the cause of medical education as Hallward had been'.[13]

The Last Year

Hallward's contract at Nottingham provided for retirement at the age of 65, which meant that he could have stayed on until the summer of 1966. In fact, he decided that he wanted to leave in March 1965, and informed the Council at the end of 1963, giving them plenty of time to find a successor, although in the end the Deputy Vice-Chancellor, Professor Norman Haycocks, presided over the summer term of 1965 before the arrival of Dainton in the autumn. A number of factors combined to persuade Hallward to leave a little early. One was that his wife's health had not been good and sunshine and fresh air had been prescribed by the doctor. Another was that he felt a new Vice-Chancellor should tackle the building of the Medical School from its inception. A third, and very important, consideration, was that he did not approve of the recommendations of the 1963 Robbins Report.

This vast, four-volume analysis of Britain's future needs in the realm of higher education made 178 recommendations based upon exhaustive research. The general argument behind the report was that there should be a dramatic increase in the number of universities, and a drastic rise in the number of students taught at all universities. Six new universities should be built immediately, all Colleges of Advanced Technology should be given university status, and between eight and ten thousand places should be made available at most higher education institutions. The State should accept the enormous increase in expenditure that all these changes would involve. Governments of the 1960's, both Conservative and Labour, accepted the main recommendations of the report, which has shaped the development of higher education ever since.

Although numerical expansion had been the keynote of Hallward's years as Vice-Chancellor, it had been expansion at a moderate pace. The most dramatic rise in the number of students had actually taken place before his arrival, from about 700 in 1944 to 2,000 in 1948. In terms of student numbers his first ten years had been a time of slow growth while the new University concentrated on building the necessary facilities to teach so many students and to accommodate most of them on campus. After 1957 Hallward had accepted that the University might grow to a maximum of 4,500 and when he left in 1965 it had actually reached 3,500. The concept of a university of twice this number did not conform to his frequently reiterated philosophy of the university with a pastoral as well as an academic role, where dons were both teachers and friends. On a more practical level, he suspected that if the State became responsible for funding higher education on such a massive scale, universities would become the lapdogs of politicians and the State might well go bankrupt.[1]

All these were good reasons why 1965 seemed to Hallward a natural break, an appropriate time to hand over to a successor. But there was a fourth reason, perhaps the most compelling of all. He had become enthused with another great enterprise, this time a personal one. He would build an ocean-going yacht, sail it to the Mediterranean with Margaret, and spend months of each year in the azure waters of the ancients. He formulated this plan early in the 1960's and, once decided, it was pursued with vigour. 'Heaven was to steer and control,' he had told an assembly of freshers in 1951, and he intended to put this to the test.

Aware of his impending retirement, the University of Sheffield hastened to honour Hallward in May 1964 by inviting him to open their newest hall of residence, Sorby Hall, and by bestowing upon him an honorary doctorate. The Public Orator told the assembled gathering that 'Hallward's main concern has

The Vice-Chancellor ice-skating.

always been with the quality and the integration of life in the University. Notable products of his vision are the University Park, enlarged nearly three-fold in his time, and the great social centre of the Portland Building. Above all, and of special relevance to to-day's festivities, is the magnificent chain of residential halls, each with its own identity and corporate life, none more than a few minutes' walk away from the centre of the University, and together translating for a modern community the best virtues of the ancient collegiate system'. 'Soon,' he went on, Hallward would be borne from 'the detergent foam of the Trent to the phosphorescence of the Aegean', leaving only a new Nottingham legend to add to Robin Hood and Jesse Boot, that of 'the youthfully athletic figure of Bertrand Hallward, striding along a yard ahead of his breathless companions, or in winter skating pensive figures on the lake, or in the committee planning, persuading, counselling and cajoling, impervious to politics and pressures, but dedicated to the creation of a great University.'[2]

'Impervious to politics' was a fair description of the apolitical stance which Hallward had adopted throughout his time at Nottingham. He was not a paid-up member of any political party and this had been a great advantage at times when his various schemes had fallen into the arena of local politics. However, in October 1964, within months of retirement, he truly threw all caution to the winds when giving the prizes away at Cheltenham Grammar School. VC SLAMS LABOUR ran the largest headline *The Gongster* had ever devoted to Hallward who, it reported, denounced the Labour Council's plans for the extension of comprehensive schools in Bristol. 'It is very wrong' he announced, 'to use a change in schools to achieve a social change which is not good for education. The parents of the children of Bristol will be repulsed when they realize the full consequences of this action. I warn the socialists that if they carry out this policy on a national scale there will be such a reaction throughout the country that their party will be swept out of power.' This produced a furious response from Robert St John Reade, the Vice Chairman of the Bristol Education Committee who had been dismissed as a master at Clifton under Whatley for standing as a Bristol Labour councillor. In a letter published in the *Times Educational Supplement* and elsewhere he wrote: 'I am amazed that the Vice-Chancellor of a distant University should think it his business to intervene in a political controversy in an area far outside his sphere of influence, and I think the matter should be reported to the Chairman of the University Grants Committee or the Secretary of State for Education and Science.'[3] Another black mark for Hallward in Whitehall.

This proved to be the last excitement before the round of banquets, speeches and presentations which marked the Vice-Chancellor's departure on Tuesday, 16th March. Council gave a dinner in his honour and the Chancellor unveiled

Hallward's bust by the sculptor David McFall, RA.

a bronze bust of him which had been executed by David McFall, RA, whose commissions so far had included the two bronze unicorns surmounting Bristol's Council House, and busts of Ralph Vaughan Williams and Winston Churchill. Hallward liked the finished product, noting that the face looked quite different on each side, which he thought true to life. As for the inscription, this 'was a challenge to me I could not resist,' he recalled. 'I remembered the epitaph the Emperor Augustus is said to have composed: *Latericiam Inveni Reliqui Marmoriam*, so I sent to the Registrar *Collegium Invenit Reliquit Universitatem* (He found a College and left a University) which Alfred Plumb accepted.'[4]

On the afternoon of this valedictory day a special Congregation was held in the Great Hall of the Trent Building, where the Duke of Portland conferred upon Hallward the honorary degree of Doctor of Law, and also presented him with a cheque representing a present from Court, Council, Senate and staff. Then followed three beautifully turned speeches from the Public Orator, Professor Barrington; the President of Council, Sir Francis Hill; and the Deputy Vice-Chancellor, Professor Haycocks. Professor Barrington began speaking of Hallward in his Cambridge days, 'a dashing figure on the tennis courts where he was to be seen "defeating" his opponents with the easy grace of a natural athlete, returning the deadliest of volleys with the effortless skill of a born chairman of a university senate'. Clifton's evacuation to Bude he described as

'Veteran Hallward Shakes Pickard' was the headline in the local press when, close to retirement, Hallward took on the twenty-one-year-old tennis ace, Tony Pickard, and made him work very hard for a victory. Hallward sported a trilby hat on this occasion.

'the only occasion on which Hallward has been known to retreat in the face of adversity, but it goes without saying that it was a fighting retreat, and he maintained a school in good heart during the years when its future must have seemed wholly dark. Indeed as we look back at those Clifton days through contemporary eyes, we see our future Vice-Chancellor taking recognizable shape. Firm in his disciplinary control, but unfailingly benevolent in his intentions, he swept despondency aside with an infectious combination of courage, energy and charm. And he threw in, we understand, for good measure, a constant stream of original ideas on every conceivable subject.' Then he turned to Hallward's work at Nottingham.

> The growth of a university is guided by the deliberations of a hierarchy of committees. The members of these bodies address themselves to their tasks with sacrificial enthusiasm, for academic communities take a professional pride in their ability to peer searchingly into both sides of every question. Indeed, they are apt to feel mortified if they fail to uncover a third side as well. Unfortunately, it has proved necessary in recent years to adapt this agreeable habit to the demands of a harsher world of competitive expansion in which universities that hesitate are irretrievably lost. Through this world our Vice-Chancellor has moved with enviable self-confidence, and at times with an air of positive enjoyment. By no means indifferent to the benefits of democratic discussion, he has yet contrived by well-timed glances at the Council Room clock to remind us of a world outside that will not be kept waiting. For seventeen breathless years the University has been swept by his impulsive energy from one major building project to the next. The experience has been unforgettable, leaving us all with the vivid realization that our Vice-Chancellor's administrative methods, like his roads, are 'Unsuitable for Pedestrians'.

> For this we have good reason to be profoundly thankful. The momentum that he has imparted to our planning, and the foresight with which he has controlled the development of our superb estate, have been of fundamental importance in securing the transformation of the College into the handsomely equipped University of which we are all so proud. It is not surprising that in 1955 the Chairman of the University Grants Committee was reporting that the buildings of The University of Nottingham had increased to an extent that had not been thought possible five years before.

> We may suspect, however, that Hallward would not wish us to remember him solely as a builder in bricks and stone. He has striven with no less vigour to realize here at Nottingham a vision of an urbane and

balanced community, inspiring all of its members to that high quality of achievement upon which any academic reputation must ultimately rest. By his imaginative grasp of the potentialities of the Portland Building, and by his vigorous advocacy of the claims of halls of residence, he has convincingly demonstrated that the influence of a modern university can be extended far beyond the limits of formal teaching hours. His deep love of music and the fine arts has moved him to give powerful support to their development, so that they now bring inspiration and refreshment to us all. These things, and much more besides, we owe to a man who would not take 'no' for an answer; to a Vice-Chancellor who insisted that if a university could finance the demands of modern technology, it could not pretend that it was too poor to buy a harpsichord.[5]

Speaking second, Sir Francis Hill, who as President of Council had worked, so amicably with Hallward for seventeen years, readily conceded that 'our high rate of expansion in every respect has been largely due to the human dynamo in the central power station at Highfield House. In those early days ... the Vice-Chancellor spent many a quiet hour walking around, planning and dreaming for both the near and the further future. Vacations were not holidays to him: they were opportunities to work with less interruptions than in term time. For us laymen who come here to Council or to committees, to take decisions, and then to return to our other responsibilities, it has been a source of contentment to know that there would be no pause or hesitation in execution of policy. Many a time, when some long-awaited development has at last become possible, the Vice-Chancellor has instantly been on the telephone to discuss how much preparatory work could be done in advance of the next Council meeting. This characteristic of the Vice-Chancellor has perhaps been most clearly seen in the Buildings Committee, which is attended by large mixed teams of experts, architects, builders, quantity surveyors and consultants of all kinds, people who are used to having ideas of their own. There they have found, sometimes with ill-concealed surprise, that they have to work as members of a team, or perhaps rather as members of an army, for the most apt comparison is with a military operation. Our reputation for finishing our buildings on time derives from this wholesome field discipline.'

'One other characteristic must be singled out for mention', the President continued. 'His tenure of office has been marked by a single-minded devotion. He could so easily have given part of his energies to other good causes but ... he has for the most part abstained from doing so, from a conviction that the University at this stage of its life required and deserved all that he could give to it. This total absorption in our affairs, this gift of all his great qualities of head and heart in some of the best years of his life, will never be forgotten here.' On a more personal note, Hill emphasized the *human* side of the 'human dynamo'. 'We shall still think of the hearty welcome, the boyish smile, the infectious optimism which have always greeted us when we came here, and we shall remember many stimulating talks and gay exchanges when he is far away in his new enterprise, planned with a zest which we have witnessed with so much admiration and just a little envy. The greatest thing that he can take with him as he leaves us is the consciousness of achievement on a monumental scale.' 'All these things that he has done,' Hill concluded, 'he could not have done without the support of Mrs Hallward. Her provision of a happy home life for him and her gracious hospitality to so many of us have been a gift to the University the value of which is beyond measure.'[6]

Sir Francis Hill was followed by Professor Norman Haycocks, the Deputy Vice-Chancellor, who spoke on behalf of the Senate.

> Out of curiosity, I recently glanced through the Senate minute-books for 1948 and a year or two after. I found that the Vice-Chancellor chaired his first Senate on the 20th September 1948, and as far as the minutes show, apart from acknowledging the welcome of his colleagues and performing the normal routines of chairmanship, he sat throughout as a silent observer. I need hardly add that this never happened again! At the very next meeting on the 11th October, he was in full action with a proposal to set up a Development Committee, which was also agreed later by Council and which started work the following month. The first Bassett-Lowke model was commissioned, an Endowment Appeal fund soon launched, and Open Days followed later during which departments displayed their work to a beguiled and sometimes astonished public. Nor was the Vice-Chancellor's fertile brain concerned only with bricks, mortar and money. In his first term he mooted with Senate the possibility of teaching the History of Science — I am afraid we are still only mooting it — and there followed quickly such varied items as discussions between members of Senate and representatives of industry about co-operation in research, a definition of the just teaching load of assistant lecturers, the creation of new Chairs and many other academic developments. Not all his proposals were welcomed; in his first term, for example, he pressed for the abolition of the Whit Monday holiday, but prudently retreated before the agonized hostility of the Senate. Needless to say, the Whit Monday holiday was quietly abolished a few years later.
>
> It is not my purpose to set out a chronological record of the Vice-Chancellor's achievements. I am merely illustrating how immediately

and with what a sense of urgency, he began to grapple with the whole range of academic, administrative and financial problems of the new University. I join with the other speakers in expressing our profound gratitude for the way in which he has continued throughout these seventeen years to guide our affairs with the same energy, power and decision. Some Vice-Chancellors have achieved fame by their exploits outside their universities; as the President of the Council has said, ours quickly decided that all his efforts ought to be concentrated here, and it is this single-minded devotion which did so much to turn a provincial University College into the vigorous and self-reliant University we have today.

I turn now to the Vice-Chancellor's work as an educationalist and to ask this question: how has he used his office to shape the education which this University offers? Many others have thought recently about the aims of university education; the Robbins Committee, for example, produced rather hesitantly and with many qualifications a set of four aims which they thought should characterize higher education as a whole though not necessarily any one institution. The Vice-Chancellor has never been hesitant. He has never deviated from the conviction that being at a university should mean belonging to a community, a community of dons and students, engaged between them in a wide range of activities, intellectual, creative, social, athletic, all pursued strenuously and to as high a standard as possible. It should be a real community, fostering good personal relationships, making it easy for friendships to be formed and for character to be shaped by the impact of person on person. It should express a way of life and a sense of values.

It is this conviction which lies at the heart of all the Vice-Chancellor's endeavours and which explains his priorities. To meet it, the academic quality of our community had to be maintained and enhanced and this meant recruiting more staff, the best staff, if necessary from the Antipodes. It meant establishing new departments, providing more flexible degree courses, encouraging research. It meant not only extending fully the ablest students, but caring also for the more average. A thoroughgoing tutorial system had to be developed and if the life outside the lecture-room and the laboratory were to be enriched, the University had to become mainly residential, the amenities of the Portland Building had to be created, and activities such as music and fine art had to be brought within the experience of everybody.

It is easy to see these as the Vice-Chancellor's memorial. I prefer — and I am sure he would prefer — to see them simply as means, means serving

a coherent educational purpose. The Vice-Chancellor's real memorial is
the conception which he leaves with us of what the experience of being at
a university ought to signify in all its depth, variety and richness. His
conception may not be an original one; what is more important is that he
has pursued it, and pursued the whole of it, in a period of rapid expansion,
with more consistency and success than has been the case in any other
British university in these post-war years.[7]

The last to speak was Hallward himself, who dismissed the foregoing
eulogies and insisted that about retiring Vice-Chancellors, *de functo officio nil nisi
bunkum*: nothing but nonsense was said. Read *The Gongster*, he suggested, if you
want to know the truth. He then launched into a fighting speech concerning the
great debate about the potential reservoir of student talent and the extent to
which it was likely to come forward for entry into the universities in the next
decade. 'My own views on this matter are already known', he said. 'I regard the
Robbins Report as a dangerously misleading document. Indeed the evidence in
its own appendices does not in my opinion support its conclusions. I therefore
believe that the projected expansion of numbers will be accomplished, if it *is*
accomplished, by offering undeserved places to the relative dimwits of the
middle classes, since there is no evidence that in the immediate future the high-
ability working-class children will suddenly change their habits, stay on at
school and become available for entry to the University.' Hallward then moved
on to ask his audience a few questions. 'Are you satisfied that our methods of
teaching and learning in this University are reasonable, efficient and satisfactory? And our systems of examinations and classing for degrees and the time we
take over this progress? Our libraries and use of books and the buying of books?
The student use of vacations and student attendance at public and general
lectures and lectures of the student's special subject? What about the problems
of student discipline and morals in a university? Has the Arts Faculty shaken
itself free from the "Ichabod" neurosis from which it suffered a few years ago?
And has it gained a new sense of purpose and obligation in a predominantly
scientific world? I have some indication that this may be so, though at the Senate
yesterday my doubts returned. I should like to conclude this part of my address
by affirming for the last time my profound conviction that high quality is the first
essential in a university and that larger numbers and greater through-put must
never be allowed to jeopardise this fundamental objective of high quality.'[8]
Then followed a more conventional sequence of thanks to groups and individuals, and he sat down.

With a kick in the groin for the Robbins Report, a slap on the wrist for the Arts
Faculty, and a bundle of testing questions for the University in general, this was

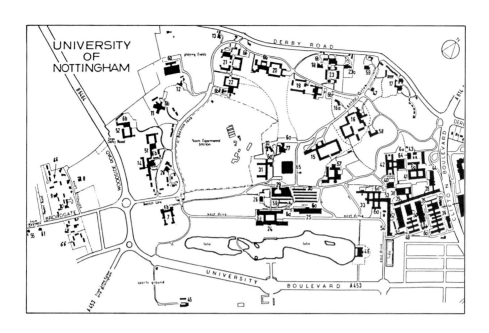

Halls and Annexes

Women
7   Florence Boot
8   Broadwood
11   Nightingale
12   Lenton Fields
13   Lenton Eaves
51   Cavendish
55   No. 8 Broadgate

Men
15   Hugh Stewart
16   Cripps
16A Lenton Close
17   Wortley
18   Lenton Hurst
19   Lincoln
20   Derby
21   Sherwood
23   Lenton
23A Redcourt

Flats
9   Oaks
10   Pines
66   Student Flats

Mixed
22   Rutland
52   Ancaster

Teaching and Research Buildings

24   Trent Building
28   Lenton Grove (Dept. of Music)
29   Old Engineering Block
30   Temporary Buildings
31   Education
32   The Orchards
33   Biology
34   Mining and Mechanical
       Engineering
35   Civil and Mechanical
       Engineering

36   Pharmacy and Metallurgy
37   Cancer Research
38   First year Applied Science T.1
39   Second and third Year Applied
       Science T.2
40   Science Library
41   Chemistry
42   Physics and Mathematics
43   Radiochemistry
44   Tower Building (Electrical
       Engineering and Architecture)

49   Production Engineering
50   Chemical Engineering
53   Cell Biology
54   Geology and Psychology
56   Copse Block (lecture rooms)
57   Social Sciences
59   Paton House (Institute of
       Planning Studies)
62   Medical Sciences
65   University Library

Recreational and Other Buildings

25   Portland Building
26   Highfield House (Vice-
       Chancellor's Residence)
27   University Club
29   Gymnasium
45   Sports Pavilion

46   Lakeside Pavilion
47   Squash Courts
48   Broadgate House (University
       Air Squad)
58   Cripps Health Centre

60   Sports Centre
61   Officers' Training Corps
63   Wolfson Institute for Interfacial
       Technology
64   Cripps Computing Centre

The campus and buildings of The University of Nottingham in 1969.

far from being, typically enough, a complacent farewell, and, while printing the other speeches in full, the *University of Nottingham Gazette* for April 1965 contented itself with the single line, 'The Vice-Chancellor replied on behalf of himself and Mrs Hallward.' True to form, Hallward went out, as he had gone in, quite happy to rock the boat.

Part Six

Safe Havens 1965-1995

Delphis

One of the young Bertrand Hallward's contemporaries in the classical sixth at Haileybury had been an amiable rogue called Stuart Perowne who was prepared even to risk balancing a heavy Latin dictionary over the door of the classroom so that it would fall upon the unsuspecting head of his headmaster. Malim duly strutted in, and the dictionary came tumbling down, but missed him. 'Not that time, Perowne,' was all he said.' Years later Perowne married the distinguished writer Freya Stark and it was she, so it seems, who filled Bertrand's head with fantasies of the sea. 'I had read a good many of Freya Stark's books, and in two of her books of travel in Asia Minor there were illustrations of a small river boat *Elfin*. I found out that it belonged to the English consul at Smyrna, David Balfour. I made further enquiries and decided to charter it from Balfour with his Greek skipper Mitsu and son Babi.'[1] This was in 1963 and it might well have brought Bertrand's career as Vice-Chancellor at Nottingham to an abrupt halt.

Margaret and Bertrand were joined on *Elfin* by their daughter Iola and her husband George who boarded at Chios. George noticed that the boat: 'had the proportions of an English canal narrow boat, but with one major difference. The stern was only a foot or so above sea level, and the saloon and bunks were protected only by swing doors from any water which came over the stern. Probably it had been designed for use on the river Thames. We set out for Skyros via Psara but had to shelter for several days in the lee side of an uninhabited island because of high wind. Eventually the wind died down and a favourable forecast persuaded Bertrand to sally forth. But soon the high wind returned, waves increased in height, and water over the stern seemed inevitable, with consequent flooding and sinking. Suddenly Bertrand decided that the best chance of surviving was to turn — a very slow business with almost inevitable flooding — and run before the wind. He gave the order. Mitsu refused to obey. "All is lost," he said, "We can't go on, we can't go back." But Bertrand could be forceful. *Elfin* was turned 90°, wallowed in a trough, pulled right round, and ran before the wind to Anti-Psara. When she was lifted out of the sea, water poured from *Elphin* for many hours.'[2]

This experience did nothing to deter Bertrand's growing resolve to spend a good deal of his retirement at sea, but it made clear to him the need for a reliable boat, and he decided that he would have one built. This was a brave decision, for he was not rich by the standards of many yacht owners. However, his daughters no longer needed his support and in his last few years at Nottingham he was able to save something of his salary and make a little money through investments. Margaret received some family legacies during this period, as did Bertrand when his mother died, aged 90, in 1964. So they decided to risk the considerable expense of building an ocean-going yacht large enough to provide a home for several months of each year. He did not have in mind a sleek and ostentatious boat: he favoured something that would look like a sturdy fishing vessel yet provide comfort below decks. Making detailed enquiries, and sifting through many catalogues and visiting the London Boat Show, he discovered the Eyemouth Boatbuilding Company in Berwickshire, and their 'Inchcape' class of yacht. In 1963 he commissioned them to build him one of these 49 foot long vessels, fitted with a Rolls Royce Gardiner engine, at an estimated cost of £17,500. He was involved in much of the planning in consultation with the naval architect and boatbuilders, and *Delphis*, as the yacht was to be named, was almost finished when, early in 1964 an accidental fire at the boatbuilder's yard resulted in its destruction. 'Vice-Chancellor's luxury yacht goes up in flames,' the newspapers announced. 'It's gone up in flames,' he told his Secretary as soon as he heard about the disaster. 'What are you going to do?' she asked. 'I don't know. I'll tell you when I've walked round the lake.' He walked round the lake with Margaret and returning to his office announced: 'I'm going to build another one!'[3]

The second *Delphis* was two feet longer than the first with a far superior inside lay-out and fitted with a Volvo Penta fishing boat standard six cylinder engine. Insurance money was recouped from the fire but the second boat cost £23,000, the relative value of which is illustrated by the fact that Bertrand bought a large family house in Aldeburgh at about the same time for £7,500. *Delphis* was not exactly a 'luxury yacht', but owning her was certainly a luxury. The 1986 sale brochure described her as 'a unique vessel, a powerful ocean-going home, built to a high specification for a vessel of her type. She has nearly all the amenities of a house. She has, at the instigation of her first owner, a generous rig, with gaff main rig, main topsail and bermudan mizzen rig. All in all, a most outstanding MFV yacht, designed by a prominent naval architect and based on the Scottish Seine Net fishing boat.'[4]

Delphis at sea.

The shock of the fire and the extra expense involved in building the second boat were certainly a worry and Bertrand was very relieved to find that all seemed well with *Delphis* when he first sailed in her on a tentative voyage out of Eyemouth on December 16th 1964. He wrote to Margaret: 'It was very exciting actually getting down the harbour under our own power and then through the mouth and out to sea with James Anderson at the controls. We were out at sea about two hours and at one point I began to feel a bit queasy! The main engine is marvellously silent and with hardly any vibration — infinitely less than many steamers you and I have been on. No carpets are down yet and no curtains in and no lino in the wheelhouse. I long to see the effect of these. I'm feeling very much more relieved and confident that after the interminable delays and difficulties our ship *Delphis* will be a really good craft to sail the seas. She certainly looks beautiful, like a white seagull. We had a party of eleven on board — electricians, carpenters, engineers: a bottle of rum was consumed and the boat still swarms with men finishing off this and that.'[5]

In February 1965 *Delphis* set out on her sea trials under the supervision of her makers, leaving Eyemouth on the 16th and sailing *via* Great Yarmouth to Ipswich where Bertrand joined her on February 20th for a weekend sail to Newhaven. From there she was taken on to Falmouth where, having been pronounced mechanically fit, she awaited her new owner. '*Delphis* is a very fine ship,' was the official view. The interior furnishings had now been completed and they included a large saloon, six berths, a galley, two lavatories and a hip bath. Given reasonably calm seas, she would provide a comfortable mobile home.

However, the Hallwards did not intend to spend *all* their time at sea, and in January 1965 Bertrand bought 52 Saxmundham Road in Aldeburgh. Looking back later he wrote: 'It is interesting to note that in the 1940's, 50's, and 60's I was quite unaware of the great importance (in an age of raging inflation) of having any savings or capital invested in a house of one's own in order to reap the benefit of capital augmentation. Highfield House was in fact a 'tied cottage'. I was a professional man, amazingly innocent of the advantages of acquiring a small pocket of wealth for retirement.'[6] This is not to say that he was financially embarrassed, especially since he had a generous pension; only that his new lifestyle was not that of the carefree rich.

To say that Bertrand lost no time in taking over *Delphis* is to put the matter mildly. The presentations and farewells took place at Nottingham on Tuesday March 16th, and on Thursday 18th he and Margaret were down at Falmouth ready for a five-month cruise that would take them to Malta, where they intended to keep the yacht in harbour. On the Friday they went for a trial trip round Falmouth, the first time that Bertrand acted as skipper and Margaret as 'mate'. Bertrand's qualifications to sail a yacht to Malta amounted to very little, despite his experience with *Elfin*. He could certainly use a sextant and had studied charts and read books on sailing, especially the invaluable guides by Henry Denham, but in truth he was a novice and would learn by experience. On the first leg of the journey, the crossing to Le Havre, the Hallwards were accompanied by Margaret and Harry Lucas as well as two students, all of whom had yachting experience. After delays in Falmouth waiting for a few last minute adjustments and a suitable tide, they crossed in thick fog on the 28th and arrived at Le Havre early on the 29th when to Margaret's delight the sun came out and she saw numerous shearwaters, gannets and puffins. Bird-watching was to be one of her chief pleasures on board *Delphis*.

Captains are required to keep logs of their journeys, and it should therefore be relatively easy to trace the voyages of *Delphis* over the next ten years or so. But this is not the case, and Bertrand has explained why in an autobiographical passage he wrote in the 1990's.

> I have very little of the squirrel in my make-up. 'Never look back but always be looking forward' has always been a basic philosophy of my life. I have never developed a love of writing or desire to earn my living or supplement my income by writing. Part of the reason for this is that as a don at Peterhouse and as a headmaster taking a VI form class in some set book of English literature I had gained a very strong critical sense and understanding of the qualities and skills which are necessary for good writing and a complete realization that I did not possess them or had never developed them. When people said to me 'Aren't you writing a book about it?' I just laughed and read Hammond Innes or Freya Stark instead.
>
> Nor am I a passionate photographer and have always thought that it was an expensive hobby; and through our lives Margaret and I had to count the cost. At Bude there was no photography and I much regret it; nor in our holidays in Wales at Tyndon and not very much from our camping holidays in France and Italy. I have quite a lot of slides and photos from our trips to America and plenty from our two visits to Christabel in Hong Kong. My own photos of *Delphis* and cruising in the Mediterranean are sparse, largely because the skipper of a yacht has such total responsibility for this extremely valuable cruising home and floating houseboat that during operations he cannot be taking photographs. However, here the four daughters who came out with their children on board have taken some excellent photographs and slides. One must also make the point that the fashion of multiple cameras snapping every meeting or event is a fairly recent one and that during the last War there really was practically no photography at all. And of course the technical developments from black

and white to colour and of automatic focusing cameras and special fast films for winter and non-sunlight have been revolutionary.

Most serious of all as I realize it now has been my lack of historical sense about my own life and as a result I have had no filing system (I always had a secretary as Headmaster and Vice-Chancellor). I have kept no letters or documents or at any rate very few. After selling *Delphis* I gave away my Mediterranean charts and still worse literally destroyed my log books of voyages. I have only come to realize what a blunder this was when I obtained a copy of the log of the professional skipper who took *Delphis* across the Atlantic to America under the new name of *Islandia*. And through my life I have kept no diary.[7]

On this first voyage in 1965, however, Margaret kept a diary and it has survived to provide the details of a considerable adventure. The plan was to travel from Le Havre to Sète near Marseilles using canals and rivers inside France, a journey that was accomplished in twenty-one days and involved the navigation of several hundred locks. First came the canal to Rouen with a good look round the old town, then along the Seine, past Château Gaillard to Paris and into the canal du Centre; on to Lyons, down to the coast at Aigues-Mortes, and eventually to Sète. Here the Lucases left and David and Phyllis Bawtree came on board. A naval doctor, David Bawtree had shared Bertrand's plans for *Delphis* and he knew the Mediterranean well. One of his dictums was that: 'to become a skipper, it is only experience with someone who has sailed that area before, and who will ensure that no risks are taken with the weather, that counts.' 'The hazards of the sea are many,' he warned; 'sudden squalls, causing severe rolling in a yacht like *Delphis*; fog — not so prevalent in the Mediterranean but dangerous in the rock-strewn Aegean; collision at night and mistaking which island is which in the Aegean.'[8]

Under the guidance of David Bawtree Bertrand struck out along the Spanish coast to Tarragona, where a few modifications were made to the steering, sailed east to Puerto Soller in Majorca and on to Port Mahon in Minorca, then back to Majorca. They particularly liked the scenic port of Andraitx which became their base for a week before the sail to Ibiza which, to Margaret's surprise, was 'most unfriendly and inhospitable'. Having thoroughly investigated the Balearic Isles, *Delphis* sailed on to Ajaccio in Corsica without the Bawtrees who had gone home, leaving Bertrand for the first time as skipper in his own right. Sardinia followed Corsica before *Delphis* could be sighted off the north coast of Sicily, tying up in the spectacular port of Cefalu while the Hallwards and their guests marvelled at the mosaic of the superb Christ 'Pantocrator' in the apse of the Norman cathedral. On round the coast to Syracuse, past Scylla and Charybdis

Delphis in the Mediterranean.

with *Delphis* ploughing through splendid whirlpools, and from Syracuse, so vital a port in the Punic Wars, to Malta, despite the *sirocco* that blew up and gave her a rough crossing. It was August 17th when the Hallwards tied up in Malta almost exactly five months since they had boarded *Delphis* in Falmouth.[9]

For ten years, until she was sold in 1975, *Delphis* was based in Malta. The pattern developed that, after she had been tied up during the winter, the Hallwards would go out to Malta at the end of February and work like slaves to clean her up and put her on the slips to be anti-fouled. Then friends would come out in April or May before the blowing of the Meltemi wind, especially violent in the Aegean. From Malta *Delphis* would make for Pylos in two nights and a day, often running deliciously before the wind while the Hallwards consumed marmite sandwiches accompanied by plenty of gin. 'Went from port to port,' Bertrand recalled, 'stopped at little creeks. Nobody else there. Elysium!' Then they would return to Aldeburgh for the best months of June, July and August, and be back again with *Delphis* in September and October, before returning to Suffolk for Christmas.[10]

The house at Aldeburgh was a handsome, modern, brick-built family home with a large garden and a fine view across to the river Alde. Bertrand had been presented with a generous cheque on leaving Nottingham and this was used to meet the cost of re-wiring the house, making a new large sitting-room, fitting a

The Hallwards' house at Aldeburgh.

modern kitchen and building on a sun room. For the first time for thirty years Bertrand and Margaret lived together alone. Bertrand's mother, who had shared a home with them since 1934, died in 1964 and all four daughters had their own homes by now. Gardening became once again one of Bertrand's chief occupations and he delighted especially in growing tomatoes. Daughters came frequently to stay, bringing grandchildren, and there was much enjoyment of the sunshine and seaside life that Aldeburgh had to offer. Bertrand attended the local church on Sundays (for Margaret's sake) and there was bridge from time to time with a few of the neighbours. But it was a quiet life, a complete contrast to the fast pace of former years. 'Oh, I remember the Hallwards well,' said the occupant of the house opposite them in 1994. 'Such a nice, quiet family. He was rather a military-looking gentleman.'[11]

Yet this was exactly the life that Bertrand sought — several months in each year cruising on *Delphis*, the rest spent enjoying the fresh air of Aldeburgh. 'My total retirement from public life', he wrote later, 'and from public service at the age of 64 in excellent health must have been noted with interest and perhaps a touch of jealousy or even resentment. When approached as an ex-Vice-Chancellor to undertake some public work as chairman of some board I was able to reply "I regret I shall be out of England", and I admit that this gave me pleasure. I had no political or other ambitions.' It is true that no public honours came Bertrand's way, whereas the three other Headmaster-Vice-Chancellors of his generation

(Morris, James, Wolfenden) all ended up in the House of Lords, as did two of his successors at Nottingham (Dainton and Butterfield). Unreasonable though it may now seem that Bertrand received no recognition outside Nottingham University for his work there, it did not concern him at the time, nor did he go in pursuit of honours. 'In this private and family life the addition of a political handle by knighthood to my name would not have been of any consequence,' he wrote. 'Nor would my wife have found any pleasure in it.'[12] All who knew Margaret Hallward would recognize the truth of this. In any case, by universal consent she had long been acclaimed as a 'lady' by nature.

As a headmaster and vice-chancellor it is not always easy to make personal friends among those on the staff of the school or university, and Bertrand never moved easily even in the ranks of his fellow headmasters or vice-chancellors. Yet he made many friends at sea, sharing the excitements and dangers of life on board a yacht; it was a return to the comradeship of those Pigou years in the mountains where exertion and occasional adversity strengthened the bonds of friendship. David and Phyllis Bawtree sailed with the Hallwards on several occasions and remember joining *Delphis* at Vouliagmeni in the Gulf of Athens and sailing to the Island of Aegina where 'Bertrand led me up the steep cliffs to see the famous temple which in typical Greek fashion had been built to form an exact equilateral triangle with Sounion and the Acropolis. We then sailed on to Poros, then on to the Central Aegean and Mykonos, Delos, the volcanic Theira

Friends aboard Delphis.

and the lovely sandy beaches of Ios. Then we visited the Gulf of Corinth which was most interesting as there is a strong current, and the yachts stay near Corinth to await the Blue Flag which gives them permission to proceed into the canal which is cut through high, rocky cliffs. At the eastern end of the canal we visited the gulf of Itea and went by ferry and coach to see the marvels of Delphi which encouraged Bertrand to give us the classical history of this beautiful site. We then anchored in the creek off Galaxidi where, as we were anchoring, we went astern forgetting that at that time we were towing the dinghy. We fouled the dinghy and managed to produce several turns of the dinghy painter round the screw, which entailed four hours of interminable diving by Bertrand and myself, which was extremely hard work.'[13]

Henry Denham was a famous figure in the yachting world, author of the internationally known Denham guides, a man who raced with Uffa Fox and whose yacht Herald was frequently in Malta. Bertrand regarded the Denham Guides as 'lifelines to amateur learning skippers like myself, but it is Henry Denham's personal friendship with Margaret and myself in Malta which I treasure so much. At 11.00 am he would appear in the wheelhouse of Delphis with a bottle of gin and splendid naval talk and advice when asked. I still remember his face when he heard that we had guests for a cruise with the names of Sir Paul and Lady Sinker.'[14] In fact the 'Sinker' cruise nearly lived up to its name because the engine of Delphis died in a squall and Bertrand, unable to revive it, had to be towed back to the safety of Malta.

The Bosanquet family were among the many who enjoyed voyages in Delphis. Dr Charles Bosanquet retired in 1968 as Vice-Chancellor of Newcastle University and his daughter Clare had first signed on as a crew member on Delphis in the summer of 1967 for a cruise round Corsica, Sardinia and Sicily. Her parents joined the yacht in Malta in 1970 for what they described as 'thirty adventurous days that saw Delphis in Syracuse, Crotone, Corfu and other Ionian Islands and the Gulf of Corinth', and in 1972 they went aboard at Heraklion and, sailing anti-clockwise through the Dodecanese and Cyclades, reached Vouliagmeni thirty days later. Charles Bosanquet kept a detailed diary of the 1970 cruise and a few excerpts from it give some of the flavour of life aboard Delphis with Bertrand as skipper.

On a bright, May morning we find Delphis tied up in the harbour of Crotone, in Calabria, Southern Italy. 'Weather forecast says anti-cyclone over East Med,' wrote Charles Bosanquet, 'so Bertrand decided to sail direct for Corfu, about 15 hours. We took on water after breakfast. I went into the town with Margaret, bought cheese, walnuts, asparagus, prosciuto and beer. We lunched early, expecting to leave at 2.30 but delayed to have a mechanic look at the dynamo

Bertrand navigating aboard
Delphis.

— batteries low in voltage and specific gravity. He checked and said it was charging OK and ampere meter was wrong. But Bertrand was not satisfied. We sailed from Crotone at 4.00, economizing in electricity in every possible way, not using "George", the automatic pilot. We stood watches of two hours each and took half-hour turns at the wheel. Weather forecast was good, and we had a northwest breeze to speed us on our way. Calabrian coast was spectacular in the red sunset, a fine half moon gave good light, and stars were brilliant. Entering the Gulf of Otranto we had an unpleasant beam sea but were able to change course to get wind astern and hoist sail. We covered the 50 miles from St Maria di Leuka to Fano Island between 2.30 and 10.28, having seen the 1400 foot peak at 7.46. We anchored in the tiny fishing harbour of Kassiopi at 13.30, having had practically no sleep since leaving Crotone. There was a lot of hidden anxiety about the electrics, the engine overheating, riding lights, etc. We enjoyed an excellent dinner of grilled fish in a restaurant under an awning. The proprietor, remembering Bertrand and Margaret's visit the previous year, welcomed them as old friends.'

The next day, *Delphis* was on the move again. 'Called at 5.00 am, we cast off warps, raised anchor and were under way soon after 6.00 — beautiful dawn over the Athenian hills. We breakfasted as we cruised slowly down towards Corfu town. Entering the beautiful little bay of Goulion we made ready to go

A family group in the wheelhouse of Delphis.

alongside but drifted onto a sandbank and stuck! A friendly Cypriot in a fishing boat tried in vain to pull us off. We put down a kedge anchor and pulled on it with no result. The Greek went away to find a second boat and then I noticed the warp to the kedge anchor was slack, pulled on it and found we had drifted free!'

After a couple of days in Corfu harbour *Delphis* prepared to leave early one morning. 'Four big caiques slid in and tied up just ahead of us, hemming us in, but they went out at 4.00 am with heavy *bonk-bonk* noises of diesels,' Bosanquet wrote. 'The skipper also got up to chase cats off the boat. Because of all the early morning disturbances skipper did not give us the promised extra half-hour's sleep. Up at 5.00, pushed out by boat hooks, motored quietly out of the west channel, passing a small chapel on the broom covered island, and a monastery or convent on the outer island with the lighthouse. We ran down the coast of Paxos and passed anti-Paxos, small bright yellow cliffs and green patches of vineyards. About 9.00 am, when we were well south of anti-Paxos a loud noise in the engine-room made Bertrand stop the engine — he found that one of the two belts driving the dynamo had broken. Half an hour was spent in cleaning up and we then proceeded south, not using "George". Never a dull day on *Delphis*!'[15]

In 1972 the Bosanquets presented Margaret Hallward with a pair of field glasses to assist her in her bird-watching, a presentation shared with the family

Margaret Hallward ready for a bathe, aged 70.

of Dr Allen Crockford, also frequent guests on *Delphis*. 'By contributing to this gift of binoculars to you, Margaret,' Dr Crockford wrote, 'we hope we are, in a way that will please you and delight the skipper, acknowledging the marvellous contribution you have made to the general enjoyment of life by all who sailed with you in those most memorable months of May 1970, June 1971 and June 1972. Success for any skipper is measured by the happiness and contentment of his crew. You, Bertrand, have given us these in abundance. Our admiration for your wide knowledge and many skills is only equalled by our gratitude for your generosity and kindness.'[16]

On another occasion Allen Crockford wrote: 'Above all it is the companion-ship and good fellowship that make life on *Delphis* something of rather special quality. These are the lubricants that oil the wheels of daily life and make everything such fun — deckwash, dinghy work, navigation, boat maintenance, sightseeing, shopping, eating, drinking ... The greatest highlights were perhaps the sheer beauty of Lindos, the magnificence of Knossos and the grandeur of Rhodes. Close on their heels are Delos with its splendid lions and vast extent, Cos with its superb view and medical associations, Sounion with its glittering temples so worthy of the great Poseidon himself ... the great monument of Polycrates, the arcades of oleander at Samos, the tree-flowering shrubs everywhere, the booted eagle, the Golden Auriole and that incredible series of sunrises, the ever constant reward of an early start.'[17]

The only item missing in this catalogue of wonders is the great bay of Carthage and the ruins of the city, lying nowadays in modern Tunisia, and a comparatively easy sail from Malta. Yet the historian of the Punic Wars never steered his yacht in that direction, content to see the city of Hannibal only in his mind's eye. Nevertheless, he and Margaret did undertake other ambitious journeys during these years, notably the long flight to Hong Kong where on two occasions they visited their youngest daughter Christabel who was senior history mistress in a large day school there, though she subsequently returned to England and in 1973 married Major John Sworder in the chapel of Selwyn College, Cambridge.

1975 was a sad year for the Hallwards in many ways because they decided that, in their mid-seventies, the strains of sailing in *Delphis* were beginning to tell and that summer they took her out on the last cruise before her sale. Long hours standing at the wheel had not been good for Bertrand's back and the family were increasingly anxious at the thought of their parents sometimes alone on the high seas. So *Delphis* was sold, and with sad farewells the Hallwards returned to a more permanent home at Aldeburgh.

Relaxing in the shade.

Gretton Court

'I was a pomologist in retirement,' Bertrand claimed, and indeed he devoted a good deal of his time to the cultivation of apples, pears and tomatoes, even going to the extent of installing undersoil heating apparatus. There were bracing walks along the front at Aldeburgh and there was the enjoyment of the music festival, the brainchild of Benjamin Britten on whom the University of Nottingham had bestowed an honorary doctorate in Bertrand's time. A family of four daughters and eleven grandchildren kept the Hallwards busy with birthdays and anniversaries and family visits and letters and telephone calls. Moreover Bertrand followed with keen interest current developments in national and international affairs, and especially the progress made at Nottingham University. Shortly after his departure in 1965 it had been forced to weather the storm

Lovers of the garden.

of student aggression which so disfigured the face of university life nationally in the late 1960s and early 1970's. Professor Dainton stayed five years as Vice-Chancellor, long enough to ensure that the detailed plans for the new medical complex had been finalized, and to set up a pilot medical school in 1968. A vast new Sports Centre, said to be the finest in the country, opened in 1969, helped by another large gift from the Cripps family.

In 1971 Professor John Butterfield was appointed Nottingham's third Vice-Chancellor and in 1973 the new University library was opened. Bertrand Hallward's own policy towards the library had gone through three stages. In his early years he suggested that another floor should be built across the existing high-roofed library in the Trent building, but this plan came to nothing. Then, as the library 'spread like a cancer down the corridors of the Trent building', he put forward a daring scheme to build a roof over the entire quadrangle, but the Senate resolutely opposed him over this. 'Quite right!' he subsequently agreed. He then realized that a new library must be built, and in 1962 turned to Sir William Holford who succeeded Sir Percy Thomas as the University's consultant architect and who also favoured the building of a new library. Unfortunately there were other priorities in these busy years when the halls of residence were still far from complete, but it was during Hallward's time, in 1964, that H. Faulkner Brown was appointed to draw up plans for the new building, and Bertrand Hallward's last address to Convocation in 1965 specifically highlighted the need for a modern library.[1]

The building that emerged from the subsequent eight years of planning, discussion and counter-discussion among all the interested parties in the University is one of the jewels in Nottingham's crown, prompting *The Gongster's* correspondent to describe it as 'a superb place to work in' and the University Librarian to consider it 'almost certainly the finest academic library in the country'.[2]

These were not entirely peaceful years for the University, however: rent-strikes and sit-ins interrupted life on the campus, though the Student President election of 1974 was considered 'the end of one of the Union's more radical periods'. All the same, the Union officers of 1975 were still disappointed 'that we made little headway in a campaign to persuade the University that the Union should have its own building and that it should operate commercial and catering outlets which seemed to be an unnecessary distraction for the University'.[3] In 1976 Professor A.C. Weedon took over as fourth Vice-Chancellor, beginning a period of office which was to last until 1988, and which saw the completion of the vast Clifton Boulevard complex, named the Queen's Medical Centre in 1977, the year of its ceremonial opening by the Queen. Bertrand, as a former Vice-Chancellor and as a member of the University Court, naturally took a great interest and pride in these developments, many of which had their roots in his day.

It was in 1980 that Bertrand came down to breakfast one morning in the house at Aldeburgh to find that Margaret had collapsed onto the kitchen floor, suffering from a heart attack. She recovered, but this incident persuaded them both that the time had come to move from Aldeburgh to the 'safe haven' of Gretton Court, in Cambridge. Lady Gray, the widow of a Vice-Provost of King's College, and Lady Lee, the wife of the Master of Corpus, had in 1966 conceived the idea of building some self-contained flats for retired Cambridge academics and others. In 1969 they bought a plot of land in the picturesque village of Girton, well beyond the parish church, and by 1974 a modern block had risen there, named Gretton Court when it was discovered that 'Gretton' was a mediaeval name for 'Girton'. Set in the centre of spacious gardens, the building contained about sixty flats with a common room and dining room where lunch was served to residents who required it, while qualified nursing staff were on hand to deal with any medical emergencies. Bertrand had heard about Gretton Court soon after its opening and had reserved a flat in anticipation of the move that now took place in 1980. At first the Hallwards occupied an upstairs flat but later moved downstairs where their living-room looked out on to well-trimmed lawns. They had a small kitchen, a bathroom, and two bedrooms; almost less than the accommodation in *Delphis*, let alone the large houses they had inhabited at other times in their lives. On the other hand the Gretton Court flats were warm and comfortable and there were like-minded residents for company. More than that, Gretton Court was near Cambridge, the Chadwicks, many old friends and Peterhouse, where Bertrand was an honorary Fellow: it was the ideal place for the Hallwards to begin their ninth decade.

For Bertrand the new life was rather like that of a retired Cambridge don. He would drive into town to dine at various Colleges or chat to long-standing friends, especially Sir Desmond Lee and Professor Nick Hammond with whom he had not only Cambridge and Classics in common, but Clifton, where all three had been headmaster. The Lees lived in Barton Close and the Hammonds on Belvoir Terrace, next door to the Hallwards' first home. Other good friends included Walter Hamilton who had done some supervising for Bertrand at Peterhouse before eventually becoming Headmaster of Westminster, then Rugby, and Master of Magdalene. The Chadwicks, too, lived very close, even after they moved from the Master's Lodge at Selwyn in 1983. There was plenty to do and to talk about. There was the continuing excitement of grandchildren and even great-grandchildren, and there was the constant comfort of a powerful, loving relationship between Bertrand and Margaret, undimmed by sixty years of marriage.

Bertrand Hallward at a party
close to his 90th year.

The Hallwards' Diamond Wedding was celebrated on September 2nd 1986 in the house at Aldeburgh, then owned by their daughter Iola and her husband, and it was marked by a telegram of congratulation from the Queen, which 'caused great excitement at the Post Office'. There was a gathering of the family, numbering over thirty in its various strata, though there were comparatively few with the surname Hallward. Bertrand's brother Philip died of a coronary on his 76th birthday, February 1st 1979, leaving two sons, David and Colin. Colin had gone to school at Clifton shortly after Bertrand ceased to be Headmaster and, later a doctor, sent his two sons George and Charles there in the 1980's. David also fathered two sons, and there was another branch of Canadian Hallwards with large families. The complexities of genealogy began to intrigue Bertrand during these years and he spent a good deal of time drawing up charts and lists and corresponding with genealogical experts. He was particularly impressed with his Gurdon pedigree which wandered through various noble houses and even touched mediaeval royalty.

During the Nottingham years Bertrand had been remarkably free from illness, bearing in mind the duodenitis problems of earlier years. Nor did he suffer much on *Delphis*, though his back began to cause problems, probably because of his constant exertions in the wheelhouse. The ear infections from which Margaret had suffered at Nottingham were much improved by the fresh

The Hallward heraldic device.

air on *Delphis* but after her heart attack of 1980 she needed careful supervision. While at Gretton Court Bertrand had to be taken for a prostate operation at Addenbrooke's Hospital and he had only just recovered from that when, six months later, he lost consciousness in the flat at Gretton Court and had to be taken for a major stomach operation and removal of the gall bladder. He managed to bounce back from both these trials, however, and after them he could still stride about energetically and talk with his usual animation. Above all he could write letters in a neat, unwavering, and wholly legible hand, and, finding himself now at the centre of a large and influential family and with a wide range of acquaintances and contacts, he channelled a good deal of his energies into writing letters. These were intended to entertain and influence their recipients, rather in the way that he had stirred undergraduates into action at Cambridge, staff and pupils at Clifton, and everyone at Nottingham.

One of Bertrand's earliest initiatives as Vice-Chancellor of Nottingham had been to commission a history of the University College from Professor Wood, which was published in 1953. In the mid 1980's he decided to give substantial sums to both Nottingham University and Clifton College for the commissioning of up-to-date official histories of both institutions. At Nottingham this led to the setting up of the History Project and the extensive researches of Dr Brian Tolley, Dr Susan Ablett and others, while at Clifton an account of the school's history

214 BERTRAND HALLWARD: A BIOGRAPHY

in the twentieth century was published late in 1990. Up to 1987 the most significant development at Clifton had been the opening of a new dayboy house in the Upper School in the 1950's which allowed numbers at the school to reach a peak of 700, while steady growth in the Preparatory School had brought it to almost unmanageable proportions with more than 550 boys. Clifton in the 1980's was therefore considerably larger than it had been under Bertrand, and the need to maintain the number of pupils, to improve, if possible, the academic standards, and to move with the times, led the Council to make the decision to become a fully coeducational school from September 1987. 'The decision of Clifton to take girls right through the school is a momentous decision, and I applaud it,' Bertrand wrote. 'It is exactly in line with the spirit of the age.' But, he warned, big changes such as this cost a lot of money, so 'masters and their wives must discreetly look for the rich widows who may be much taken by the "brother-sister idea".'[4]

In 1988 Professor Weedon was succeeded as Vice-Chancellor at Nottingham by Professor Colin Campbell who, on making contact with Bertrand, was impressed by his personality and valued his thoughts on a number of issues. Like many other people who had seen Nottingham University develop as a place of high renown he felt that the contribution of Bertrand Hallward deserved wider public recognition. In May 1989 the University's Estates and Buildings Committee considered the following proposition: 'Informal consultation among senior academic, academic-related and lay members of the University community has shown a strong desire to acknowledge formally the great debt the University owes to its first Vice-Chancellor, Dr Bertrand Hallward. It is considered appropriate to name a major building after him, and it is therefore proposed that the University Library should be named "The Hallward Library". The Librarian strongly supports this move.'[5] Subsequently the Vice-Chancellor was able to write to Bertrand that 'the Library is the heartbeat of the University and we wanted a central and general facility — not something tied to one Faculty — to bear your name ... Our strong feeling is that we want the name of Hallward visible and prominent in the University to betoken the magnificent service you gave in shaping the University and the campus as Vice-Chancellor.'[6]

The naming ceremony took place in the foyer of the Library on 6th October 1989, when Bertrand and Margaret together unveiled a commemorative plaque and Bertrand said: 'In gratitude, pride and affection I name this much-praised University Library "The Hallward Library". I repeat I name it the *HALLWARD* Library' (here he emphasized the correct pronunciation). 'May it be not only a power-house of learning and knowledge but also a temple of wisdom. The coat of arms of the University has on it an open book between the

Bertrand and Margaret Hallward at the naming ceremony for the Hallward Library, 1989.

The Hallward Library.

two castles of Nottingham City which now signifies the Hallward Library with the other libraries of the University both public and private and it stands for the learning and knowledge of the scholars of the University. And I read the motto *Sapientia urbs conditur*, "on Wisdom a City and University are founded". Finally I prophesy in the words of a writer who wrote in 1662 *Magna est veritas et praevalebit*, "Great is Truth and it shall prevail".[7]

Though Margaret Hallward accompanied Bertrand on this occasion she looked very frail, and indeed for several years her health had been a constant worry to her husband and family. She died on New Year's Day 1991, at the age of 90 and was cremated after a funeral service in Girton church on January 7th, which Bertrand was too ill to attend. Owen Chadwick wrote: 'From her girlhood to the end she remained a deeply Christian woman, who had the most delicate green fingers in a garden, saw good in everyone, loved the human race and especially its children and grandchildren ... and drew out the best in other people by her care for them and by the charity and intelligence of her conversation.'[8] Few have the experience to know what it is like to be deprived of a marriage partner of sixty-four years, and the early months of 1991 were a bleak time for Bertrand who, alone in the flat at Gretton Court, had come to reflect upon the extent to which his own achievements had depended upon the unfailing support of his wife. Now that he had to live without her he came to see — more, perhaps, than ever before — how indispensable she had been. Letters and tributes to Margaret poured in from family, friends and companions stretching back across the vigorous years of a long lifetime.

'A month before Margaret died,' Bertrand wrote, 'I said to her — "You know I've tried all our lives together to be a perfect lover — one flesh, as the marriage service enjoins. Have I succeeded?" — and she gave me one long, passionate kiss and then fell asleep. The careers of Headmaster and Vice-Chancellor are preeminently ones where the contribution of the wife may match that of her husband. The tributes that were paid to Margaret after her death were full of testimony to this. Looking back I can only hope that Margaret had a full sense of success and self-realization in our partnership. Our wonderful happiness together gives me grounds for confidence in this hope.' 'Bertrand, how do you manage to look so young and happy?' someone asked him in the full flood of the Nottingham years. 'Four prunes a day and a marvellous love life' was his answer. 'You are doing a Margaret,' her daughters would say to one another, meaning 'you are behaving in an almost impossibly unselfish manner like your mother.' 'Bertrand, did you listen,' Margaret would enquire gently on his return from a meeting, 'or talk all the time?'[9]

Bertrand's 'modernist' religious views did not shake the simple faith of his wife. 'With my Margaret until she died,' he recalled 'I would discuss points she raised as she read her Bible and I would refer to a Commentary and read out passages from the text. Margaret knew my dangerous and heretical views but she would laugh and say "I wish I had my father here to see what he would say". Thinking back after her death, I am quite certain that I did not worry her or damage her faith because I never quarrelled with her nor tried to oppose her views.' Indeed quarrelling between husband and wife was rare in the Hallward household. As Bertrand wrote in 1993, 'looking back it seems to me quite amazing that I should have met the most perfect girl in the world and persuaded her to marry me for the most wonderful sixty-four years of married life. If this wasn't Guidance or Providence or Astounding Fortune, what was it? I watch now the modern grandchildren who go through such stresses and strains to find the right partner for life. It was given to me on a plate.'[10]

Yet there was to be, for Bertrand, a life after Margaret, and he faced a tenth decade alone with the same resilience that had characterized his approach to other challenges. Partly as a tribute to Margaret he composed some autobio-graphical reminiscences, several of which have been quoted in this book. He produced and edited a video of his life with Margaret for the entertainment of his family. Indeed, ever in tune with the latest developments, he had long been Gretton Court's video expert, running the residents' video club and collecting hundreds of films. This prompted him to commission the construction of a special cabinet to house them, and in December 1991, at a small ceremony in

The Hallward video library
at Gretton Court.

Twenty-five years on.

Gretton Court, he was able to announce: 'I have pleasure in handing over to you today into your possession and custody ... my Hallward collection of videos. It is housed in a cabinet of oak with locked glass-fronted shelves. This cabinet has been designed and made for me by the distinguished master craftsman Giles Munby. The collection contains between four or five hundred films; there is a manuscript catalogue and also the key film encyclopaedias.'[11]

Bertrand took a special interest in the progress of The University of Nottingham and in 1990 presented some silver tankards to the University Club. The Chairman, Dr D. McKay, wrote in reply: 'I remember the founding of the Club in 1953 and the great part you played in that, and also that you chaired the committee that appointed me in the same year as a very junior lecturer in Engineering ... I always remember with particular pleasure the period when you were Vice-Chancellor, the great changes that occurred to transform a College to a University and the energy, the vitality and the great good humour with which you went about your business.'[12] In 1993 Bertrand founded the Hallward Prizes for Musical Composition and Fine Art at the University, and he was an enthusiastic supporter of the new University Arts Centre that opened in 1994, a year that saw him in excellent form at a special Senate Dinner at Nottingham, as well as at Guest Night in Peterhouse. 'Dr Hallward!' exclaimed one of the ladies at the Peterhouse dinner: 'They had told me how good-looking you were, but I didn't really believe them.' And he laughed, and inclined his profile slightly to the right, and did his best not to look too pleased.

Bertrand Hallward in the garden of Gretton Court in the Summer of 1995.

Notes and Sources

Abbreviations used in the Notes

BLH	Dr Bertrand Hallward
MH	Margaret Hallward
DOW	The Author
v.	Verbally
G.	*The Gongster*
Ibid.	In the same place
Op. cit.	In the work cited

Part One: Youth 1901-1919

Parents and Family (pp. 3-8)

1   BLH autobiographical notes.
2   Ibid.
3   Ibid.
4   Ian Anstruther, *Oscar Browning*, p.88.
5   Memoirs of Bertrand Hallward and other papers (henceforth *Memoirs*),
      p.2.
6   Norman Hallward (NLH) to Oscar Browning (OB), 16 Jun. 1898. King's
      College Library, Cambridge.
7   NLH to OB, 31 Aug. 1898.
8   NLH to OB, 23 Dec. 1899.

9   NLH to OB, 29 Aug. 1904.
10   Quoted in Anstruther, p.116.
11   Anstruther, p.1.

Warden House (pp. 9-12)

1   *Memoirs*, p.3.
2   Ibid., p.7.
3   Ibid., p.7.
4   Extracts from the Warden House School Magazine, 1914.
5   *Memoirs*, p.6.
6   *Memoirs*, p.3.
7   *Memoirs*, p.4.

Haileybury (pp. 13-28)

1   *Memoirs*, p.11.
2   Quoted in *A Brief Guide to Dunsfold Parish Church*.
3   *King's College Annual Report*, 17 Nov. 1934.
4   *Memoirs*, p.2.
5   *Memoirs*, p.11.
6   Ibid.
7   *Memoirs*, p.8.
8   Imogen Thomas, *Haileybury 1806-1987*, p.24.
9   Thomas, p.27.
10   Thomas, p.159.
11   Thomas, p.141.
12   R.L. Ashcroft, *Haileybury 1908-1961*, pp. 17, 18.
13   Thomas, p.43.
14   Thomason House Records, Haileybury.
15   *Memoirs*, p.8.
16   BLH to DOW, v.
17   *Memoirs*, p.8.
18   Thomas, pp. 135, 136.
19   Ashcroft, p.25.
20   *Memoirs*, p.10.
21   Ibid.

22 Thomason House Records.
23 *The Haileyburian*, vol. xxii, pp. 120, 121.
24 Ibid., p.339.
25 Ibid., p.340.
26 *Memoirs*, p.9.
27 *Memoirs*, p.13.
28 *The Haileyburian*, vol. xxi, 24 Jun. 1915.
29 *The Haileyburian*, vol. xxi, 5 Apr. 1916.
30 Ibid., p.292.
30 *Memoirs*, p.9.
31 *The Haileyburian*, vol. xxi, 26 Oct. 1916.
32 Thomas, p.146.
33 *The Haileyburian*, vol. xxii, 3 Apr. 1918.
34 Ibid., 20 Jun. 1918.
35 Ibid., 21 Nov. 1918.
36 Ibid., p.219.
37 *Memoirs*, p.9.
38 *Memoirs*, p.10.
39 Ibid., p.8.
40 Ibid., p.14.
41 Ibid., p.10.

Part Two: Cambridge 1919-1939

Undergraduate at King's (pp. 31-47)

1   *Memoirs*, p.14.
2   *Memoirs*, p.15.
3   George Eliot, *Romola*, vol. I, p.120.
4   *Memoirs*, p.15.
5   See Peter Turner, *Film Stars don't die in Liverpool*, p.72.
6   *Memoirs*, p.15.
7   *Memoirs*, p.16.
8   *The Sketch*, 9 Mar. 1921, p.351.
9   *The Ladies' Field*, 12 Mar. 1921, p.28.
10 *The Sketch*, 16 Mar. 1921, p.399.
11 *Memoirs*, p.16.

12 L.P. Wilkinson, *A Century of King's 1873-1972*, p.92.
13 *Memoirs*, pp. 19, 20, 21.
14 Patrick Wilkinson, *Frank Ezra Adcock: a Memoir*, p.4.
15 Ibid., p.8.
16 *Memoirs*, p.16.
17 C.R.B. Elliott to DOW, v.
18 *Memoirs*, p.16.
19 *Memoirs*, p.17.
20 *Memoirs*, p.21.
21 *Memoirs*, pp. 23, 24.
22 BLH to NLH, 13 Feb. 1923.
23 BLH to NLH, 6 May 1923.
24 *Memoirs*, p.24.
25 BLH to NLH, 3 Jul. 1923.
26 *Memoirs*, p.25.
27 BLH to NLH, 8 Jul. 1923.
28 *Memoirs*, p.26.
29 Prince Chula of Thailand, *The Twain have Met*, p.130.

Fellow of Peterhouse (pp. 48-68)

1   BLH *Memoirs*, p.22.
2   T.A. Walker, *Peterhouse*, p.114.
3   *Peterhouse Society Annual Record*, vol. I, p.4.
4   BLH to DOW, v.
5   *Peterhouse Society Annual Record*, vol. I, p.6.
6   The Diary of Hilary Macklin, vol. III.
7   Margaret Tait to Alice Tait, 29 Jun. 1926.
8   *Memoirs*, p.27.
9   Alison Pollock, 3 Jul. 1926.
10 Ibid.
11 *Country Life,* 12 Oct. 1992, p.42.
12 Margaret Hallward to Alice Tait/Macklin, 16 Sept. 1926.
13 *Memoirs*, p.30.
14 *Memoirs*, p.30.
15 BLH to MH, 26 Mar. 1927.
16 BLH to MH, 28 Mar. 1927.
17 BLH to MH, 8 Apr. 1927.
18 S.A Cook et al., *Cambridge Ancient History*, vol. VIII, p.484.

19 In the late 1980's three scholars rejected BLH's assertion that the ruins of Carthage were sown with salt. See *Classical Philology*, vol. 81, 1986, pp.140-146 and Jan. 1988, pp.39-42.

20 S.A. Cook et al., *Cambridge Ancient History*, vol. VIII, p.485.,

21 F.W. Walbank, *B.L. Hallward, Peterhouse 1923-39*, p.1.

22 F.W. Walbank to BLH, 14 Aug. 1994.

23 F.W. Walbank, op. cit., p.4.

24 *Memoirs*, p.33.

25 BLH to DOW, v.

26 *Memoirs*, p.34.

27 N.G.L. Hammond to DOW, v.

28 S.C. Alexander, *Autobiography* (MS), p.8.

29 Rt. Hon. J. Enoch Powell to DOW, 13 Oct. 1994.

30 *Letter of Application and Testimonials of B.L. Hallward, M.A.* 1932.

31 *Memoirs*, p.35.

32 *Memoirs*, p.40.

33 *Memoirs*, p.38.

34 *Memoirs*, p.40.

35 *Memoirs*, p.35.

36 BLH to MH, 'Thursday, 8.15'.

37 BLH to MH, 'Thursday, 4.15'.

38 BLH to MH, 'Friday, 7.00 am'.

Part Three: Clifton 1939-1948

A New Headmaster (pp. 71-78)

1 See DOW, *John Percival, the Great Educator*.

2 *The Cliftonian*, vol. 22, p.337.

3 *The Times*, 25 Apr. 1933.

4 *The Cliftonian*, vol. 31, p.373.

5 Norman Whatley, *Memoirs*, p.52.

6 *The Bristol Mirror*, 29 Mar. 1939.

7 DOW, *Clifton after Percival*, p.121.

8 Telegram from Sir Robert Witt, Clifton College Archives.

9 *The Daily Mail*, 19 Jan. 1939.

10 Quoted in *The Bristol Evening Post*, 29 Mar. 1939.

The Bombing of Bristol (pp. 79-93)

1   Norman Whatley, *Memoirs*, p.64.
2   DOW, *Clifton after Percival*, pp. 86, 87.
3   Ibid., pp. 94, 95.
4   See DOW, *Henry Newbolt and the Spirit of Clifton*.
5   S.C. Alexander, *Autobiography* (MS).
6   J.H. Arrowsmith-Brown to DOW, 20 Oct. 1994.
7   *The Western Daily Press*, 26 Jun. 1939.
8   *The Bristol Evening Post*, 1 Jul. 1939.
9   *The Western Daily Press*, 22 Jul. 1939.
10 *The Cliftonian*, vol, 35, p.351.
11 Ed. N.G.L. Hammond, *Centenary Essays on Clifton College*, p.171.
12 *Bristol in World War II*, Historical Association document pack.
13 S.P. Beachcroft in *Centenary Essays*, p.171.
14 Clifton College Council Minutes (CM), vol. 13, p.147.
15 DOW, *Clifton after Percival*, p.124.
16 Ibid., pp. 126, 127.
17 *Bristol in World War II*, Historical Association document pack.
18 Letter from 'Tim' in Clifton College Archives, undated.
19 Letter from 'Tim', 7 Dec. 1940.
20 Clifton College Council Minutes, vol. 13, p.158.
21 Telegram from Sir Robert Witt in Clifton College Archives.
22 *The Cliftonian*, vol. 40, p.39.

Evacuation to Bude (pp. 94-102)

1   *The Bristol Evening Post*, 1 Apr. 1942.
2   *The Western Daily Press*, 30 Jun. 1942.
3   DOW, *Clifton after Percival*, p.135.
4   A Clifton pupil to BLH, 19 Dec. 1941, 19 Dec. 1941.
5   Denis Mack Smith to DOW, v.
6   B.H. Polack to BLH, 20 Oct. 1991.
7   Sir Peter Newsam to DOW, 9 Nov. 1994.
8   A Clifton pupil to BLH, 19 Dec. 1940.
9   BLH to DOW, v.
10 Letter (anonymous) in BLH archives.
11 Letter in BLH archives.
12 D.F. Mackintosh in *Fugitive Pieces*.

After the War (pp. 103-112)

1   DOW, *Clifton after Percival*, pp. 144-150.
2   *The Western Daily Press*, 30 Jun. 1945.
3   BLH to A.H. King, 5 Nov. 1945.
4   DOW, *Clifton after Percival*, p.134.
5   *The Cliftonian*, vol. 38, pp. 89, 90.
6   Clifton College Council Minutes, pp. 5, 6.
7   *The Western Daily Press*, 27 Feb. 1946.
8   *The Bristol Evening Post*, 9 Nov. 1946.
9   *The Daily Mail*, 30 Jun. 1947.
10 W.H. Alexander to DOW, 27 Sept. 1994.
11 Revd. J.M. Burgess to DOW, 1994.
12 A.H. King to DOW 6 Oct. 1994.
13 Revd. J.M. Burgess to DOW, 1994.
14 BLH to DOW, v.
15 C.R.B. Elliott to DOW, 1994.
16 Ibid.
17 L.L. Cohen to DOW, 4 Oct. 1994.
18 W.H. Alexander to DOW, 27 Sept. 1994.
19 J.D. Marsh to DOW, 1994.
20 BLH to DOW, v.
21 BLH to DOW, v.
22 Revd. J.M. Burgess to DOW, 1994.
23 N.T. Hardyman to DOW, 26 Nov. 1994.
24 Quoted in DOW, *Clifton after Percival*, p.171.
25 *Centenary Essays*, p.190.
26 *The Cliftonian*, vol. 38, p.352.
27 *The Daily Mail*, 19 Jan. 1939.

Part Four: Nottingham 1948-1957

A New University (pp. 115-130)

1   Frank Barnes, *Priory Demesne to University Campus*, p.144.
2   Christabel Sworder to DOW, v.

3   See Stanley Chapman, *Jesse Boot of Boot's the Chemist*, and Christopher Weir, *Jesse Boot of Nottingham*.

4   A.C. Wood, *A History of University College, Nottingham*, p.117.

5   *The Gong*, 1947, p.4.

6   Nottingham University Charter of Incorporation, in *University of Nottingham Calendar 1994-5*, pp. B5 to B11.

7   A.C. Wood, op. cit., p.129.

8   Nottingham University Report of the Council to the Court, December 1949.

9   BLH to DOW, v.

10 *The Gongster* (G.), 3 Nov. 1948.

11 C.Weir, op. cit., p.69.

12 *Conferment of an Honorary Degree on the Chancellor*, pamphlet in the Special Collection, Hallward Library, p.37.

13 G., 20 May 1949.

14 Union of Students' Presidents 1913-1993 (pamphlet).

15 Geoffrey Sayer to Dr Susan Ablett in *Miscellaneous Quotes* (MS).

16 G., 23 Jun., 1949.

17 G., 11 Oct. 1949.

18 G., 4 Nov. 1949.

19 G., Sayer to S. Ablett in op. cit.

20 G., 2 Dec. 1949.

21 BLH to DOW, 20 Jan. 1995.

Development Plans (pp. 131-134)

1   Vice-Chancellor's Report to Council, 1950.

2   Council Report, 1949.

3   G., 3 Feb. 1961.

4   Percy Thomas, *Pupil to President*, p.53.

5   BLH to DOW, 18 Oct. 1994.

6   See p. 83.

7   Percy Thomas, op. cit., p.52.

8   Vice-Chancellor's Report to Council, 1950.

9   Ibid.

American Journey (pp. 135-138)

1   Two notebooks of Margaret Hallward in BLH's archive.
2   BLH to DOW, 11 Oct. 1994.
3   BLH to DOW, 19 Oct. 1994.
4   Council Report, 1954.

Portland and Cripps (pp. 139-146)

1   Council Report, 1953, p.8.
2   BLH to DOW, 18 Oct. 1994.
3   BLH to DOW, Jan. 1995.
4   Slide Script in BLH archives.
5   G., 30 Jan. 1953.
6   G., 13 Feb. 1953.
7   G., 27 Feb. 1953.
8   G., 9 Nov. 1956.
9   Council Report, 1958, p.18.
10 Council Reports, 1953, 1954.
11 Council Report, 1954, p.10.
12 BLH to DOW, 22 Oct. 1994.
13 BLH to DOW, 15 Oct. 1994.
14 Sir Humphrey Cripps to DOW, v. 1994.
15 Council Report, 1954.
16 Council Report, 1956.
17 G., 12 Feb. 1959 and 27 Feb. 1959.
18 G., 23 Oct. 1959.
19 Sir Humphrey Cripps to DOW, v. 1994.

Student Opinion (pp. 147-151)

1   G., 10 May 1962.
2   Christopher Dodd to DOW, 2 Oct. 1994.
3   *The Gong*, Easter 1949, pp. 4, 5.
4   G., 28 Apr. 1950.
5   G., 6 Oct. 1950.
6   G., 6 Feb. 1951.

7   G., 11 May 1951.

8   G., 11 Oct. 1951.

9   G., 23 Oct. 1952.

10 G., 2 Oct. 1953.

11 G., 22 Jan. 1954.

12 G., 29 Oct. 1954.

13 Union of Students' Presidents (pamphlet).

14 G., 26 Oct. 1956.

15 G., 9 Nov. 1956.

16 G., 25 Jan. 1957.

17 G., 1 Feb. 1958.

18 G., 9 Nov. 1956.

19 Union of Students' Presidents (pamphlet).

20 G., 25 Oct. 1957.

Part Five: Nottingham 1957-1965

Science City and the Halls of Residence (pp. 155-165)

1   Council Report, 1957.

2   Council Report, 1956, p.17, and 1959.

3   BLH to DOW, v.

4   Council Report, 1955.

5   Lord Murray to Dr Susan Ablett, 5 Mar. 1987.

6   BLH to DOW, 19 Oct. 1994.

7   G., 29 Jan. 1960.

8   G., 29 Jan. 1960, p.5.

9   Council Minute 299, 23 Oct. 1957.

10 Ibid.

11 Council Minute 4, 22 Oct. 1958.

12 Frank Barnes to BLH, 18 Dec. 1993.

13 Council Minute 149, 26 Oct. 1960.

14 G., 11 Mar. 1960.

15 Ibid.

16 Frank Barnes, op. cit., p.429.

17 G., 13 May 1960.

18 G., 19 Jun. 1959.

19 BLH to DOW, 18 Oct. 1994.

20 BLH to DOW, 19 Oct. 1994.

21 *University of Nottingham Gazette* No. 40, p.709.

22 Council Report 1962, pp. 9, 11, 22.

23 G., 25 Jan. 1963.

24 G., Jan. 1924.

25 G., 9 Oct. 1964.

26 BLH to DOW, 19 Oct. 1994.

27 Don Varley to BLH, 11 May 1989.

Renaissance Prince? (pp. 166-172)

1   Professor A. Willcocks to Dr Susan Ablett in *Miscellaneous Quotes* (MS).

2   G., 7 May 1994.

3   Sir Harry Pitt to DOW, 1994, v.

4   Sir Joseph Pope to DOW, 1994, v.

5   J. Rich, in his funeral oration for E.A. Thompson, Jan. 1994.

6   Professor Brian Tate to DOW, 1994, v.

7   G., 29 Oct. 1954.

8   BLH to DOW, 11 Oct. 1994.

9   Dr Barbara Reynolds to Dorothy Sayers, 11 Jul. 1956.

10 Dr Vera Daniel to Dr Susan Ablett, 9 Jan. 1987.

11 T.E.B. Howarth, *Cambridge Between Two Wars*, p.182.

12 George Spafford to DOW, 13 Feb. 1994.

13 A. Smith to Dr S. Ablett in *Miscellaneous Quotes* (MS).

14 Professor Chesters to Dr S. Ablett.

15 Ralph Townley to BLH, 1991.

16 Alistair Smart to BLH, 1991.

17 *Chattanooga News-Free Press*, 25 Aug. 1958

18 *University of Sheffield Gazette*, 1964, p.18.

19 Union of Students' Presidents (pamphlet).

The Nottingham Playhouse (pp. 173-176)

1   J. Bailey, *A Theatre for All Seasons*, p.4.

2   BLH to DOW, v.

3   *Nottingham Guardian Souvenir Journal and Supplement*, 11 Dec. 1963.

4   Ibid., p.2.
5   Ibid.
6   Sir Hugh Willatt to DOW, 30 Nov. 1994.
7   *Nottingham Guardian Souvenir Journal and Supplement*, 11 Dec. 1963.
8   *The Guardian Journal*, 12 Dec. 1963.
9   *A Theatre for All Seasons*, p.86.
10 Ibid., p.83.
11 Ibid., p.95.

A Medical School (pp. 177-180)

1   Dr Susan Ablett, *The Medical School of the University of Nottingham: Origins and Development*. Nottingham Univ. Ph.D. thesis, 1992, pp. 47 and 97. All subsequent references in this section are to Dr Ablett's thesis.
2   p.14.
3   pp. 49 to 55.
4   p.55.
5   p.57.
6   p.57
7   pp. 57, 58.
8   p.58.
9   p.79, 80.
10 p.80.
11 p.80, 81.
12 p.82, 83.
13 p.97, 98.

The Last Year (pp. 181-192)

1   BLH to DOW, v.
2   *University of Sheffield Gazette*, 1964, pp. 18, 19.
3   G., 6 Nov. 1964.
4   BLH to DOW, v.
5   *University of Nottingham Gazette*, Apr. 1965, pp. 1023, 1024.
6   Ibid., p.1025.
7   Ibid., pp. 1025, 1026.
8   From the text of BLH's speech in his archives.

Part Six: Safe Havens 1965-1995

Delphis (pp. 195-208)

1   BLH to DOW, 1994, v.
2   George Spafford, *An Incident at Sea* (MS), 1994.
3   Rosemary David to DOW, 1994, v.
4   *Interyacht* sales brochure 1986.
5   BLH to MH, 16 Dec. 1964.
6   BLH, *Memoirs*, p.46.
7   *Memoirs*, p.28.
8   David Bawtree, *Memorandum*, 1994.
9   Diary of Margaret Hallward (BLH papers).
10 BLH to DOW, 1994, v.
11 Mrs Stebbings to DOW, 1994, v.
12 BLH to DOW, 19 Sept. 1994.
13 David Bawtree, *The Vice-Chancellor puts to Sea* (MS), 1995.
14 BLH to DOW, 23 Jan. 1995.
15 Diary of Dr Charles Bosanquet, May 1970.
16 Dr Allen Crockford to BLH, Jul. 1972.
17 Allen Crockford to BLH, '30 Jun.'.

Gretton Court (pp. 209-219)

1   *Nottingham University. Report of Council to Court*, 1965, p.20.
2   G., 16 Oct. 1973.
3   Union of Students' Presidents (pamphlet).
4   BLH to DOW, 12 Apr. 1987.
5   Extracts from Nottingham University: Buildings Committee Agenda item 2 May, 1989.
6   Professor Colin Campbell to BLH, 3 May, 1989.
7   Text of BLH's speech in BLH papers.
8   Revd. Professor Owen Chadwick: Obituary notice for Margaret Hallward.
9   BLH to DOW, v.
10 BLH, *Memoirs*, p.17.
11 BLH, *Memoirs*.
12 Dr D. McKay to BLH, 27 Apr. 1990.

Sources

Archives

Clifton College Council Minutes, 1939-48.
Nottingham University: Reports of the Council to the Court, Council Minutes, Senate Minutes. 1948-1965.
Thomason House Records, Haileybury, 1914-1919.

Institutional Magazines

The Cliftonian, 1939-1948.
The Gong, 1948-65.
The Gongster, 1948-1980.
The Haileyburian, 1914-1920.
King's College, Cambridge, Annual Report, 1934.
Peterhouse Society Annual Record, vol. I.
University of Nottingham Gazette, 1965.
University of Sheffield Gazette, 1964.
Warden House School Magazine, 1910-1914.

The Hallward Papers

Letters to Dr B.L. Hallward.
Diaries of Margaret Hallward and Hilary Macklin.
Memoranda by BLH on various subjects.
Memoirs of Bertrand Hallward and other papers (MS).

Letters

a) *c.* 180 letters and memoranda from BLH to the author.
b) Letters to the author on BLH's years at Clifton from:
    S.C. Alexander
    W.H. Alexander
    J.H. Arrowsmith-Brown

Revd. J.M. Burgess
L.L. Cohen
C.J. Dodd
C.R.B. Elliott
R.N. Exton
N.T. Hardyman
A.H. King
J.D. Marsh
Sir Peter Newsam
R.J. Newton
Professor F. Ursell
I.U. White

c) Letters to the author from Michael Knight, J. Enoch Powell, Sir Hugh Willatt.

d) Letters of Norman Hallward to Oscar Browning, in King's College Library, Cambridge.

Interviews

Notes or transcripts of interviews or conversations between the author and:
Sir John Anstey
John Bailey
Professor Sir Colin Campbell
Revd. Professor and Mrs Owen Chadwick
Mr and Mrs David Corder
Sir Humphrey Cripps
Rosemary David
Dr and Mrs Colin Hallward
Professor and Mrs N.G.L. Hammond
Lord Jenkin of Roding
Denis Mack Smith
Sir Harry Pitt
Sir Joseph Pope
Mr and Mrs Jeremy Potter
Ernest and Pat Polack
Alfred Plumb
Professor Sir John Smith
Mr and Mrs George Spafford

Mr and Mrs Ralph Stockbridge
Mr and Mrs John Sworder
Professor and Mrs Brian Tate
Sir John Meurig Thomas
Professor Frank Walbank
Sir Hugh Willatt

Newspapers

Relevant articles from:

The Bristol Evening Post, The Bristol Mirror, The Daily Mail, The Ladies' Field, The Nottingham Guardian, The Sketch, The Times, The Western Daily Press.

Photographs

The Hallward Family Collection
Haileybury
Clifton College Archives
Peterhouse, Cambridge
Martin Golding
The Hallward Library, The University of Nottingham, Department of Manuscripts and Special Collections
John Laing plc
The Nottingham Playhouse

Books, etc.

Ablett, S., *The Medical School in the University of Nottingham: Origins and Development*. Nottingham University Ph.D. thesis, 1992.

Ablett, S. and Johnston, D., *Campus Collection: A Photographic Record of The University of Nottingham* (Nottingham University Library, Department of Manuscripts and Special Collections, 1989).

Cook, S.A., Adcock, F.E., and Charlesworth, M.P., *Cambridge Ancient History* vol. VIII (Cambridge University Press, 1930).

Alexander, S.C. *Autobiography* (MS).

Anstruther, I. *Oscar Browning* (John Murray, 1983).

Ashcroft, R.L., *Haileybury 1908-1961* (1961).

Bailey, J., *A Theatre for All Seasons* (Alan Sutton, 1994).

Barnes, F., *Priory Demesne to University Campus* (University of Nottingham, 1993).

Chapman, S., *Jesse Boot of Boot's the Chemist* (Hodder & Stoughton, 1974).

Chula of Thailand, Prince, *The Twain have Met*.

Dunsfold Parish Church, a brief guide.

Eliot, George, *Romola*, 2 vols (Smith, Elder, 1880).

Hammond, N.G.L. (ed.), *Centenary Essays on Clifton College* (Bristol, 1962).

Howarth, T.E.B., *Cambridge between Two Wars* (Collins, 1978).

Lee, K., *The Origins of Gretton Court* (Cambridge, 1993).

Mackintosh, D.F., *Fugitive Pieces* (London, 1989).

Saltmarsh, J. and Wilkinson, P., *A.C. Pigou, A Memoir* (Cambridge, 1960).

Thomas, I., *Haileybury 1806-1987* (1987).

Thomas, Sir Percy, *Pupil to President* (1963).

Tompkins, J.C.H., *Clifton at Bude and Butcombe* (Bristol, 1945).

Turner, P., *Film Stars don't die in Liverpool* (Penguin, 1988).

Union of Students' Presidents 1913-1993 (pamphlet) (Nottingham University, 1993).

Walbank, F.W., *B.L. Hallward, Peterhouse 1923-39* (MS).

Walker, T.A., *Peterhouse* (Cambridge).

Weir, C., *Jesse Boot of Nottingham* (Nottingham, 1994).

Whatley, N., *Memoirs* (MS), Clifton College Archives.

Wilkinson, L.P., *A Century of King's 1873-1972* (Cambridge, 1980).

Wilkinson, P., *Frank Ezra Adcock: a Memoir* (Cambridge, 1969).

Winterbottom, Derek, *Henry Newbolt and The Spirit of Clifton* (Bristol, 1986).

Winterbottom, Derek, *Clifton after Percival* (Bristol, 1990).

Winterbottom, Derek, *John Percival, the Great Educator* (Bristol, 1993).

Wood, A.C., *A History of University College, Nottingham* (Nottingham, 1953).

Index